'BOMBAY BUCCANEERS'

Royal Indian Navy

'BOMBAY BUCCANEERS'

MEMORIES AND REMINISCENCES

of the

Royal Indian Navy

collected and edited by

Commander D J Hastings RINVR

BACSA
PUTNEY, LONDON
1986

Published by the British Association
for Cemeteries in South Asia (BACSA)

Secretary: Theon Wilkinson
76½ Chartfield Avenue
London SW15 6HQ

ISBN 0 907799 15 9

Cover designed by Rosemarie Wilkinson

Printed by The Chameleon Press Ltd
5-25 Burr Road
Wandsworth
London SW18 4SG

Contents

Illustrations

---

* Courtesy of National Maritime Museum, Bombay

Foreword

This is the eighth of a series of books published by BACSA for BACSA members with a wider public in mind and particularly those with an interest in the maritime activities of the British Raj.

The title, "Bombay Buccaneers", comes from a nick-name of pre-war days, sometimes shortened to the "Bombay Bucks", which gives a flavour of this dashing Service. It contains the memoirs compiled and edited by Commander DJ Hastings RINVR under the aegis of the Royal Indian Navy (1612-1947) Association.

There is a record of the early history from the days of the East India Company, the reminiscences of general service as told by ex-officers spanning the period 1927-47, and separate accounts of the many and varied Branches of the Service particularly during the Second World War.

It is a story that needs telling as many who spent their lives in one of the other services in India or in trade and commerce within the sub-continent, will admit to only a very hazy knowledge of the Royal Indian Navy.

Over thirty ex-officers, including some WRINS, who served in the Royal Indian Marine and Royal Indian Navy contributed to this collection of reminiscences and in the words of one of them, it was:

> ... a personal excavation of memories, without recourse
> to records. In war, personal diaries at sea or in operational
> areas were strongly discouraged and such notes, sets of my
> orders etc which I was able to retain, have been destroyed
> over the years in order to reduce the amount of clobber carried
> round from place to place while serving since the war.

It is therefore timely that they are preserved for posterity as a record of a unique Service.

Hon. Sec. BACSA

Acknowledgements

I wish to place on record my grateful thanks to the many people who have assisted with the preparation of this volume. In particular my thanks are due to:

* Mrs PPS (Pat) Wright, who was Hon. Editor of the Journal of the Royal Indian Navy (1612-1947) Association for nearly 30 years, for her help and encouragement.
* Mr AJ Francis of the Naval Historical Library, (MOD), for his help with the story of the Calcutta Naval Volunteers.
* The Rev Gordon Taylor RNVR, for his help with the same story.
* Lt. Colonel Patric Emerson, the Hon. Secretary of the Indian Army Association for providing me with material which he had 'unearthed' during researches at the National Army Museum.
* Commander AB Goord, DSC, RIN, for the time he spent reading numerous drafts and for many helpful suggestions.
* Arthur Grant of Wareham, for copying and printing the photographs.
* Those who helped the contributors of particular chapters:

    - the many ex-Signals Officers who contributed to the completion of The Communications Branch, after the death of Commander HC Bird in 1983; among them Commander J Mansell RIN, Lieutenant Commander EM Shaw RIN, Lieutenant Commander E Lodge RINVR, Lieutenant Commander KC Cornish RINVR and Lieutenant AGS Bryson RINVR.

    - the information given to Commander (E) PC Card RIN for RIN Engineering Memories, from Mrs MS Trenoweth, Mrs R Lifton, Mrs EC Harvey, Captain WR Shewring, CIE, RIN, Commander (E) GW Watson RIN, Commander (E) A Briggs, OBE, RIN, Lieutenant Commander (E) G Taylor RIN and Lieutenant (E) GN Forbes RIN.

* Many other people who sent me personal records and reminiscences, too numerous to mention individually.

To all who have provided this material I owe an immense debt of gratitude.

Wareham   DJH
1986

To
those who
served

Preface

When I started to write my 'History' of the Royal Indian Navy, 1612 to 1950*, I had access to the reports and journals of the Royal Indian Marine Club and the Royal Indian Navy (1612-1947) Association from 1934 to the present day.

These reports and journals contained many an interesting story which helped considerably in compiling the History.

I wrote, also, to many ex-officers, to their widows and families to 'scrounge' archival material and 'memories' which would help me in my task.

The present volume is largely a collection of personal memories, from which I extracted material for the writing of the History, but which, clearly, could not be included in full. It presents an unusual cross-section of history and reminiscences, provided mainly by those who served in the Royal Indian Marine and the Royal Indian Navy.

Wareham, Dorset.
October 1985.

DJ Hastings.

* "The Royal Indian Navy - 1612 to 1950, a definitive History", due to be published in 1987 by McFarland and Co. Inc., Jefferson, North Carolina, USA

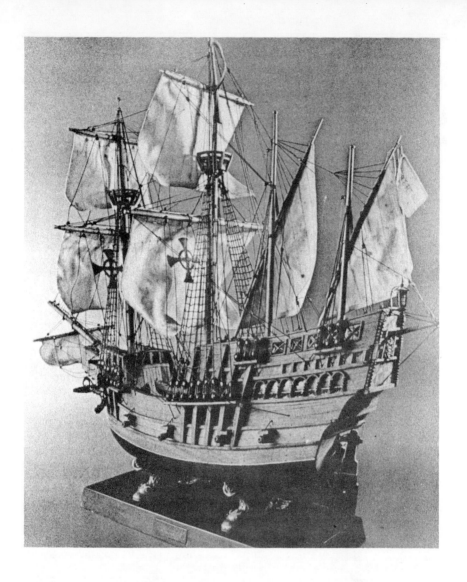

Portuguese Galleon – c.15th century

These four-masted warships, of approximately 200 tons, were noted for their sturdiness, a pre-requisite for trans-oceanic voyages.   It is on one such galleon, the SAN GABRIEL, that Vasco da Gama landed in Goa in 1498.

1
A Brief History

On the 31st December 1600 Queen Elizabeth the First granted a Royal Charter to the Honorable East India Company, then called the Honorable Company of Merchants Trading to the East Indies. The first two voyages of the Company's ships were to the East Indies; the third voyage of the HECTOR, carrying Captain Hawkins, was to Surat. From there Captain Hawkins travelled to Agra, arriving on April 16th 1609, bearing a letter from King James to the Emperor Jehangir, asking permission to trade. Jehangir promised trading facilities, but the Portuguese, who were by that date well established in India, made it clear that they would resist any encroachment on what they considered their special preserve and the Company's ships, on their subsequent voyages to India, were prevented from trading by the presence of the Portuguese in all the principal ports and by the Portuguese fleet at Surat.

As a counter-measure, the Company sent a squadron of four vessels - DRAGON, HOSEANDER, JAMES and SOLOMAN - under the command of Captain Thomas Best, which arrived off Surat on September 12th 1612. This may be regarded as the foundation of the Indian Navy.

Best obtained a 'firman' (mandate) confirming Jehangir's permission to trade and, on the 29th September, the Indian Marine engaged in its first action with the Portuguese fleet, which had arrived to challenge their right to trade. A battle of several days' duration ensued which, though not decisive, nevertheless left the British masters of the situation and the Company's first 'factory' was established at Surat.

Best remained on the west coast of India for three months without further challenge from the Portuguese and then sailed for Sumatra; the Indian Marine was then established, the Company having received permission to open other 'factories' and to maintain a fleet of small craft, known as 'grabs' and 'galivats', to protect the Company's commerce from the Portuguese and the pirates of the west coast.

Grabs were craft of about 300 tons, mounting up to six, nine or twelve-pounder guns; galivats were smaller craft of up to 70 tons, mounting six, two and four-pounders. They were manned by volunteer officers from the Company's ships and Konkani fishermen - the first Indian employees of the Company.

Four of the Company's ships, under Captain Downton, arrived at Surat in 1614 and these ships, together with the grabs and galivats, inflicted a decisive defeat on the Portuguese fleet.

The Emperor Jehangir was well pleased with the result of this action, for the Portuguese had been endeavouring to force him to break off relations with the English and, though powerful on land, Jehangir had no navy and had, therefore, been at the mercy of the Portuguese at sea.

The Indian Navy has continued in existence, as a British force, ever since the arrival of Thomas Best's squadron in India and, during the 338 years until its final demise in 1950, when India became a Republic, it operated under various titles and, though at times reduced to small proportions, it was invariably found necessary to maintain a sea service. From 1612 to 1686 it was known as the Honorable East India Company's Marine; from then until 1830 as the Bombay Marine; from 1830 to 1863 the Indian Navy; thence until 1877 again the Bombay Marine; from 1877 to 1892 His Majesty's Indian Marine; from 1892 til 1934 the Royal Indian Marine and, from 1934 onwards, the Royal Indian Navy.

Almost continuous warfare was waged against the Portuguese from 1612 to 1630 when, following their defeat at Ormuz in the Persian Gulf in 1617, the Portuguese were again defeated at the third battle of Swally. Four years later, a truce was declared, followed by a formal convention, under which a limited number of the Company's ships were admitted to Portuguese ports.

On the marriage of Charles II to the Infanta Catherine of Braganza, the Portuguese ceded to Charles 'the Port and Island of Bombay', as part of Catherine's dowry. In 1668, Bombay was leased by the Crown to the Company, at a yearly rental of £10. Bombay was far superior to Surat as a port and soon replaced the latter as the Company's Headquarters.

After settling its differences with the Portuguese, the Marine turned its attention to the pirates. By this time, the west coast of India and the Persian Gulf were hunting grounds for these gentlemen of fortune and the rich 'Indiamen' proved a lucrative source of profit. Amongst the most notorious were Captains Kidd, Avory and Chivers - they operated under British colours, which naturally led to misunderstandings.

The Emperor Aurangzeb demanded indemnity from the Company for the depredations of the pirates and, when Avory took a Mughal ship with a cargo valued at 26 lakhs of rupees, the Emperor threw the President and 63 of the Company's servants into prison. Thus encouraged the Company took active steps against the pirates, both renegade British and native.

The most formidable of the west coast pirates were the Mahrattas, of whom the Angria clan was notorious. They held sway over the whole coastline and had no hesitation in attacking the Company's ships. The first outstanding success against the Angria pirates was won by Commander, (afterwards Commodore Sir William) James, when a convoy from Bombay to Tellicherry under his command was attacked by pirates, who were repulsed with heavy losses.

Subsequently, in 1755, James, in conjunction with the Mahratta Peshwa, attacked the Angria stronghold of Severndrug and reduced it. The following year a squadron of the Royal Navy under Admiral Watson arrived at Bombay and the opportunity was taken to attack Gheria, (Viziadrug), the main base of the pirates. After a personal close reconnaissance by Commodore James, a combined Royal Navy, Bombay

Marine and Mahratta force, with 1,400 infantry under Lieutenant Colonel Clive, carried out the attack, in conjunction with a Mahratta army operating from landward and reduced the fort, which had until then been considered as strong as Gibraltar and regarded as impregnable.

During the protracted wars with the French in the latter half of the eighteenth century, Marine ships, serving with the Royal Navy under Admirals Boscawen and Pocock, fought in many engagements; they also took part in successful actions against Hyder Ali and the Mahrattas, who were operating with the French. There were constant actions against French privateers and, when Holland was absorbed into the new Republic, the Marine assisted at the capture of Ceylon and the Dutch East Indies. Five of the Company's ships took part in the capture of Mauritius and eight in the reduction of Java in 1811.

The Marine next turned its attention to the Joasmi pirates, a powerful Arab tribe who had established themselves in the Persian Gulf, with their headquarters at Ras-el-Khaima. At first the Company, in an endeavour to avoid hostilities, issued instructions to captains that they were not to attack the Joasmis, but only to act in self-defence. The pirates soon took advantage of this state of affairs and, sending a fleet to Sind and the Gulf of Kutch, captured twenty Indian ships. The captain of the FURY, having beaten off a strong attack, was reprimanded for disobeying the Company's instructions not to 'molest the unoffending Arabs'. At last, the depredations of the pirates compelled the Company to take action against them. Their force by this time comprised thirty-six large ships and eight hundred-odd small ones, manned by 19,000 men.

In 1809, a fleet of two of His Majesty's ships with ten Marine ships and four transports was sent to the Persian Gulf. This fleet cleared up Ras-el-Khaima, went on to Lingeh and carried out a cruise round the Gulf, destroying the pirate ships wherever they could be found and reducing fortifications.

In 1816, the Joasmis again became troublesome and, after the Company had suffered loss of merchandise worth well over ten lakhs of rupees, a second expedition was despatched against them in 1819. This force comprised three of His Majesty's ships and six of the Company's ships, together with eighteen transports, in which 1,600 British and 1,400 Indian troops were embarked. They were joined in the Gulf by three more of the Company's ships and a Muscat force of two frigates and 600 troops, while 2,000 Muscati troops operated from shoreward. This force destroyed Ras-el-Khaima and the fleet then visited other Joasmi strongholds and reduced them all. Early in January 1820, a treaty was concluded with the maritime Arab tribes, which was faithfully observed.

In 1824, war broke out in Burma, in which the Company's ships played a prominent part. The main force comprised four of His Majesty's ships, six of the Company's ships and twenty-three transports. There were also on the Arakan coast three of the Company's ships, eighteen brigs and schooners and twenty row-boats under Commodore John Hayes. The Company's paddle steamer DIANA, the first steam vessel in eastern waters, (built at Kidderpore the previous year), was also present. The senior British naval officer was Captain Frederick Marryat.

In 1830, the title of the Service was changed to the Indian Navy. Under the new title, the Company's ships took part in the capture of Aden in 1839, the war with China in 1840 and operations against the Maori chiefs in New Zealand in 1845-46. In the second Burma War, 1851-1853, a force of six Indian Naval ships took part.

The Indian Navy next saw service in the Persian Gulf in 1852-53, the naval side being provided entirely by the Indian Service. After preliminary operations to capture Bushire, the force proceeded up the Shatt-el-Arab to attack the fortifications at Mohammerah. Here the Indian Navy distinguished itself conspicuously. Sir James Outram, the Commander-in-Chief, describing the action, wrote: 'The gentlemen in blue had it all to themselves and left us naught to do.'

Over a century and a half ago, many fine vessels were built in India, both for the Company's Marine and for the Royal Navy.

In 1670, Warwick Pett (a descendant of the great Elizabethan shipbuilder Phineas Pett) arrived in India to build two ships and two brigantines for the Bombay Squadron of the Marine and Shipbuilding at Bombay were started. Larger vessels were mostly built at Surat until 1735, when the Master Attendant persuaded a Parsi shipwright, Nusserwanjee Wadia, to go to Bombay, where a building yard had been established on the site of the present Dockyard.

In 1754, the first dry dock was constructed and, shortly afterwards, a wet basin was added. In 1775, Abraham Parsons wrote of Bombay:

It boasts such a dry dock as perhaps is not to be seen in any part of Europe, either for size or convenient situation. It has three divisions and three pairs of strong gates, so as to be capable of receiving and repairing three ships of the line at the same or separate times . . . Ships built at Bombay are not only as strong, but as handsome as ships built in any part of Europe; the timber and plank of which they are built so far exceeds any in Europe for durability that it is usual for ships to last fifty or sixty years.

Another authority remarked:

It is universally admitted that a Bombay teak-built ship is 50 percent superior to vessels built in Europe.

In 1823, the first steamship, the Honorable East India Company's paddle steamer DIANA was built at Kidderpore and, in 1829, the steamer HUGH LINDSAY was launched at Bombay making the first steamer passage from Bombay to Suez the following year. In 1830, a steam sloop of 705 tons and 250 horse-power was launched at Bombay and, in 1840, a steam frigate of 946 tons, 220 horse-power, mounting six eight-inch guns, was built, a second frigate being completed two years later.

In a little over a hundred years, 115 men-of-war and 144 merchant vessels were built in the Dockyard. These included four 84's and five 74's for the Royal Navy, of which His Majesty's ship TRINCOMALEE, (now

Castle Barracks – Bombay

Built by the Portuguese in the early 16th century, this majestic quadrangular fort came into British hands in 1662 when Charles II married Catherine of Braganza

called FOUDROYANT), built in 1817, is still in use as a training ship and is the oldest British warship still afloat. The ASIA, launched in 1824, carried Sir Edward Codrington's flag at Navarino. Admiral Sir Pulteney Malcolm wrote:

> Tell my old friend Nowrojee (Wadia) what a glorious part the ASIA sustained in the battle of Navarino and how proud I am of his success as a builder . . .

The last ship built by Wadias was the INVESTIGATOR, launched in 1881.

When the Sepoy Mutiny broke out in 1857, the Indian Navy formed a Naval Brigade of seventy-eight officers and seventeen hundred-odd men. In these operations, the Indian Navy won its highest awards – two Victoria Crosses; one to Mr Midshipman Mayo and the other to Mr Acting-Master Chicken. Mayo's VC was subsequently presented to the Service and remained in the RIN Mess at Bombay until Partition, when it was apparently stolen and has not been heard of since.

After the Mutiny, the Government of India was taken over by the Crown and, in 1863, the Honorable Company's Indian Navy was abolished and a reduced service was re-formed as the Bombay Marine. This period of eclipse lasted for fourteen years, after which Admiral Bythesea, VC, re-organised it as His Majesty's Indian Marine. It was divided into Western and Eastern Divisions, with dockyards at Bombay and Kidderpore. Its duties were the transport of troops and stores; maintenance of station ships at Aden, the Andamans, the Burma stations and the Persian Gulf; maintenance of gunboats on the Irrawady and Euphrates; the Marine Survey and various miscellaneous duties, including the maintenance of Government vessels and launches.

In 1871, the Government purchased two coast defence vessels, the MAGDALA and ABYSSINIA and, in 1889, seven torpedo-boats were added to the strength. Three years later, two torpedo-gunboats were acquired. This force was manned by personnel partly from the Royal Navy and partly from the Indian Marine and was commanded by a Captain of the Royal Navy.

The Indian Marine took part in the Abyssinian War of 1871, the Egyptian Campaigns of 1882 and 1885, the third Burma War of 1885 and the Chin-Lushai Expedition in Burma in 1889. Its services were recognised in 1892, when Queen Victoria authorised its name to be changed to the Royal Indian Marine. Under this title it took part in the Suakin Expedition of 1896, the Expedition to Mkwelo (East Africa) in 1896, the Boer War, the Boxer War in 1900 and the Somaliland Expedition in 1902-04. The Royal Indian Marine's next spell of active service was in the suppression of gun-running in the Persian Gulf and the Gulf of Oman, in conjunction with the Royal Navy, during the period 1909-14. The Naval General Service Medal was awarded for these operations.

The Royal Indian Marine took part in World War I and the three troopers, DUFFERIN, HARDINGE and NORTHBROOK were converted into auxiliary cruisers and the station ships were employed as patrol vessels. HARDINGE and DUFFERIN took part in the search for the KOENIGSBERG and EMDEN after the latter had bombarded Madras and HARDINGE was later in action in the Suez Canal when the Turks made their attack on Toosoum. The Royal Indian Marine was also represented at Dar-es-Salaam and in the operations of German East Africa.

Many ships and small craft were requisitioned or built and the Service was represented in every Indian expeditionary force throughout the war. The largest of these was the Indian Expeditionary Force 'D' to Mesopotamia, in which at one time as many as 500 officers and 13,000 ratings of the Royal Indian Marine were serving. This force distinguished itself at the Battle of Kurna, known as 'Townshend's Regatta'.

In the retreat from Ctesiphon, RIMS COMET and HMS FIREFLY were detailed to cover the rear of the army. After a gallant fight, both were severely damaged and had to be abandoned. COMET was the only Royal Indian Marine vessel lost by enemy action during the war. After the Great War, Admiral of the Fleet Lord Jellicoe visited India and made recommendations concerning the re-organisation of the Royal Indian Marine. A Flag Officer of the Royal Navy was appointed to command the Service and all appeared to be set fair. The next turn of fortune, however, brought a severe reverse.

As a result of the Inchcape Commission in 1923/4, the Service reached its lowest ebb. The three troopships were sold and the station ships were practically reduced to lighthouse tenders. Failing to obtain what he considered a reasonable hearing from the Government, Rear-Admiral Mawby made the strongest protest a serving officer can make; he resigned his appointment as Director of the Royal Indian Marine and went home.

Motto of the Royal Indian Marine and the Royal Indian Navy

Bunting — c.1892

This strong line of action was followed by the appointment of a committee headed by Lord Rawlinson, then Commander-in-Chief in India, to re-examine the whole question. The naval members of this committee were Admiral Sir Herbert Richmond, Commander-in-Chief, East Indies and Captain Headlam, Director of the Royal Indian Marine. There were also two civilian representatives of the Government. The Rawlinson Committee recommended the complete re-organisation of the Service as a combatant force and an Indian Navy (Discipline) Bill was introduced for the new Service. The Bill was defeated in the Legislative Assembly by a single vote, not because the Legislature objected to a navy, but as a protest against the Government's policy towards the Indian coastal shipping question.

The work of re-organisation was nevertheless started in 1928 and the White Ensign was hoisted on board all Royal Indian Marine ships. The Bill, on reintroduction six years later, was passed; it received the Governor General's assent on September 8th 1934 and the Royal Indian Navy came into being.

Unfortunately, the following decade was a period of financial stringency, due to the world economic depression and, in consequence, all new measures were seriously delayed by restrictions on expenditure. Six of the eight trawlers built during the Great War were sold out of the Service and little progress was made with the provision of new equipment which was so badly needed.

Two sloops were built during this period - HMIS HINDUSTANI and INDUS in 1930 and 1935 respectively. The former visited Australia to take part in the Victoria Centenary celebrations in 1934 and the latter remained in the United Kingdom to represent the Royal Indian Navy at the Jubliee Review. INDUS subsequently took the King's Colour out to India. The King's Colour was formerly presented in India by Lord Brabourne, the Governor of Bombay.

In 1938, the Headquarters of the Flag Officer Commanding, Royal Indian Navy was moved to Delhi, to be in close touch with the Government and the headquarters of the other two Services. Originally, Naval Headquarters returned to Bombay for the hot weather season - the move was discontinued during the first two years of the war, owing to lack of communication facilities, but in 1941, it was transferred to the seat of Government and this time the move was permanent.

In 1938, the Commission headed by Admiral of the Fleet Lord Chatfield arrived in India to make recommendations concerning the three Services. Virtually all measures proposed for the Royal Indian Navy were accepted: formation of the Reserves, which had been outstanding for many years, was started; the supply of essential equipment from the United Kingdom was agreed; the construction of modern ships was authorised - all this on the eve of hostilities.

The situation at the outbreak of war was by no means satisfactory - expansion measures had barely been started and the Service was feeling the effects of the lean years. The RIN comprised five sloops, one surveying vessel, (which was converted to a sloop) and two patrol vessels. The strength of personnel was around 2,000.

8

During the war, the strength increased to about fifteen times the original figure and the fleet included a number of modern sloops as well as many smaller vessels designed for convoy escort work, minesweeping and anti-submarine patrol. There were also a large number of auxiliary vessels, coastal craft and landing craft. The sloops were built in the United Kingdom; some of the fleet minesweepers in Australia and some in the UK and others in India. Most of the smaller vessels were built in India. Of the officer personnel, about half were European and half Indian. Ratings were 100 per cent Indian. Recruitment was on an all-India basis and men were drawn from all sections of the community.

The initial training of regular officers of the RIN was carried out in Royal Navy ships and establishments on exactly the same lines as the training of officers for the Royal Navy. On completion of their courses, for the rank of Lieutenant the officers proceeded to India, where they were required to qualify in Urdu. Subsequently, officers selected for specialist courses returned to the UK and qualified in the appropriate naval establishment. Officers were also lent to HM Ships from time to time, to keep themselves fully acquainted with modern developments and practice.

The Royal Indian Navy like other Services, expanded very rapidly in the early years of the war, and in consequence, had a relatively low proportion of fully trained and experienced personnel. Every endeavour was made to improve the standard of training and to overtake the deficiencies of earlier years. Training establishments were brought up to date with modern equipment and new ones. Altogether, there were sixteen training establishments which catered for approximately 4000 ratings undergoing instructional courses, as well as a large number of officers under training.

HMI Ships served in most theatres of war. They took part with the Royal Navy in the reduction of Mussolini's African Empire and had plenty of minesweeping in the Red Sea, Burma, Singapore and Java. One of HMI ships was first to enter Massawah. Ships of the RIN took part in the capture of Axis vessels at Bandar Shapur and other operations in the Persian Gulf; they served in the Atlantic and in the Mediterranean, where two sloops took part in the invasion of Sicily.

HMI Ships JUMNA and SUTLEJ were serving in Eastern waters when Japan entered the war. Both ships had plenty of thrills and JUMNA is believed to have been the last Allied ship to leave Batavia.

The RIN's most spectacular engagement was fought by one of the minesweepers, HMIS BENGAL, when on her maiden voyage from Australia to Bombay, in company with the Dutch tanker ONDINA, in November 1942. They were attacked by two Japanese raiders of 8,000 to 10,000 tons, armed with a relatively heavy broadside of four five-inch guns. The spirited action which followed resulted in the sinking of the larger raider. The second, after torpedoing the ONDINA and shooting her up, sheered off. The tanker, although severely damaged, managed to make port under her own steam and HMIS BENGAL, despite the odds, got off remarkably lightly.

Coastal Forces, including units of the Landing Craft Wing, had been actively employed with military forces ever since the Japanese occupation of Burma and did sterling work in the Arakan Operations, leading to the re-capture of Rangoon. Another branch of the Service which deserves special mention is the Communications Branch, which built up a network of W/T communications in India and formed the Indian link with the Admiralty's world-wide system. HMI Dockyard was greatly expanded during the war and worked at high pressure fitting out and repairing Royal Navy, RIN and Allied ships.

The war services of the Royal Indian Navy were recognised and a great honour accorded to the Service when His Majesty King George VI visited the sloop GODAVARI while she was attached to the Home Fleet. On October 21st 1944, General Sir Claude Auchinleck, Commander-in-Chief, India broadcast a tribute to the Royal Indian Navy in which he said:

> The foundations of the Royal Indian Navy were laid three hundred and thirty-three years ago . . . . Since 1939, His Majesty's Indian ships have been in action all over the Seven Seas . . . . I should like to see India becoming navy-conscious and sea-minded, as befits a great nation with a great length of coastline . . . . This matter of sea power is all-important to the India of the future and I hope this Navy Day will focus attention on it . . . .

Just how well India took up this challenge is clearly demonstrated by the modern Indian Navy.

Crest of the Royal Indian Navy

Gunmetal casting – 1937

The Calcutta Naval Volunteers – c.1899

2

Naval Volunteers in India

D J Hastings

It all started in October 1983 when Archie Bryson arranged for a friend, Ian Munro, to send me an old photograph for which he was 'trying to find a home'. When it arrived, the photograph showed a gun team of the 'Naval Volunteers', said to have been taken in Calcutta early this century, and which showed Ian Munro's father as a rating. In his letter, Ian Munro said: 'My father, TM Munro, (who seems to be the only member of the gun team to wear his cap at a rakish angle!) was the prize-winning cadet in the old CONWAY at Liverpool. He then joined the Hooghly River Survey, which he left at the outbreak of war in 1914 to join the RNVR in Scotland. He served under Captain DJ Munro, RN in installing the boom defences at Scapa Flow. He was later posted to the Dardanelles to instal boom defences there.'

The photograph intrigued me from a number of points of view:-

a)   The Royal Naval Artillery Volunteers existed only from the 21st May 1874 to the 31st March 1891, when they were disbanded.

b)   The Royal Naval Volunteer Reserve was not created until 1903.

c)   The Commanding Officer of the gun crew, (Commander Petley) is shown wearing 'wavy' stripes (with the curl 'going astern').

d)   One officer, an Engineer, is shown wearing a single thin wavy stripe without a curl.

e)   Several of the officers and ratings (including the CO) are wearing large moustaches!

f)   On consulting the History of the RNVR, written by J Lennox Kerr and Wilfred Granville in 1957, I could find no record of any RNAV or RNVR Division or section in India at the turn of the century.

I turned first to the Revd. Gordon Taylor, who was Chaplain to the London Division of the RNVR for many years and whose excellent book on the history of the Division 'London's Navy', was published by Quiller Press Ltd. early in 1983.

Gordon Taylor went to immense trouble and in the January 1915

Navy list he found Temporary Lieutenant Thomas Mathew Munro, RNVR as being attached to HMS IMPERIEUSE. Lieutenant Munro is shown as 'Assistant Harbour Master'. In the same 1915 Navy List Commander (Acting Captain) DJ Munro is shown as 'appointed to COLUMBINE additional for service at Cromarty and as King's Harbour Master.' He had retired as a Commander on the 11th January 1910, so he had been dug out for further service. Since he was in command at Cromarty, he must have requested that his RNVR relative be appointed as his Assistant. There was, however, no mention of Commander Petley or of the Calcutta Naval Volunteers.

By a remarkable coincidence a week later, Gordon Taylor wrote to me to say that out of the blue, somebody who had read 'London Navy' had sent to him an old Navy Week brochure of HMS PRESIDENT produced in 1938, about the world's RNVR Divisions and Branches, including India. On the Calcutta Naval Volunteers it says:-

> First raised 1883 as Naval Artillery Volunteer Corps, the designation of 'Calcutta Naval Volunteers' being authorised 1889. The Corps all European. In 1896 they were the senior Volunteer Corps in India. Establishment comprised: 12 commissioned executive officers; 1 Seaman Instructor; 1 Gunnery Instructor; 2 CPOs; 6 1st Class POs; 4 Quartermasters; 6 2nd Class POs; 4 Shipwrights;20 leading Seamen; 4 Buglers and 278 Seamen; organised in 4 divisions. The Corps possessed a steam launch with Hotchkiss and Nordenfelt machine guns and 6 9-pounder field guns. In 1896 the officers were:
> Hon. Captain - The Lieut. Governor of Bengal.
> Commander - Eaton Wallace Petley RN ADC to the Governor.
> 3 Lieutenants; 6 Sub-Lieutenants; 1 Chief Engineer; 1 Medical Officer; 1 Honorary Captain.
> They are now (1938) disbanded.

Here, then, was our Commander Petley.

I then turned to the India Office Library and Records Section of the British Library, where a very helpful Mr AR Levett sent me a photo-copy of page 533 of the Indian Army List, dated 1st December 1908. From this it becomes clear:-

i   That the correct name of the force was 'The Calcutta Defence Volunteer Corps' and that it was a composite force of Naval and Army personnel.

ii   The force was under the control of the Indian Army.

iii   That Commander Eaton Wallace Petley was Navigating Lieutenant RN (Retd); that he joined the Corps on the 17th August 1888 and that he attained the rank of

Commander on the 1st April 1899.

iv   Commander Petley's rank was attained after the disbandment of the RNAV, but before the formation of the RNVR - whence, then, his wavy stripes?

v   The Naval cadre of the corps had been somewhat changed since 1896.

vi   Thomas Mathew Munro was commissioned as a Sub-Lieutenant in the Corps on the 13th November 1900. Commander Petley's rank dates from the 1st April 1899 and since Munro is shown as a rating in the photograph, this must have been taken sometime between 1st April 1899 and 13th November 1900.

Also of interest is that, among the staff listed, there appears Commander Edward Jackson Beaumont RIM, who joined the Corps on the 8th February 1895, with the rank of Honorary Lieutenant. The Royal Indian Marine List for 1922 reveals that EJ Beaumont retired as a Captain on the 1st October 1911.

I was still not completely satisfied and I therefore turned to Mr AJ Francis of the Naval Historical Library, (MOD), in Fulham. Mr Francis was immensely helpful and he produced a mass of information for me including:-

i   A photo-copy of a page from 'British Naval Dress' by Dudley Jarrett, published by JN Dent and Sons Ltd., London, in 1960 which gives details of the dress worn by officers and ratings of the Royal Naval Artillery Reserve.

ii   A photo-copy of a page from the Royal Navy List of January 1917, which says:-

Munro DJ FRGS served through the Burma war of annexation from 1885 to 1887, in the river flotilla and was present at various engagements throughout the war; took part in the suppression of the Sandoway revolt in the Province of Arakan in 1889 and received the thanks of the Commissioner of the Province for the prompt manner in which reinforcements were brought to the front: in 1890 took command of the geological surveying expedition to the Siam frontier by the Burma Government.

Mr Hughes, Superintendent, Geological Survey of India, in his report to the Indian Government, said: Mr Munro made two main reconnaissances in the interior, one to Mowdaung and another up the Meungoo Chaung. Both of these journeys have resulted in adding to our topographical knowledge of this part of the country. He also surveyed Kissering Island and the valleys of the Sungei Baleih and the Packchang which have resulted in greatly extending our geological knowledge of these parts.

Lieutenant of HMS FOX during the Sierra Leone rebellion of 1898. Landed at Manoh Salya when that place was shelled and destroyed and eighty refugees rescued. Qualified interpreter in Burmese, Hindustani and Swahili. Inventor of 'Munro's tactical speed and distances card', for which he received the thanks of the Admiralty for 'an extremely ingenious invention'. Received the 3rd Class of the Royal Crown of Prussia, 1907. Inventor of a ferro-concrete clamp, trunk buoy shackle, all the above introduced into the Service.

Appointed first King's Harbour Master at Rosyth, 14th July 1911; Admiralty Representative on the Dundee Harbour Trust, December 1911.

iii Further information on the career of Captain D J Munro:-

Captain Donald John Munro CMG RN died on the 11th July 1952. His seniority dates were: Lieutenant (Supplementary List) 31st October 1895; Commander (Retd.) 11th January 1910 and Captain (Retd.) 11th November 1918. He had previously served in the RNR (Sub-Lieutenant 1st September 1892; Lieutenant 3rd September 1894).

Commander Munro was appointed to HMS COLUMBINE on the 1st July 1913 as King's Harbour Master at Cromarty.

His wartime appointments, as an Acting Captain, were:-
HMS COLUMBINE as King's Harbour Master, Cromarty, 1st July 1913; HMS PRESIDENT (for service under Director of Naval Equipment) 20th October 1915; HMS ARROGANT (for Special Service) 26th March 1918; HMS ATTENTIVE III (Later ATTENTIVE II) 24th March 1919.

He is last shown on the Active List in the Navy List for October 1919 - still serving in ATTENTIVE II.

iv Details of the Service career of Thomas Mathew Munro:-
Thomas Mathew Munro first appears as a Temporary Lieutenant RNVR, serving in HMS IMPERIEUSE in the Navy List for December 1914. He was appointed to IMPERIEUSE as Assistant to King's Harbour Master on the 20th October 1914. HMS FISGUARD (ex AUDACIOUS) was renamed IMPERIEUSE in October 1914 and was a depot ship at Scapa Flow from 1914 to 1919. Munro's later appointments were:-
HMS INFLEXIBLE, 18th February 1915; HMS THALIA, (storage hulk at Cromarty), 3rd August 1915 and HMS WALLINGTON, (Immingham Depot), from 11th July 1916

until demobilised in September or October 1919. He was awarded the Volunteer Decoration and it is noted in some of the Navy Lists that he was formerly a Midshipman, RNR.

v   A photo-copy of 'Who was Who', 1897 to 1916, which reads:-
PETLEY, Eaton Wallace CIE, b Woolwich 23 May 1850; 3rd son of Capt. JE Petley RN and Jane, d of Edward Riddle, FRS; m Ida, 2nd d of CA Stuart, Postmaster of Bombay; Educ. Christ's Hospital, London. Joined Navy 1865 and served in Mediterranean Fleet and China Sea Survey; passed for Lieutenant 1871; after joining East Indian Squadron, flagship GLASGOW, was appointed navigating officer of corvette WOLVERINE and afterwards gun-vessel MAGPIE; present at attack on Fort Souik in Persian Gulf 1873; Transferred to Marine Survey of India 1874; Deputy Conservator, Port of Calcutta, 1881; VD; ADC to Viceroy of India; Commander of Calcutta Port Defence Volunteers; Lieutenant RN retired; Deputy Conservator of the Hughli River; retired from India 1910. Died 28th Feburary 1913.

vi An obituary, published in 'The Times' on Saturday, 1st March 1913:-
The death took place at his residence at Southsea on Thursday of Commander Eaton Wallace Petley CIE, RN, who for many years held executive charge of the conservancy of the Hooghly and supervised the special Pilot services of that most wayward of tidal rivers. Commander Petley, who was born at Woolwich in 1850, was the third son of Captain John Eaton Petley RN. He was educated at Christ's Hospital and joined the naval service in his 16th year as a cadet in the BRITANNIA. In 1871 he joined the East Indies Station in the hydrographic department and, incidentally, when navigating officer of the gun vessel MAGPIE, took part in active operations against Persian Gulf pirates. In 1874 he was transferred to the Marine Survey of India and did excellent work, both in the Bay of Bengal and along the Western seaboard. The Calcutta Port Commissioners appointed Commander Petley in 1881 their Chief Executive Officer under the title of Conservator to the Port and River Surveyor and he subsequently held the post of Port Officer and Master Attendant. He remained until his retirement in March 1909 - that is, for 28 years -the officer-in-charge of the conservancy and survey of the Hooghly from Calcutta to

False Point and fulfilled duties, made arduous by the vagaries of the river, with zeal and efficiency.

To the Volunteer movement he gave up most of his limited leisure. From the nucleus of the old Naval Artillery Volunteers, he organised the Calcutta Port Defence Volunteers and was the commandant for more than a quarter of a century. The Military Department for a long time, hindered, rather than helped the movement and Petley met with obstacles which would have driven a less determined and enthusiastic man out of the field. But recognition ultimately came from the Admiralty; the force being constituted as the Royal Naval Volunteer Reserve.

Petley was made honorary ADC to the Lieutenant-Governor of Bengal and, in 1901, Lord Curzon appointed him to the same post on the Viceroy's staff. He was created CIE in 1897. His good-heartedness and charm of manner gave him great popularity in Calcutta society.

Such, then, is the story - which serves to show just how involved one can get in researching just one old photograph.

Footnote on the moustaches seen in the photograph

In their History of the RNVR, Lennox Kerr and Wilfred Granville say, of the disbandment of the Royal Naval Artillery Volunteers in 1881:

The young zealots of the disbanded RNAV did not accept the Admiralty verdict as final. They knew, even if the Navy did not, that there ought to be a Naval Volunteer Force and, if the Admiralty would not support one, these young men would form a Navy of their own. . . .

As a symbolic gesture of hopelessness, one of the ex-Volunteers, Edmund Wildy, who had joined the Artillery Volunteers as a rating, passed to Petty Officer's rate and then to Commissioned rank, grew a moustache.

Did Wildy's action perhaps spark off the crop of moustaches which are seen on both officers and ratings in the photograph?

POSTCRIPT

After writing this article, I sent a copy to Ian Munro and I have since received a most interesting letter from him, extracts from which I give below:-

While I am sure that my father would have been flattered at being taken as an RNVR relative of Donald Munro, such was not the case. I think they met in India and both had Inverness connections, but not close ties....

Donald wrote three very interesting books - 'The Roaring Forties and After'; 'Scapa Flow - a Naval Retrospect' and 'Convoys, Blockades and Mystery Tours'. . . .

Another penny has just dropped! I have among my father's medals, two service medals of the Volunteer Force in India - one as a rating and the other as an officer. . . .

3

Birdie Bowers
of the Antarctic

Henry Robertson Bowers, only son of Captain Alexander Bowers, FRGS, RNR and Emily, (nee Webb), his wife, was born at Greenock on July 29th 1883.

From his father he inherited a short, stocky build, powerful physique and a passion for seafaring and exploration and he shared with both his parents the fine moral qualities of fearlessness, integrity, independence and devotion to duty which were based on a deep and broad religious feeling.

His forebears had been Master Mariners for generations on the east coast of Scotland and his father was Captain of his own ship in the Mercantile Marine at the age of nineteen. His father had been closely associated with the first developments of British trading and shipping in China and ran his own ship further up the Yangtse Kiang than any other British ship had ever penetrated in those days.

He was also one of the pioneers of trading in the Malay Archipelago and Burma and, in 1869, was appointed to represent the interests of the mercantile community of Rangoon in the Bhamo Expedition under Sir Edward Sladen. He navigated the difficult waters of the Irrawady as far as Bhamo, a feat in which he was afterwards followed by his son.

His father's death, on one of the Malayan islands, deprived young Bowers of the direct influence of a character whom he would certainly have admired and in many ways grew to resemble.

After school at Sidcup in Kent and at the Streatham High School, under Dr John Stanley FRGS, where he received a good grounding, he was entered as a cadet in HMS WORCESTER in September 1897. He was lucky in his Captain-Superintendent, Commander, (now Captain Sir David), Wilson-Barker, RNR, in whom he found a life-long friend and whose influence was behind every position to which he was afterwards appointed.

Sir David notes him as, 'the only cadet I ever had in 27 years in the WORCESTER who took a real interest in the Natural History.' Bowers' special hobby was butterflies and moths, of which he had made a fine collection and his Commander taught him how to skin and preserve skins of birds.

His chief scientific interests lay in geography, meteorology and astronomy. Sir David describes him as:

an average boy, whose steady application in work and play took him to the quiet pursuit of his duty in and out of school work - storing his mind with knowledge and his body with strength which, at the right time and under the right incentive, called forth his latent energies. His gentle temper made him a friend of all his fellows and his tubby figure and large nose earned him the nickname 'Kinky-boke'.

He passed out of the WORCESTER in July 1899 as Gun-Cadet Captain, with a First Class Extra certificate in both School and Seamanship. Preferring sail to steam, he joined as apprentice the four-masted ship LOCH TORRIDON, bound that winter for Australia and returning via the Horn.

In this vessel, he made four voyages by the same route until he had served his indentures and was listed Midshipman RNR, when, in order to gain experience in steam, he was transferred to the CAPE BRETON as 3rd Mate, though holding a 1st Mate's certificate.

Recalling his experiences in the LOCH TORRIDON some years later, he wrote:

I can hardly realise the times when, with all hands aloft and chilled out of all feeling, we positively cried with cold, or rather, tears came from somewhere in one's head which, till then, one had imagined was a block of ice.

In October 1905, he was appointed, (on Captain Wilson-Barker's recommendation), Sub-Lieutenant in the Royal Indian Marine and posted to the DUFFERIN at Bombay, but, in February 1907, was transferred to the SLADEN, (named after the Commander of the Expedition in which his father had served).

This appointment gave him a new experience (for he was always, at heart, a blue water sailor) of navigating the Irrawady from Rangoon to its uppermost reaches and in this he soon became so expert that, after four months, he was placed in temporary command of the BHAMO, his handling of which astonished experienced pilots.

Relinquishing his command in February 1908, and having creditably passed both his examinations in Hindustani, he was posted to the MINTO as navigating officer - pending leave.

He spent his leave at his mother's home in Ardbeg, Bute, where he revelled in the natural beauties of loch and mountain. His recreations were cycling, climbing, tennis and especially swimming. The water was his natural element, whether on it or in it and he astonished even the hardiest bather by his powers of endurance and immunity from cold - it was nothing for him, for instance, to swim from the point of Ardbeg to the Craigmore pier and back before breakfast! Already he was showing signs of possessing that exceptional physique and constitution which was to call forth the admiration of his comrades in the south.

Of tireless energy, he was never happy unless actively occupied, either in work or play and his happiness was infectious. His fund of high spirits and zest for life seemed inexhaustible and he had a rare gift for seeing the comic side of situations. His pleasures were simple and, though he entered to the full into whatever social festivities there were going, he was at heart a 'home bird' and the society he loved best was his mother's and his sisters'.

Returning to the Service in February 1909, he was again posted to the DUFFERIN in Rangoon river; but only a month later, received an appointment with the rank of Lieutenant to the cruiser HMS FOX, (Captain, later Admiral, Sir AT Hunt), on duty in the Persian Gulf, disarming gun-running dhows between Arabia and Baluchistan. On one occasion, he earned fame by boarding a dhow and holding up the entire crew with nothing but an unloaded revolver.

When granted a fortnight's leave off Colombo, he spent it touring Ceylon alone on his bicycle and covered an almost incredible mileage in the time, visiting the ancient Buddhist ruins in the interior and writing a very interesting diary of his travels.

In October, he was specially selected, with two Lieutenants RN of the FOX, for dhow chasing and was given his own cutter. But his most important contribution to the ship's record was his survey of the coast - a very arduous task which he deliberately set himself to do under conditions of torrid heat. His maps and charts were acknowledged as models of their kind and his fixings of some cardinal points were sent to the Hydrographic Office in London.

He had kept on terms of friendship with the Commanders of each ship in which he had served and his conscientiousness and efficiency had won high recommendations in every case. He had climbed the ladder of promotion in very quick time and was due for his Commander's examination in 1911. But his roving propensities were as strong as his ambition to succeed in the Service and his thoughts were always in the south.

He had followed with intense interest the stories of Scott's voyage in the DISCOVERY and that of Shackleton's in the NIMROD and, when on leave, he had been introduced by Captain Wilson-Barker to Sir Clements Markham, the 'Father' of Scott's Expedition.

When Captain Scott's second projected attempt on the South Pole was made public, Bowers was surprised to receive a letter from Sir Clements, offering to recommend him for a place in the TERRA NOVA.

'I was at first opposed', says Sir David Wilson-Barker, 'to his leaving the Persian Gulf for the Antarctic, but his enthusiasm overcame my objections.' Being a friend, also, of Captain Scott, he now supported Sir Clement's recommendation and placed Bowers' credentials before Scott personally. The result was a telegram from Scott in March 1910, offering him a place on the expedition and the Government of India put no obstacle in the way. Bowers' appointment was, thus, confirmed without any direct application from him.

It came to him as fulfilment of his dreams. No cloud had ever dimmed his fortunate star and now it seemed to be well in the ascendant. He was appointed store-keeper to the expedition, at first as a Ship's Officer only but, before the ship had left for New Zealand Scott was so impressed with his capacity, mental and physical, that he decided to keep him with the shore party.

The world knows the sequel: the Depot Journey, when, with Cherry-Garrard and Seaman Crean he was marooned on the ice-flow; the Winter Journey when, with Dr Wilson and Cherry-Garrard he went, in mid-winter, to the emperor penguins' rookery on the 'weirdest birds-nesting expedition ever invented' and survived a series of hardships and hazards unparalleled in Polar history and, finally, the Polar Journey itself, in the final stages of which, with Scott and Wilson, he won through to within eleven miles of almost certain safety, only to be defeated by the last final blizzard. This tragic and heroic story need not to be repeated here – it lives in English history.

They had done what they set out to do – they had reached the Pole, but only to find themselves forestalled by the Norwegian expedition, which had started earlier from another base.

Scott's own appreciation of Bowers is the considered judgement of a man not prone to exaggerate:

> I believe he is the hardest traveller that ever undertook a polar journey, as well as one of the most undaunted. His untiring energy and astonishing physique enabled him to continue to work under conditions which are absolutely paralysing to others.

That is a tribute of a commander to his subordinate. But, his last word, written to Mrs Bowers from the tent of death on the Great Ice Barrier, is the tribute of one friend to another:

> He has come to be one of my closest and soundest friends and I appreciate his wonderful upright nature, his ability and energy. As the troubles have thickened, his dauntless spirit ever shone brighter and he has remained cheerful, hopeful and indomitable to the end. The ways of Providence are inscrutable, but there must be some reason why such a young, vigorous and promising life here is taken . . . . To the end he has talked of you and his sisters. One sees what a happy home he must have had and, perhaps, it is well to look back on nothing but happiness. He remains unselfish, self-reliant and splendidly hopeful to the end, believing in God's mercy to you.

Captain Lancelot Sanderson, CIE, RIN

4

"A Lifetime"

L Sanderson

It is now sixty-eight years since I started my seafaring life and, if I were asked why I went to sea, my reply would be that I was brought up on Captain Marryat's novels, 'Midshipman Easy', 'Masterman Ready', 'Peter Simple' and others. In fact, I still have some of them in my library today.

After the usual amount of trouble to my parents, I went in due course, to a preparatory school and in 1902, at the age of thirteen, found myself on board the Training Ship WORCESTER, moored off Greenhithe, with Captain Wilson-Barker in command. There, for two-and-a-half years, I was instructed in Mathematics, Navigation, Astronomy and other subjects, including the art of seamanship, to fit me to be a sailor.

In 1905, at the age of fifteen-and-a-half, I joined the barque AULDGIRTH as an apprentice, together with Lionel Greenstreet, another cadet from WORCESTER. In 1914, Lionel Greenstreet went with Sir Ernest Shackleton in the ENDURANCE to the South Polar regions, intending to cross the Antarctic continent by way of the South Pole. The ship was crushed in the ice and the party eventually landed on Elephant Island, where they camped below vertical ice cliffs until Sir Ernest rescued all his men several months afterwards. This episode reminds me of Lieutenant Bowers, Royal Indian Marine, who, in 1910, went with Captain Scott and three others to the South Pole, which they reached in January 1912 - but the heroic journey ended in death to the whole party.

In the AULDGIRTH, I was one of six boys in the Half-deck; two had already served for one voyage round the world and were known as 'old hands', which left four of us as first voyagers - but we were soon driven to be tough by the mate and to know our job.

The AULDGIRTH belonged to the Village Line of Glasgow, owned by Guthrie, Macdonald, Hood & Company, all of whose ships were named after Scottish villages: Ecclefechan, Dunvegan etc. They had a white House - flag with a diagonal bar and two red balls - known to us as two biscuits and a bone! The AULDGIRTH was a three-masted barque of about 1,200 tons, with double topgallant sails, but no royals, therefore known as a 'bald - headed' barque. She carried twenty-two hands all told.

My first voyage took me round Cape Horn and north to British Columbia to discharge a general cargo, then we loaded grain at Seattle and again rounded the Horn, through fog and icebergs, bound to Cork for orders. During this voyage, some grain got into one of our two fresh - water tanks owing to the tank cover being insufficiently secured, after which our water ration was severely cut and we could only wash in salt water, without soap - or, perhaps, not at all! When becalmed in the tropics, we had to catch as much rain water as possible to supplement our drinking water.

My second voyage was to Perth, in Western Australia and, during this passage, I was sent aloft on the mizzenmast about four o'clock in the morning watch, to pass over the gaff-topsail tack. Unfortunately, I must have slipped and fell fifty-five feet on to the poop skylight; this awoke the Skipper, but I did not hear his curses as I was unconscious. I fell on the softest part of my body and did not break any bones, but was badly bruised all over and had to spend several weeks lying on a mattress on the saloon deck. The Captain, to prevent my limbs becoming stiff, worked them to and fro, night and morning, against my shouts of pain. This was my medical treatment, which did the trick and, as soon as I had sufficiently recovered, I was sent aloft to do the same job.

From Perth, we sailed round the south of Australia in ballast and sometimes made eleven knots. Then up to Newcastle to load black diamonds, (coal), for Chile. I found the Australian people very kind and helpful and we were frequently invited to their homes for meals and social activities. I should also like to mention the Flying Angel, (or Missions to Seamen), who do such excellent work in many ports, at home and abroad. I still give support to the Mission here.

While in Newcastle, our Captain married a barmaid from one of the public houses and, to our dismay, brought his wife on board for the voyage home. This gave a lot of extra work for the apprentices in carrying coal to the saloon for fires and helping the Steward with food from the galley in bad weather.

The voyage to Valparaiso, Chile, was uneventful, but one incident which occurred during this time may be of interest. My shipmate, Lionel Greenstreet and I were studying books in our watch below, to help us to qualify for our 2nd Mate's Certificate in London, so we brought out a sextant to shoot the sun at noon and obtain our latitude. Unfortunately, we were spotted by the Captain, who let out a roar and sent us aloft to grease down the topmast - so that was the end of our practical navigation!

After discharging our coal into lighters by hand winch, we proceeded north to a port near Iquique to load saltpetre. This cargo came in 180 lb sacks by lighter; was hoisted aboard and lowered into the hold, where it was stowed by one stevedore sent off by the Agent. He took the sack on his shoulder and dumped it in its correct position in the hold. Being expert, he seldom had to move it again, so the whole cargo was stowed by one man.

After completion of loading, it was customary for crews of other ships in the port to lend a hand to break out the anchors of the departing ship. As the anchor came to the cathead, you heard the shanty 'Time for us to go' - or something similar. These men were given a tot of rum for their voluntary labour.

We were soon homeward bound and, rounding the Horn for my third and last time, it was not many days before we were in flying-fish weather. Then began the time for cleaning, painting and dolling up the ship, (spit and polish), for our arrival at a home port. After some delay in the doldrums, we picked up the north-east Trade wind and everyone was in good humour, including the Captain's wife, now that the end of the voyage was in sight.

After passing the Board of Trade examination for 2nd Mate of a square rigged ship, I was nineteen years of age - so what plans could I make for the future? My father had been in India for many years in the East India Railway Company, until invalided home. After making enquiries, he found that a great prospect lay open to me of securing a commission as a Sub-Lieutenant in the Royal Indian Marine, a Service officered by experienced seamen who had all served in sailing ships. I therefore tendered my application to the India Office.

In the meantime, I obtained an appointment as 2nd Mate in a ship belonging to the City and Hall Line, sailing out of London to the Mediterranean and Black Sea ports - good training and hard work; watch and watch, with about fifteen ports on the outward voyage.

After qualifying and passing for 1st Mate, I signed on again in the same Company and soon got promotion to 1st Mate. It was usual to carry a general cargo outward and to bring home grain from the Black Sea. On one occasion, in the River Danube, we loaded grain in bulk at Braila. It was essential to see that the grain was trimmed well under the beams to prevent shifting in bad weather. I was in the after-hold with six trimmers, with the grain pouring in from the elevator. As there was little space left, I stopped the trimming until the foreman on deck stopped the elevator, then the grain had to be moved into the 'tween decks so that I and the trimmers could get out. My language to the foreman will not bear repeating!

After two years in this trade, I began thinking about my future career. I thought that my application to the India Office had been forgotten, as it was two years old, so my surprise was great when a letter arrived at my home, offering me a commission in the Royal Indian Marine. I was appointed Sub-Lieutenant in August 1911, on the princely salary of Rs.100 per month, from which I had to pay Rs.30 for messing and Rs.15 for a servant and refund Rs.25 per month to pay back the advance I had received to purchase white uniform.

On arrival in Bombay in the troopship DONGOLA, I was appointed to the HARDINGE, with Luck in command, and, in December of that year, I had the privilege of seeing the arrival of King George V and Queen Mary in Bombay. In 1913, I was appointed to the Marine Survey of India under Commander Hickman, in the old INVESTIGATOR, a ship without double bottoms and experienced my first season of hydrographic work in the Mergui Archipelago.

During the First World War I had various appointments : towing river boats from Colombo to Bombay and also to Basra, patrolling off Calicut and Cochin and between Karachi and the Gulf of Kutch, to prevent arms being landed from dhows and one had always to remember to go alongside a dhow on the weather side, or you could be smothered when they lowered their sail. This was in the Bombay Harbour launch TAMIL, my first command. In 1916, I was appointed for surveying duties under the Director General, Port Administration and River Conservancy, Basra and surveyed Hamar Lake and, later, the Shatt-el-Arab River with Captain

Maundrell - then a Lieutenant Commander.

Now for a small diversion. While serving on the Rangoon station in the MAYO, I was a junior Sub-Lieutenant with John Corser as Navigator. We had bicycles in Rangoon - cheaper method of transport to the Gymkhana than the tikka-ghari. On one memorable occasion, we carried out an escapade by changing the name plates at the gates of various houses in the residential part of the town and, fortunately, we were not discovered! In 1919, I was appointed to the Naval Transport Office, Bombay, under Captain Sir Ernest Huddleston and he told me the following yarn, which he later wrote, in more detail, in Blackwood's Magazine:-

He was appointed MTO, Aden before the First World War and the British Resident at Berbera informed him that King Edward had sent a magnificent elephant as a gift to the Emperor of Abyssinia, but the Resident had been unable to get anyone to land it at Berbera. It had been in Aden for three months and cables had come asking why the elephant had not been landed and sent up country, so the matter was urgent. Could the MTO do the job? But on no account is the elephant to swim ashore - he must land dryshod and march up country to Addis Ababa.

The MTO agreed and arranged for a lighter at Aden to carry the eight ton elephant and to be towed across by the Aden Station ship; also sheer legs and tackle to hoist the elephant from lighter to pier. In Berbera, it was found that there was not enough drift on the wharf to carry the sheers, so the MTO obtained 100 Somalis and 2,000 sand bags, which they filled with sand on the beach. The depth in the lighter's hold was ten feet, so the elephant's shoulders were about level with the deck. Two tiers of sand bags were laid along the floor of the lighter; then the mahout walked the elephant from his open pen at the after end to the bows, while the tiers of bags were continued - then back the elephant went while two more tiers were laid and the process repeated until the elephant was raised to deck level. The pier was not strong enough to take the weight of the elephant, so the MTO obtained several baulks of timber and, using the sheer legs on the pier, lifted the baulks up and formed a solid gangway from the lighter to the back of the pier. When all was ready, the mahout spoke quietly to the elephant and got him to cross the gangway on to the causeway and so he was ashore dryshod.

The year 1919 finished very happily for me as, in December, I was married to dear Anne in Bombay Cathedral and my Best Man was Lieutenant Commander Robin Melhuish.

Between the Wars, I was employed on hydrographic work, for which there were two surveying vessels, the INVESTIGATOR and PALINURUS. The system was seven months at sea surveying. Then four-and-a-half months in the hills at Coonoor, where we were known as the 'Nilgiri Mariners'. There we drew up the charts which, when completed, were sent to Poona to be photographed before the original was sent to the Admiralty for engraving.

I remember one occasion in 1924 at Coonoor - Captain Dauglish, the Surveyor-in-Charge, was celebrating his birthday and brought a bottle of champagne to the drawing office, with which to drink his health. In the

28

middle of this, in walked John Cameron, who was on leave in Coonoor and, after some sarcastic remarks, joined in the celebration!

In January 1925, I was No 1 of the INVESTIGATOR, with Dauglish in command. The other officers were Caws, Jefford, Thomson, Atkins and Paine; also Major Seymour-Sewell, Marine Biologist, for his last season afloat. We were surveying the western approaches to Nankauri and Tilanchong in the Nicobar Islands. On the morning of January 29th we received an SOS from ELPHINSTONE, Garstin in command, saying she had struck an uncharted rock when leaving her anchorage in Castle Bay, so we proceeded at once to pick up all the Officers, passengers and crew, (including the ship's cat) and all their boats and then took them to Rangoon. The wreck of the good ship ELPHINSTONE is still visible under water in Castle Bay and was found by the underwater explorers, Hans and Lotte Hass, in January 1960.

During my thirty-five years service in the RIM and the RIN, I served in many ships and saw many changes. I enjoyed a very happy life in all my appointments and the four years I served in Calcutta, 1939 to 1943, as Naval Officer-in-Charge, are filled with many memories, humorous and otherwise. I recollect an incident with John Farnfield, the Paymaster, who listed an item for cups of tea in the monthly accounts, which I was unable to approve. He was surprised and said it was allowed in civilian offices!

It was during these years that I met many RINR and RINVR Officers. Both Anne and I treasure the silver salver presented to us by my brother officers on our departure from Calcutta. If I had to start my seafaring life again and put the clock back, I would be pleased and glad to repeat my service in the Royal Indian Navy.

Our Service, of which we are all very proud, was taken over in August 1947 by the Indian and Pakistani Governments. I am sure that the two Navies will continue in the head of the line with the Army and Air Force of the two respective countries.

5
In the Royal Indian Marine
C O B Temple

When I was seconded to the Royal Indian Marine, for technical duties, in August 1926, the Director and Officer Commanding was Captain Sir EJ Headlam, CSI, CMG, CBE and the Chief Constructor of the RIM Dockyard was Mr WGJ Francis, with whom I closely liaised.

I was of the British Army, so the learning of Hindustani was not obligatory, as with members of the Indian Army, but, fortunately, I had studied it voluntarily for six months before I reported to the RIM HQ, where I was allotted fitters and labourers who could not speak or understand English. I found the fitters very good and the labourers most loyal, but sometimes stupid.

My first need was an office, which we designated the 'Armament Office' and which was the upper floor of a small two-storey wooden building, fronted with verandahs and on the dockside overlooking the double drydock. Like many Service establishments in India, I learnt that finances were not too readily available and this was in evidence in some instances in the lack of modern equipment. For example, there were no dockside cranes to serve the double drydock and if any major (heavy) component was needed to be raised from the floor of the dock, sheer legs were rigged up and the means of hoisting was by wire rope and capstan, manually operated by masses of Indian labourers on the hand – spikes.

I mention this as an example of a number of difficulties which were surmounted and I was amazed at the marvellous things which were performed in that Dockyard with dedication and skill.

I commandeered part of a dockside shed where chain lifting tackles were being repaired and settled my fitters in there. The charge-hand responsible for the lifting tackle repairs was an overweight Parsi and, like all I met in the Dockyard, a great admirer of the Royal Navy. On the wall, he had a large board with pictures of quite a dozen British warships and he enthusiastically drew my attention to them, remarking 'HMS BENBOW very good ship – HMS 'Invegetable' (INFLEXIBLE) very good ship'!

I recollect that the Troopship RIMS DUFFERIN, went through its conversion to a Training Ship for Indian Merchant Navy Cadets, which was eventually commanded by Sir Henry Digby-Beste RIN and from which, with the approval of Mr Francis, I was able to use a fine Italian marble bath out of one of her staterooms, which otherwise would have been broken up.

The cadets on their Training Ship were a good crowd of fellows and edited their own Ship's Magazine in English and I would occasionally be given a copy. Some of the articles were quite amusing - one I recollect was headed 'Sleep' and its author expounded the unique values of sleep - that it taught equality, because ten fellows sleeping had no advantage over each other - and how one could happily escape the boredom of waiting an hour to keep an appointment by enjoying a sleep!

The RIM seamen were trained on the Depot Ship RIMS DALHOUSIE and were recruited from along the Malabar Coast. I was invited to join a recruiting trip along that coast on one occasion and I was appalled to witness the poor physical condition of those lascars - six out of ten suffering from enlarged spleens and, out of about eight hundred medically examined, only around sixty could be accepted.

All this changed when Rear Admiral Walwyn took over the Directorship in 1927 - to initiate the conversion to the Royal Indian Navy. He aspired to enlist the tougher Punjabi boys despite many advising him that the Punjabi was more attracted to the Army than going to sea. As a result of nation - wide advertisements, he obtained quite a number of Punjabis - or, rather, north country Indians. I will not describe the conflicts on board DALHOUSIE once the Punjabis were housed with the unfortunate lascars! I did hear that a mutiny in later years was mainly initiated by those Punjabi boys who had become mature seamen.

Joining the RIM with Admiral Walwyn, was Lieutenant Commander Holstrom, RN who became the first Squadron Gunnery Officer and was responsible for all the initial training of the RIN Gunnery Branch and Lieutenant Inigo-Jones, (the late Captain HR Inigo-Jones, CIE, RIN), became his assistant.

One of the first things Lieutenant Commander Holstrom initiated was the building of a Gunnery School and the installation of teacher equipment for the QF 4" semi-automatic gun, which was to be the main armament of the RIN ships. Because the cost of the Whale Island-type of rocking platform was prohibitive, we made a system by pivoting the rear end of a beam above the centre line of the trunnions of the gun, the forward end of that beam carrying a cross-piece, to the ends of which were suspended the silhouette of a ship. This forward end was supported by thin, flexible, wire rope, which was run over pulleys above, down to a rotating arm driven by an electric motor. Thus, the 'target' silhouette ships were moved in a circular track - one to be trained upon by the elevation gun-layer and the other for traverse.

I became involved in the training of the first Indian Ordnance Artificers. Being the only one qualified to do so, I assisted in the selection of candidates, all of whom spoke or wrote in English, except one and I was persuaded, on principle, to accept this one because, during the initial interview, I found him to be quite a bright mathematician. At the time, of course, I had no idea of the difficulties I had made. However, during the twelve-month course, I found it necessary to indulge the class in more diagrams on the blackboard for the benefit of the non-English speaking candidate.

There was a three-day written examination at the end of the course and I interpreted the English questions to the non-English speaking candidate in oral Urdu. The shock came when, on collecting the completed papers, those handed in by the non-English speaking candidate were in a script unknown to my official interpreter at HQ. We searched around for someone who could interpret it and were saved by a Chief Writer in DALHOUSIE and, although it was 'all Dutch' to him in its technical nature, it was not to me and the candidate had done very well indeed.

It was gratifying that, when eventually, in 1929, the Squadron steamed out of Bombay on exercises, flying the White Ensign for the first time, (the RIM did not formally become the RIN until September 1934, because of delays in passing the necessary legislation by the Government of India), the gunnery trails proved a great success, with only one QF 4" suffering from a readily corrected breech defect in RIMS CORNWALLIS (the flagship).

In 1930, Lieutenant Commander Learmont, (the late Captain Percy Learmont), took over as Squadron Gunnery Officer and Lieutenant Commander Holstrom left for the UK. I believe that Engineer Captain Phillips was Chief Engineer of the Dockyard, assisted by Engineer Commander Trenoweth. I left in April 1931, as the first new sloop, HMIS HINDUSTAN received an enthusiastic welcome in Bombay - with pictures of her in the 'Times of India'.

6

In the Royal Indian Navy
A B Goord

On the 10th July 1935, I was appointed Lieutenant in the RIN, one of four recruits from the RNR to make up a deficiency in junior officers. After years of indecision, the Royal Indian Marine had been 're-militarised' and the Service, which had existed under various names since 1612, had become the Royal Indian Navy. Under the vigorous command of Vice-Admiral Sir Humphrey Walwyn, who was on loan from the Royal Navy, a new era had commenced.

At this time, the officer cadre, with one exception, was entirely British; there were, however, four Indian Sub-Lieutenants under training – all of them attained Flag Rank in the post-Independence Indian Navy. It is of interest to note that, at my Selection Board, I was told of the policy to introduce increasing numbers of Indian officers as part of the political objective of India obtaining Dominion status.

Most of the executive officers had received their initial training in WORCESTER, CONWAY or, more recently, the Nautical College, Pangbourne. There were also a few Dartmouth trainees, axed from the RN for budget reasons – much to the loss of that Service. Some had then entered directly into the RIM, others by way of the Merchant Service. Most of the older officers had seen service in the 1914-1918 war, some in the Army uniform of the Inland Water Transport in Mesopotamia.

In 1935, the elite of the RIN were the Hydrographic Surveyors, who had a real job of work to do. They had a fine ship in INVESTIGATOR, arduous months of marine surveying and some less arduous months in the Nilgiri Hills making up their charts.

Now, however, the opportunities in general service were beginning to look more attractive and, in the next few years, the 'H' Branch was gradually to take its place as part of a more balanced Service. A large number of officers, both Executive and Engineer, were employed in the Commerce Department of the Government of India, where they performed duties similar to those of the Board of Trade in the United Kingdom. They were seconded from the Service and did not serve afloat, but a number were recalled after war broke out in 1939.

While many of the older Executive Branch officers had become professionally stale as a result of the indeterminate nature of the Service in the 1920s this did not apply to the Engineer Branch. Most of these officers had come up the hard way through apprenticeship and Merchant vessels and they were competent mechanics as well as engineers. With relatively unskilled and uneducated lower deck personnel, these officers had to do much of the work of artificers as well. Having been fully employed professionally through the doldrum years, their efficiency had not suffered. We of the Executive Branch were to be thankful for this when war came, though I doubt if their contribution has ever been fully appreciated.

As well as manning the sea-going ships, engineer officers ran most of the Dockyard departments. The Dockyard was, of course, the heart of the RIN and then contained virtually the whole of its command, administrative, supply and training services, as well as carrying out its basic function of maintaining and repairing HMI Ships. The Dockyard proper was under the command of Engineer Captain George Annett, a powerful personality of ability and, I believe, intransigence.

Executive and Engineer were the only Branches. Doctors were provided from the Indian Medical Department and wore, somewhat incongruously, Army uniform. A diminutive, much loved civilian, 'Pat' Patterson, ran the electrical section of the Yard. The Naval Store Depot - contiguous to the Dockyard - was manned by Indian Army personnel.

The Flag Officer Commanding was Rear-Admiral Arthur Bedford, on loan from the RN. He was a kind and pleasant man, of no great personality, a good nose for sherry and with a kind and capable wife. In short, quite the wrong man to put life into the newly constituted Service which had experienced the dynamic leadership of Vice-Admiral Sir Humphrey Walwyn. He was, however, backed by a staff, mainly of Commander rank and including some p.s.c. officers, which was forward looking and competent. The 'major' ships were commanded by Post-Captains, soon to be retired or fade away. This, then was the pattern of the officering of the Service which I entered.

The four of us selected in 1935, all had a number of years' experience in the Merchant Service and had received RNR training. On the day of the Selection Board, I was still serving in the RN destroyer CRESCENT, as an Acting/probationary Sub-Lieutenant RNR. A few weeks later, at the Jubilee Review, I boarded her as a guest with two brand new straight stripes! The warmth of my welcome on that day is one of my pleasanter memories. CRESCENT made a lasting impression on me - a highly efficient ship, run with that easy form of discipline which comes from mutual trust from top to bottom and a minimum of 'bull'.

Also at the Review was INDUS, a new sloop recently taken over from the builders and similar to HINDUSTAN - already in Indian waters. They were the only modern ships in the RIN, but with a speed of only sixteen knots and an armament of two 4.7" guns, (HINDUSTAN, two 4"), and conventional mine-sweeping gear. They were very inadequately equipped compared with the Black Swans, whose similar hulls housed infinitely greater fighting capacity. Nevertheless, they were the pride of the Service, which saw in them hope for continued expansion and progress.

The remainder of the RIN Squadron comprised two clipper - bowed, yacht-like vessels, CLIVE (flagship) and LAWRENCE, each with two 4" guns and M/S gear and CORNWALLIS, an old coal-burning sloop, similar to the Flower Class. There was also a 'P' boat, PATHAN, two trawlers, of which only one was in commission and the immobile Boys' Training Ship, DALHOUSIE, moored inside the Dockyard breakwater.

After a leisurely passage out in the CITY OF BARODA, and a brief stay in the new Officers Mess, delightfully situated in the historic Dockyard, (but cursed by the presence of a peacock with ghastly screech and a penchant for scratching any polished motor car), I was appointed to PATHAN. This small ship, of queer design, was, with nineteen knots, the fastest ship in the Service, armed with a twelve-pounder gun and depth charges. Having poor sea-keeping qualities, she was employed mainly in training duties. PATHAN suffered a sad fate, being lost after an unexplained explosion at sea off Bombay in the early days of the war. Her Captain, Karl Durston, who was CO of the Gunnery School and a very fine officer, was killed in the explosion. There were few other casualties.

When I joined her in 1935, PATHAN was commanded by a senior Lieutenant, Eric Streatfield-James, later to be a key figure in recruitment and in the wartime expansion of the Service from 110/1250 to 3300/33,000 officers and men. Streatfield-James had fluent command of Hindustani and a great affection for the 'troops'. Until recently, the lower deck had been manned by seafaring Muslims of the West Coast, known as Ratnagiris. Well liked and competent seamen though they were, they lacked the education and martial tradition necessary for a modernised fighting service. Hence, the Punjabi Muslim, backbone of the Indian Army, had been introduced and was rapidly overtaking the 'Rat'. Later, recruiting was extended to all classes and creeds, (not without complication), in order to meet both educational needs and political pressures.

The official language was Urdu, the lingua franca of the Indian Army, but all the technical and nautical terms were those used in the Royal Navy - an odd mixture at times! Many of the older officers knew only 'Ratnagiri bhat', but there were some fine linguists amongst the younger cadre. John Cornish was one who spent much time and trouble teaching me the elements and, above all, the professional importance of being able to communicate freely with the men. All officers were now required to pass both the Lower and Higher Standard Urdu, which included, inter alia, literacy in the Arabic script, prior to promotion to Lieutenant Commander.

It may be appropriate to mention here that we new boys were welcomed into the Service with every possible encouragement from all quarters and were made to feel at home by hospitality which, on the miserable pay of those days, could often be ill-afforded.

In September, I was appointed to HINDUSTAN as Navigation Officer. She was commanded by a Post-Captain, a dear chap, near retirement at fifty and professionally quite useless. Fortunately, he had a first class Number One in JEN Coope and a competent team of officers, all much attached to the 'Old Man'. All pilotage, manoeuvre and navigation was left to me - an invaluable experience. In his kindly way, the Captain once remarked to me that, whereas he had only achieved command at the end of his career, we youngsters would make it in ten years. For many of us, it was to be much sooner.

Squadron exercises took place in the autumn; all the usual Naval drills, combined Service exercises, minesweeping and, of course, the eternal shore parades. Apart from the last, all were carried out with the greatest enthusiasm. Yet it was on the Parade Ground that the men really excelled. At about this time, a new King's Colour was presented and the public spectacle laid on in Bombay was extremely well done. In December, the Squadron visited the Kathiawar coast. I recollect John Lawrence, as Squadron Navigator, as well as 'Flags', taking us into Salbet and anchoring the ships perfectly in confined waters. I noted, in my journal, that 'an excellent harbour could be made if required'. Some years later, I was to make a preliminary survey for this very project. Kathiawar in winter was both bracing and beautiful and the hospitality of the Maharajas memorable.

After Christmas 1935, the Squadron, which had been held on the west coast due to the Abyssinian crisis, (the 2nd Destroyer Flotilla was also in Bombay at this time), split up and HINDUSTAN proceeded on an independent cruise to the Coromandel coast, the Laccadives and Colombo. Here came the news of the death of King George V. At the ensuing Proclamation, an impressive affair held on the maidan, HMI Ships provided the greater part of the Guard of Honour.

There followed more exercises, a refit period in Bombay and a new Captain in the person of Commander Percy Learmont, a Whale Island specialist of fierce repute. With Gunnery the order of the day, HINDUSTAN rejoined the Squadron in Trincomalee. In this idyllic spot we enjoyed six weeks' intensive training with absolutely no social distractions. There was much sailing in whalers and cutters, with Fleet regattas. It must be said that the men were not at their best at boat work and for the PO's in particular, this training was much needed. Few, however, learned to sail a boat - possibly the officers hogged it!

In June 1936, I transferred to CLIVE in Colombo. She was a beautifully built strong ship, though a pig in a sea. She was flagship of Arthur Bedford. Learmont took over as Flag Captain and, despite endless ceremony and socialising, always ran a tight ship. The Admiral, family and staff spent a month on board, mainly in Karachi, where they eventually left us to breathe more freely.

Karachi was a great station, even in summer, (if one were lucky enough to be afloat). As my Journal reflects:-

... the sailing is magnificent and the little Yacht Club a great spot. We sailed in Service boats and in 'Tom-Tits'. I was appointed amanuensis to the Governor (Lancelot Graham) but it was not quite his thing and we usually finished last. There was a Rowing Club Regatta, cricket, tennis and hockey. The RAF scared the daylights out of us, turning us inside out in Wapitis. Last, but not least, there were whaler expeditions to Sandspit, with the youth and beauty of Karachi - one, being tide-bound, finishing very late indeed.

In November 1936, CLIVE returned to Bombay for refit and, with

Commander Rattray and two other officers, I was sent to Quetta for the annual Combined Ops. exercises at the Staff College. The journey from Karachi by train took twenty-four hours, with the country becoming increasingly barren and mountainous. The old city was a heap of rubble as a result of the great earthquake, but the College was not seriously damaged. Our contingent, with nine officers from NORFOLK and some RAF, lived in tents. The soldiers were a great lot and pulled together marvellously; also contributing to give us a very good time. Memorable was a duck shoot on a jheel many miles distant, to which we travelled overnight. There was ice on the water, but the sunrise was a miracle, as was my first experience of the morning flight. (Afterwards, we walked up snipe, when one of my more experienced colleagues managed to pepper a 'Paybob' in the bottom - not popular!)

So, we worked hard, (Monty was on the Directing Staff), and played hard for a fortnight, when the whole party, soldiers and all, entrained for Karachi and made camp on NORFOLK's quarter-deck. There followed main armament bombardments, demonstrations, beach surveys and so on - most of them underlined the utter inadequacy of resources and equipment, (there were, of course, no Landing Craft at that time). However, it **was** educational and completely revised my ideas of the British Army Officer.

NORFOLK seemed a slack ship, but the Royal Marines created a tremendous impression, particularly on the soldiery. From my Journal:

> . . .most impressive were the Royal Marines . . . they make themselves so useful as to be indispensible; a splendid disciplined lot, ready to do anything. The sailors seemed to be of a very good type; appeared to know their work, but went about it more like factory hands . . . one and all, **our** ships were smarter.

In those days, all the average civilian saw of the Navy were games and parties. Both were enjoyable to the officers, but parties imposed a considerable strain and often led to some misjudgement of the sea service. However, showing the Flag was a duty like any other and could often be combined with more serious work. Thus, CLIVE, after spending Christmas in Karachi, sailed on an independent cruise with the Admiral and his lady, very idle Midshipman son and staff. Numbered amongst the last was the Squadron Engineer Officer, Winky Wale - nearly as round as he was tall. No one could remember when Winky had last descended into an engine room, but he was a cordon bleu cook and much loved. On this cruise, his art was much in demand.

Christmas had brought a pleasant surprise in the form of a thirty-three percent pay rise, actually back-dated to July. I believe that marriage allowance was introduced at this time - for officers over thirty. In 1935, a junior lieutenant had only some £300 p.a. and married officers were obliged to live in conditions sometimes almost squalid. Marriage under thirty was frowned upon and, as a result, even the senior ranks contained some bachelors.

Eleven pages of my Journal go on to describe the succeeding three months. Colombo, Calcutta, with a visit from the Viceroy (Willingdon), amongst a hundred others. Chittagong - a disaffected area where officers went ashore with an armed escort of sailors. (The Admiral, however, was considered a serious target and had somewhat more competent Gurkhas. Some of these were subsequently embarked and landed hundreds of miles south to make their way back independently to base, as an exercise in initiative). The unrest seemed to have little effect on European social life. After a Durbar, there followed parties and picnics, including a regatta on a 'tank' in unrigged 'sit-on' boats about seven feet long, (ancestors of today's beach boat?)

There followed Oyster Island, Akyab and Rangoon. I noted much easier racial relationships in Burma, then a happy and beautiful country. Then followed Mergui, where we met up with a flight of RAF flying boats returning from exercises in Singapore. Rangoon again, our Navigator, Bill Moger, once more taking us up the tricky river without a Pilot. A night landing exercise with a bitterly cold night march and bivouac, followed by a devastatingly professional ambush by the Kings Royal Rifles, which showed up our utter inadequacy in field training.

Thence to Penang - FOCRIN and the Commander-in-Chief China exchange calls, the latter flying his Flag in the sloop FALMOUTH, with CUMBERLAND in company - she seemed a taut ship. Victoria Point, Hastings Harbour, where a colony of sea-gypsies hastily embarked in a large sailing craft and made off - wisely, we did not interrupt their way of life. Cocos Islands, Ford Bay, Port Cornwallis - here, glorious beach, sand and coconuts - no people. I nearly sat on an armadillo, or something similar!

Port Blair, in the Andamans, was still a penal colony under Indian administration, where 'non-criminal' murderers led a relatively free existence in idyllic surroundings. In the Nicobars, where there was no proper landing, our football team landed in outriggers, to meet abject defeat by one of Commissioner Scott's thirteen teams. The ball seldom touched the ground. Scott and his wife had spent nine years in the Islands, the only Europeans. Nancowrie's charm defied description. Alas, all these lovely islands were to fall to the Japanese and are today little known, even to globe-trotting yachtsmen.

After Colombo, the last treat in store was a visit to the Laccadives, where the whole community lived on the economy of the coconut. This marvellous tree provided food, drink, houses and much of the material for shows, one of which was launched during our stay. Ashore, one was followed by swarms of children in a sort of 'conga', all mimicking every movement and gesture. And so back to Bombay.

A change of scene was in store. I was due for Privilege Leave, supposedly two months' furlough to be taken in India for the good of one's health and to gain some knowledge of the country. In the RIN at this time it certainly was a privilege and seldom granted. However, it happened that my father had been very ill and was unlikely to live long, so I approached Percy about the possibility of taking this leave in England. The return fare was about £70, which I could just manage. I don't think it was permitted to draw one's quota of Lee Commission passages for short leave. In the outcome, Percy Learmont was kindness itself and prevailed upon the Admiral, not only to grant the leave, but also to give me a berth, 'additional' in INDUS, which was about to sail to attend the Coronation celebrations.

Jack Rattray commanded, but effectively the ship was run by Martin Nott, then a Lieutenant Commander and undoubtedly the most brilliant officer produced by the Service. His great pre-war achievement was the establishment of Bombay Fort as a major Naval communications link. Later, he was to earn the DSO for superb and determined handling of RIN and RN sloops as mobile artillery in support of the Army in the Arakan, manoeuvering and warping the ships in narrow muddy creeks. In the years to come, I was to serve under him only briefly, but knew him well. His grasp of detail was immense, as was his ability to surmount all obstacles. As may be imagined, he was constantly at odds with his seniors, (who nevertheless, marked him as the man to be sent for in time of trouble), and not over popular with juniors, however much they admired him. Professionally, he was utterly competent, though his judgement was not infallible. Born a few years earlier, he would have done for the RIN what Jackie Fisher, to whom he bore a strong physical resemblance, did for the Royal Navy pre-1914.

The voyage was uneventful, calling at Aden, Port Said and Malta. In the Straits of Gibraltar, the Spanish Civil War was the cause of much naval activity. Ancient Spanish warships, British destroyers, Dutch submarines and a German seaplane all contributed to the scene, but nothing of note transpired. Nevertheless, it was in fact quite exciting and we were at cruising stations, with battle ensigns flying, throughout the day.

On arrival in the Pool of London, it became apparent that a very full programme lay ahead. Commander Rattray asked if I would stay on until the ship sailed for Spithead and what followed I was glad not to have missed. First, there were visits by the Lord Mayor, the Secretary of State for India and other notables. We were entertained ashore and had a cocktail party aboard. There were more unusual visits, with soldiers and sailors of the Indian forces to Lord Rayleigh's farms in Essex. The troops enjoyed this immensely and insisted on their officers making speeches of thanks. 'Rab Butler', the Under-Secretary of State for India, replied appropriately, after which, to my great embarrassment, the sailors insisted that they should not be outdone by the Army and that I, too, should make a speech. It was not a very long one!

Came the occasion of the Coronation itself. There was great disappointment that the RIN contingent were not to be represented in the procession proper, which contained many Dominion and Colonial units. We were, however, given a prime viewing position on the corner of Green Park, facing the Palace. Scotland Yard ordered that we should be in position by 0700 and gave us a route by Underground. Nott said that he would be in position by 0800, a full hour before anything was to happen and certainly was not going by Underground. The men were going to **march** from Westminster Steps in drill order, along the route of the Procession.

As there were no haversacks, the problem arose as to how they were to be fed. I spent an hour at Scotland Yard proposing a scheme to get a lorry into Green Park with food and drink. As usual, Nott found an answer - somehow, we got an Army lorry from Knightsbridge Barracks, loaded it with sustenance, drove it into the Park overnight, persuaded the driver to disappear and put two of our own men as sentries over it until the following morning.

Meanwhile, at around 0400, the greater part of the Ship's company on board INDUS in the Pool, were waiting for the arrival of a large launch, specially hired to carry them to Westminster. The hours passed, but it failed to appear. There was nothing for it but to use the Ship's boats. We had only one motor boat, not very reliable, a cutter and two whalers, making a long tow. It was also quite a long haul, with a foul tide and we were only able to inch through the bridge arches. By a miracle, we made it, landed at 0830, formed up and marched through the lined streets. At Admiralty Arch, the gates were shut and the NO in charge was in an obvious state of indecision. Not so our leader, who unhesitatingly marched us on. The gates were opened and the RIN party swung down the Mall to enthusiastic cheers from the populace and took up its position. Hence, it could be said that the first event of that great day was the march past of the Royal Indian Navy.

A few days later, I went on leave and my last duty was to go down to Portsmouth to represent the RIN at a Navy League luncheon in honour of the Dominion Navies. I was met at the station by a car, my fellow passenger being no less than the Guest of Honour, Sir Roger Keyes. He told me that, when First Sea Lord, he had been largely responsible for the creation of the Royal Indian Navy. His speech at the luncheon was overdone. He was an MP at the time and had probably got into an electioneering style. One's encounters with the great are frequently disappointing.

At the end of June 1937 I travelled out with Nott. As usual we went by train to Marseilles, thence by P & O. We were able to fit in a morning at the Paris Exhibition, where Nott introduced me to another 'great'. Uffa Fox **was** a character and a pleasure to listen to. Martin, himself, was one of the best boat sailors in the Service, but, from that time, was to put his powers of concentration on higher things. The Exhibition was magnificent, with the German and Russian pavilions vying with each other in size and impressiveness. By comparison, the British pavilion was positively homely.

In Marseilles, we embarked in the RAJPUTANA and, after an uneventful passage, I left in Aden to join CLIVE as Gunnery Officer and Squadron Recreational Officer. The Squadron was spending the monsoon based in Aden, with much minesweeping, gunnery and other exercises. Once July was out, the weather became reasonable. Strangely, as many of us confirmed, Aden was quite a popular station, with the Services and civilians alike, though predominately a male society.

September 1938 found us in Karachi again, where I was given my first and very brief command. The trawler MADRAS was in use as a target towing vessel and was in charge of a Gunner having no navigational

HMIS INDUS in the Thames for the Coronation of George VI

qualifications and was now due to return to Bombay. We had a filthy passage down in pouring rain and, by the timely use of the lead, narrowly avoided stranding on Prongs Reef. However, all ended well and so, on the arrival of the Squadron, I rejoined CLIVE as Number One.

There followed a most enjoyable independent cruise down the west coast to Goa, (sherry and cake with the Portuguese Governor and favourable impressions of local conditions), Karwar and Cochin. Here were building, by Brunton's Yard, four Victory class day boats - the first one-design to be adopted by the newly-formed RNSA. They were in teak and cost £120 complete. One was mine. Many Victorys are still sailing - notably in Gibraltar.

There followed another session of Combined Ops. in Quetta and after a brief spell as Number One in LAWRENCE I sailed for the UK in the P & O RAWALPINDI. With war now a distinct possibility, it was considered desirable that as many as possible of the younger officers should specialise, in order to form a training nucleus for Reserves who, though not yet formed, might be expected to expand the Service in emergency. While the wisdom of this was never in doubt, I never understood the thinking whereby I and, I think, one other officer, were sent to do **two** Long courses. The Chief-of-Staff, Milne-Henderson, an ex-Surveyor, able but rusty in Naval affairs, told me that he thought that Navigation and Anti-Submarine courses 'went together', so who was I to argue. I was engaged to be married and the two courses, with my six months' leave now due, would take two years if war did not intervene.

The Specialist courses proved very enjoyable, though even as a relatively experienced Navigator, I found the Navigation course quite a slog. High spots were the survey of Dartmouth Harbour and a ship handling cruise in the very tidal waters of the Channel Islands. The course finished in August, when war seemed imminent. I married in haste on the eve of the Munich reprieve and had three blissful months in France and Italy - all on about £100. The French were clearly dreading the prospect of war, but in Italy slogans and para-military activities were evident on all sides. I sent a report of my impressions to the DNI, but never received an acknowledgement. No doubt, he had better sources.

The Long A/S course started on the 1st January with an introductory visit to OSPREY at Portland, prior to three months at the Royal Naval College, Greenwich. This period was a complete waste of time. Half of us were ex-RNR and had left school at fifteen or sixteen, at least ten years previously and there were no Mountbattens among the rest. The mathematical and scientific lectures were way above our heads and given by professors who seemed to have no sense of practical application. Another peculiarity about this course was that, at the time when the U-boat was obviously going to be the principal threat the Navy would have to cope with, it comprised only a dozen or so officers, including three from the French Navy. However, with Greenwich out of the way, we got down to the nitty-gritty at OSPREY and a very good course it was too, embracing experience on, under and even over the sea, as well as nuts and bolts and basic electrics.

In August, the Reserve Fleet was mobilised, leaving only six of us to finish - even before the Passing-out results had been declared, the rest were on their way.

All Indian Service personnel were to return to India at once and the last day of August found hundreds of us on Chester railway station. (Other centres of concentration were York and Edinburgh.) An RTO in civilian clothes had stationed himself in the ticket office and, despite the fact that some other authority had very efficiently allocated us accommodation in the town, he then obliged us to queue for two-and-a-half hours, finally to be told, one by one, where to leave our baggage and the time we were to entrain for our embarkation port. The Generals, Colonels and Senior Civilians were not amused.

September 1st, a fine sunny day, saw Chester crowded with uniformed officers, many with their wives, and the atmosphere in the old town on that occasion is not easily forgotten. At 0830 the next day, we again mustered at the station to receive, over the loudspeaker, an hour's instruction from our RTO on how to board the train. We were told to stand on that part of the platform specifically marked, in accordance with the initial letters of our names. And, 'when I blow the whistle, you will entrain' - which, with a roar of derisory laughter, we duly did. There followed one of the earlier 'mystery' rail journeys - the train passed through no major towns and every station sign had already been removed. After much guesswork over a considerable period of time, we finally arrived at Greenock, from which Clydeside port we embarked, by tender, to various liners.

I found myself aboard the White Star liner BRITANNIC - to end a hilarious day, it was found that, (in their anxiety that the ship should not capsize), the military staff had loaded all the top brass at the bottom of the ship, while the junior officers luxuriated in the higher deck cabins. Needless to say, the arrangements were speedily reversed.

On the following day came Neville Chamberlain's momentous words over the radio and, at 1700 on the 3rd September, our convoy of eleven ships - ORION, (Commodore), ORCADES, ORFORD, BRITANNIC, DURBAN CASTLE, CLAN FERGUSON, REINA DEL PACIFICO, DUCHESS OF BEDFORD, MONTCALM, STRATHAIRD and SYNTHIA, escorted by a division of destroyers, sailed for points eastwards - we were at war.

*   *   *

Our convoy was escorted, initially, by a flotilla of 'V's and 'W's and on the following morning, was joined by an 'R' class battleship. A modern flotilla relieved the old destroyers and the convoy, now in five columns, made a magnificent spectacle as it sped southwards.

BRITANNIC carried about 2,000 personnel for India, mostly Army officers, with a fair number of civilians. A somewhat smaller total was crammed onto the DUCHESS OF BEDFORD. Sinkings by U-Boat, including that of the ATHENIA, were being reported and the convoy had one alarm when four days out. Several on board BRITANNIC claimed to have seen a periscope just before the destroyers dropped depth-charges but nothing further transpired.

At Gibraltar the battleship and SYNTHIA left and the destroyers were relieved by a division of 'H' class and five French boats which, with the cruiser GALATEA, escorted us to Malta. Here DURBAN CASTLE and the French destroyers dropped off, while the rest of us zig-zagged on to Port Said. Life on board fell into a routine of queues for everything, interspersed with news broadcasts, talks and many rumours. The nights, due in part to the blackout, were stifling and most took to sleeping on the upper deck. Everywhere we toted our lifejackets. More fortunate than most I was employed as Navigator, the ship's officers being fully stretched with organisational problems. Several of ours, (RIN) who had been doing courses, gave broadcast talks but, for security reasons, could not be very enlightening. (The Chief Engineer of an Indian Railway was less inhibited, giving us definite information of a secret ray with which the RAF were currently devastating the Luftwaffe!).

The sloops EGRET and LIVERPOOL escorted us through the Red Sea, where Italian submarines were reported - one being put down near Perim. After a brief stop in Aden, we reached Bombay about the 26th September where, to the great envy of our fellow passengers, the naval contingent were whisked away to hotel billets - four to a room - it seemed like heaven.

Bombay Dockyard was seething with activity, largely in fitting-out requisitioned coasting vessels as minesweepers. I was astonished at the scale and efficiency of all this, which reflected credit, not only on the Dockyard staff, but also on the planning work of previous years. Nevertheless, it appeared to me that the mine weapon was being greatly over-estimated. Apart from an odd surface raider, what enemy ship would carry them? - certainly not U-Boats, which required all their capacity for torpedoes. However, it appeared that several of the faster ex-passenger ships were being fitted with Asdics as equipment became available - of the original RIN Ships, only PATHAN and INVESTIGATOR were fitted for the A/S role.

The first RIN officer to qualify in A/S was Lieutenant Commander Joe Jefford, then serving as Commander-of-the-Yard and supervising the embryo A/S school in a minute building in a corner of the Dockyard. The one and only instructor was an RINVR Lieutenant named Collier, who had once served as a PO telegraphist in the RN. Unfortunately, although quite a good teacher, Collier had little knowledge of his subject beyond basic electrics and much of his work had later to be undone.

In a private letter, Jefford had told me that, on arrival in Bombay, I would be appointed to take over and build up the A/S school, concurrently with command of PATHAN as its sea-going tender. However, for some reason, probably because the Gunnery School had pre-empted PATHAN, I was now to go to INVESTIGATOR, operating from Calcutta, as Number One and 'Flotilla A/S Officer'.

Needless to say, there was no war going on in these waters, nor was there any anti-submarine flotilla. There were, however, a number of requisitioned river vessels already fitted with conventional mine - sweeping gear and operating at the mouth of the Hooghly.

44

INVESTIGATOR, (Commander HR Inigo-Jones), was Senior Officer. Operations were conducted under the orders of Commander Percy Learmont, the Extended Defence Officer, who brought his usual urgency and vigour to what really was a training exercise. NOIC was the shrewd, kindly and capable Captain L Sanderson, whose responsibilities in this great port went far beyond the activities of our small force.

INVESTIGATOR would spend about two weeks patrolling off the mouth of the Hooghly, returning briefly to fuel and provision and then off again. Although there was no enemy within thousands of miles, this was not as boring as it sounds. We did most of our pilotage, there were the minesweepers to exercise and, for me, my first experience as Executive Officer. Inigo was kindly and capable and believed in devolving responsibility - in short, a pleasure to serve with. Moreover, my great concern was to gain experience of Asdic operating, as I was convinced that the U-boat would be our major antagonist in the time to come.

The A/S training problem was that we had no practice target, other than passing merchant ships, which were often detected miles away owing to the freak temperature layers in these waters, but which were, of course, useless for carrying out dummy attacks. However, while at Portland, our course had been shown a substitute 'Submarine Target', bearing the name of 'Johnson', after its inventor. It was a small electric torpedo which ejected a stream of bubbles which gave off an echo. The snag was that it had a habit of getting lost - permanently. It occurred to me that we had a perfectly good method of blowing bubbles, using the diving pump and hoses. All that was needed was to devise an 'otter' which would run at a suitable depth and spread a curtain of fine bubbles on which to 'ping'. Thus was born the 'Goldfish', (made with the co-operation of ship and shore Engineer Officers, Nutall and Watson, I believe), which, towed behind the motor cutter, with the crew toiling at the pump, provided an excellent target which lacked only doppler effect in realism.

The 'Goldfish' was used extensively by the Royal and Dominion Navies, as well as our own and brought forth a complimentary letter from their Lordships and a small financial reward. It was later improved and simplified by Martin Nott, who used a small power compressor (or air bottle) instead of the diving pump. The order for a Johnson target was cancelled, or, perhaps, it just got lost.

In November, my wife arrived in Calcutta, having somehow got herself a passage in the Italian CONTE ROSSO. Welcomed by the Jeffords in Bombay and escorted by train across India by my bearer, Lakhi Zeman, who would hardly let her out of his sight, she now faced the horrors of Chowringhee and the Howrah Bridge. Happily, in the excitement of the moment, she hardly noticed them, but I took the taxi twice round the maidan to give a better impression. I had been lucky enough to find a minute but habitable flat, with a kindly Anglo-Indian landlady and just managed to ensconce Freda there before we were off to sea again. By the time INVESTIGATOR returned, I had a comfortable home and a wife speaking quite fluent domestic Hindustani.

At this juncture, Inigo-Jones was transferred and I found myself in command, not only of a ship, but of a flotilla of variegated craft posing as minesweepers, soon to be joined by SONAVATI and PANSY, which were Asdic fitted. For the next two months, we were able to carry out concentrated training down at Sandheads, in addition to routine patrols. Carrying out Oropesa sweeps with 7-knot river steamers in cross tidal streams of up to three or four knots, the relatively inexperienced Reserve officers manning them performed wonders. I must confess to having enjoyed playing at Commodore, but it was exhausting, as I had to cope as well with the technical problems of the Asdic sets and even to correct the compasses of a merchant ship. As an 'N', I was supposed to be able to do this. Fortunately, I had the right book.

In the midst of all this, I had rather lost sight of the fact that my command was temporary and was abruptly deflated by the appointment of Lieutenant Commander Martin Nott and my demotion to Number One. However, I learned that this situation would only last until the new Captain had found his feet. I believe that this was his first command too, but needless to say, it did not take him long to shake down - or indeed, to shake us all up. However, he was not as critical as I had expected and my worst reprimand, (that I can remember), was that the tea-pot spouts and saucepan handles were not all pointing forward during Captain's rounds.

Nevertheless, I felt, after two patrols, that I could be spared for ten days leave, before taking up my new appointment. It was rather naughty and Percy Learmont was not slow in telling me so, but I think he took pity on my wife, who had been cooped up in Park Street (albeit receiving much kindness from the Sandersons and others of the Service), and granted me leave. We went to the BN Railway hotel in Puri. The weather was perfect and we spent our days surfing. The waves were quite strong and it was the custom to employ a surf-boy and to wear little pointed straw hats for diving through the breakers. At the end of this idyll, we entrained for Waltair, near the port of Vizagapatam, to await the arrival of DIPAVATI, which was to dock there. She was ten days late - bless her - another ten days of sun, sea and surf - this time at Government expense.

DIPAVATI was a fine little coastal steamship, ideal for A/S work. Like all similar conversions, she was fitted with the Type 123 or Trawler set, it being impracticable to fit a retractable dome, (which housed the transmitting oscillator). A conversion ship was given a bolt-on dome, which naturally had to be removed before docking. This involved raising the oscillator, blanking off the hole in the ship's bottom and lowering the dome clear on two permanently rove flexible wires and finally recovering it by a pennant secured to it externally and led to a derrick. Removal was comparatively simple, replacement and the final alignment of the bolt holes often exasperating.

Having removed and subsequently replaced DIPAVATI's dome and checked the Asdic installation, I was then ordered to report to Bombay for instructional duties. I found the Dockyard as busy as ever. In retrospect, it would seem that the staff work which had ensured the supply of material for fitting out so many ships so promptly must have been admirable, as was the work of the Dockyard itself.

The new (to me) Flag Officer Commanding, RIN, Herbert Fitzherbert, was a stimulating change and one learned of ambitious plans for the expansion of the Service and orders for modern sloops with six HA/LA 4" guns and escort minesweepers.

After an A/S instructional cruise in RAMDAS to Madras and back in DIPAVATI, I relieved the Captain of the latter for a month while he took his leave. We were patrolling up and down some fifty miles off Bombay Harbour, alternating with other ships which had neither Asdic nor W/T nor, of course, in those days, Radar. The same thing was happening outside all major ports and was not only deadly tedious, but appeared utterly pointless. An Examination Vessel to challenge and report approaching surface vessels made sense, but we were meant to be an anti-submarine patrol.

In a report to the Chief Staff Officer, I proposed that the port A/S force should consist of three Asdic ships, two always on station in or near the harbour at instant readiness, but employed primarily on training duties and that the useless patrols be abolished. This would have been tactically sound and of immense value to training and to operational efficiency but, whether for political or other reasons, no change was made.

It must be remembered that, in the dark summer of 1940, the RIN was preponderantly an untrained force. The initial Reserve officer intake was of a very high calibre but few knew much of the sea or of the technical aspects of naval warfare. Lower-deck recruits were also of a high standard, but local defence vessels were manned largely by Hostilities Only ratings of no great ability. If Britain were to survive the Axis assault, and few of us believed she would not, the war would be long and the RIN vastly expanded. Training of personnel to man this Navy was of paramount importance.

After taking through the first course of HSDs in our 'cottage', we moved to the new A/S School in November. This was in Castle Barracks. An Attack Teacher arrived from Britain, was installed and demonstrated to VIPs, including HRH the Duke of Gloucester and, more importantly, was brought into constant use. Courses for officers and ratings were stepped up and a Reserve Officers' Long course passed out, to provide instructors and Port A/S Officers for the future. (A group photograph shows, among others whom I cannot place, Parkinson, Rose, Braund, Rashleigh, Kells, Ramdas and Pollard - all RINVR).

Excellent though the Attack Teacher was, it could not take the place of practical exercises at sea. These we carried out in various small vessels, using even smaller ones as targets. In some ways, this was more realistic than using the 'Goldfish', but every attack had to be aborted before running down the target vessel. The conflict of purpose in carrying out an effective attack and avoidance of actually hitting the target was hair-raising, but somehow, a major accident never occurred.

In April/May 1941, I was granted three weeks leave and it is an interesting sidelight that, at the time Britain was suffering terrible reverses, with neither Russia nor the USA yet engaged, in India there was still no petrol rationing - or, if there was, it must have been pretty liberal. My wife and I drove an ancient Ford V-8 down to the Nilgiris, consuming no less than one gallon every sixteen miles, plus innumerable tyres destroyed by cast bullock-shoes, and relaxed in the old home of the

RIN hydrographers.

On return to Bombay, I was not at all pleased to find myself in a new appointment. Navy Office was moving to New Delhi as NHQ and Jefford was moving there as SO (O). I was to relieve him as Staff Officer, Bombay and SO (A/S). Domestically satisfying - we had a pleasant flat and Freda was enrolled in the Air Defence system (and once transmitted to me a classic observer's report of sighting an 'aircraft with a rubber balloon tied to its tail'), but a desk job at such a time was most frustrating. However, in early 1942, I managed to shed the Bombay responsibility and, with Commander Kendall, RN, drew up plans for a combined RN and RIN Anti-Submarine School at Varsova. We took these to Delhi, where they were approved. But my days as a specialist A/S officer were over. I was to be Staff Officer to the newly-appointed Captain, Coastal Forces (John Ryland). Chatterji, enthusiastic and ebulliant as ever, would relieve me, with Parkinson still ably running the A/S School.

It seems that GHQ believed, after the devastatingly successful Japanese raid on Ceylon and the subsequent humiliating withdrawal of the Eastern Fleet to Mombasa, that the Japs would mount a seaborne invasion of India - what was the Navy going to do about it?

The Singapore experience suggested that MTBs might be a deterrent and two flotillas had been ordered, to be manned by RN personnel and expected to arrive in late summer. In addition MLs, (Fairmiles) and HD MLs were to be built in Indian yards and a separate administrative organisation set up.

My task was to lay out the first base at Trombay. It was a rush job and not very well done, but the RE officer who had to build it was dogmatic as to where he could and could not do it and that was that. In retrospect, it was extraordinarily lavish and included a number of bungalows for married officers. The RIN obviously intended to establish roots there.

Next, I was ordered to join Commander 'Jumbo' Paine in carrying out a land reconnaissance for fuelling bases on the east coast of India and to expedite the building of CF bases at Vizagapatam, Cochin and Mandapam. By October, when I did the next tour, these were well under way, but we still had no boats.

Being temporarily jobless, I was able to get a month's leave, spent with my wife on a pony trek from Simla up the old Tibet road. The November weather was crisp and perfect; the mountain scenery superb.

Arriving back in Delhi on the 16th December 1942, we found the whole war scene altered by the success of the landings in North Africa and the advance of the 8th Army. Yet, despite this, (which would appear to have eliminated any threat to India's west coast), I was now despatched, with a Captain IE, to site and plan CF fuelling bases.

Working from Tuticorin in the south, we visited every possible harbour, finishing with Salbet as guests of the Dewan of Nawanagar. It was a most interesting experience. We produced a report which was of no value whatsoever. Probably, Vice-Admiral Godfrey, who took over as FOCRIN in the Spring of 1943, squashed the project. Certainly no 'great naval base' in the Gulf of Kutch was 'planned and partly prepared'.

At the end of 1942, I was given an acting half-stripe and command of CHEETAH, the Coastal Forces base at Trombay, where CCF also established his HQ. CHEETAH was to be the main CF base in India. The old salt-barge jetty had been extended, but in the wrong direction in relation to the tidal stream. From knowledge gained during peacetime sailing forays, I foresaw, in the planning stage, that this would result in a violent trip on ebb tides, but for technical and financial reasons, no change was made. The result was that berthing in a spring ebb was virtually impossible.

We soon had HDMLs, up to a flotilla, all officered by keen young men anxious to get to war. To maintain these boats, the base absorbed some 200 men and many good officers. Tommy (THL) Macdonald was my Number One.

There was no friction with CCF, who was, for all his fiery temper, reasonable and considerate, but, in the base, we could not feel that our efforts were having any effect on the prosecution of the war. The Trombay project seemed wasteful and its purpose was never quite clear. As a training base, it had possibilities, but we were never given the facilities for proper maintenance. If not for training, what were the boats doing there anyway? With hindsight, I believe that it was a grab for post-war expansion and I understand that it is indeed now a major naval establishment.

It was a relief therefore, when in mid-July I was appointed to command the new base at Vizagapatam, HMIS CIRCARS CCF and staff followed shortly afterwards, Captain Ryland doubling as NOIC and, to my astonishment, I was given an acting brass-hat!

Vizagapatam was very different from Trombay. On the right side of India in relation to the enemy, well laid out and with easy access to the sea, CIRCARS was a main naval base, as well as for Coastal Forces. It was still incomplete, but by the time I left nine months later, we had forty to fifty craft alongside the jetties. Throughout, we had a flotilla of MTBs, nominally RIN, but manned by about 150 RN officers and men. With their short range, the MTBs were only of use as a defensive deterrent and by now, the threat of Japanese invasion was no longer real. With little to do except maintain their boats, the officers got very browned off. The RN contingent administered themselves and, apart from problems with their (Army) rations, gave me no trouble. As a result, I think I paid insufficient interest towards them.

We had some 350 RIN by the spring of 1944 and nearly 100 officers in the Mess. I was very fortunate in having an excellent Base staff. Hawley, an RINR officer, who had been a Port Officer in Burma, was an exceptional Executive Officer. Mukerji, now Commander, was Base Engineer Officer.

Our MLs were now operating in the Arakan and, sad to say, our base was far too distant for us to be of much help to them. Ryland went off to direct the operations there, but I learned little of what was going on until two years later when, serving on a desk alongside Tommy Macdonald, who wrote up some of the exploits. In the Base, our only experience of enemy activity were moonlight reconnaissance raids by solitary aircraft, presumably keeping an eye on what we might be doing. They dropped an odd bomb, ineffectively. Much more exciting, was a confirmed report of a large unidentified convoy approaching the port. All ships went to action stations, rifles and field equipment issued to all Base personnel. Hasty arrangements were made for the evacuation of families and there was fear that this was the real thing. However, someone had blundered - the convoy, was one of ours. Just as well, as the local Army was very thin on the ground. Only the MTBs must have been disappointed.

Navy Office was situated on the other side of the water from the Base and was now occupied by Commodore Scrygemour-Wedderburn, RN, with the title of Commodore, Bay of Bengal. His right hand was Harry Morland, whose father and grandfather had distinguished themselves in the Indian Naval Service, but who had himself, I believe, failed to gain promotion on account of lack of linguistic ability. He had entered the Service some years before me, but was now my junior; nevertheless, we worked well together in ironing out the differences 'over the water'. COMBAY ran the Communications Centre in the Base, where the Service wives were mainly employed. The wives also ran canteens and other amenities for merchant seamen.

Admiral Godfrey paid us two visits, the second being in the Flagship, NARBADA. Of him I wrote: 'He is a large man with a friendly smile which can turn to steel in a flash. I feel him to be shrewd and broad-visioned, with an inflexible will'. Another visitor to lunch was Sir Claude Auchinleck, known as 'the Auk' now Commander-in-Chief, India. He was held in great esteem.

The entertainment commitment was considerable and much of the responsibility fell on my wife, who was the only woman actually living in the Base. She was, by 1944, in real need of a rest in a milder climate, but knowing that I must soon get a sea-going appointment, would not leave me. Thus, when I received a DO (demi-official) letter from the Admiral, advising me that I could expect command of one of the new sloops in May, ('This is the most considerate act I have received from on high' - Journal), it was something of a relief, as well as an exciting prospect. Two months later, Aubrey Todd, Commander RINR, relieved me and, after a brief leave in Kotagiri, where I left my wife, I joined GODAVARI in Bombay on the 3rd May 1944 - at last I was to see something of the war.

*   *   *

My pierhead jump to join GODAVARI on the 2nd May 1944 marked the fulfilment of a lifetime's ambition - command of a man-of-war. Moreover, not only was GODAVARI, (A Bitterne class sloop with six 4" HA/LLA guns), one of the most modern ships in the Service, but under Joe Jefford, now acting Captain, (with George Watson as 'Chief'), she had been worked up in the Atlantic and elsewhere into a highly efficient unit. I counted myself extremely lucky - a luck to be held through the nine months to follow, after which, ashore again, all was anti-climax. It is, therefore, somewhat ironic to find that these months, recorded with some

HMIS GODAVARI

51

detail and frequency, possibly make the least readable of these recollections. Ships, squadrons and fleets were in movement on every ocean and GODAVARI's activities were not particularly noteworthy relative to the scene as a whole. Nevertheless, to those on board, they were exciting, absorbing and memorable.

There was no time to take over. We sailed immediately as SO Escort to an Aden bound convoy of five important ships, the STRATHAIRD, VOLENDAM, EMPIRE VICTORY, OTRANTO and DILWARA. The other ships of the escort were HMSs ROEBUCK, REDOUBT and TAY.

On arrival, we did the usual count of Confidential Books, then Joe sat back while we escorted a lone merchantman back to Bombay. The fortnight spent under his guidance was invaluable and gave me a lasting sense of confidence.

In Bombay, we were inspected by FOCRIN, Vice-Admiral Godfrey, in his usual impersonal way. Afterwards, he sat down in my cabin and chatted. I wrote: 'Conversation jumps all over the place - most odd. He has a bee in his bonnet about health'. Another visitor was Captain Baker-Cresswell, RN to whom I took immediately, as Captain ABCEF (Arabian Sea, Bay of Bengal and Ceylon Escort Force), he told me that GODAVARI would be joining the 60th Escort Group, operating with two 'pocket' carriers as an A/S striking force (Force 66).

The ten days in Bombay, I noted in my Letter of Proceedings, were very welcome to the ship's company, coming as they did after a month of almost continuous steaming. It was also the first harbour spell in Indian waters with defects, drafts and storing to be attended to. We were, in fact, overwhelmed with attention. COMRIN, NOIC, Captain Escort Group and CSD all had technical staffs, which tended to make co-operation difficult and must have been bewildering to ships unfamiliar with the port. There were also instructional establishments, only too eager to help and to send their trainees aboard. We even had a party of Women's Army Corps (India), presumably those later to become WRINS and a party of Indian gentlemen from the UP, who came under Government auspices and stayed to tea. All in all, it was a relief to get to sea again.

Bound for Trincomalee, escorting the dockyard repair vessel HMS WAYLAND, I found myself the Senior Officer of the escort, which included the destroyer RELENTLESS and the frigate NADDER. For some reason, our sloops were always commanded by captains or commanders - this was a peacetime custom in both the RN and the RIN, as the ships were frequently employed, individually, in a semi-political role. Destroyers, on the other hand, usually had Lieutenant Commanders in command, often quite senior. At this time, I was a substantive Lieutenant Commander of less than a year's seniority but, as an acting Commander, had already been twice in charge of escorts having captains of greater real seniority and experience. Happily, I never had any problems on this account. It did however pose problems for Baker-Cresswell, whose Group SOs were Commanders and veterans of the Battle of the Atlantic, when he was given RIN ships, commanded by acting post-captains, relatively green to the U-Boat war.

However, all this was by the way. On securing to the oil jetty in Trincomalee, we received work-up orders and commenced the same day two weeks of strenuous exercises, culminating in one aptly called 'Frenzy', involving the whole of Force 66, of which we now formed a part. The Force consisted of BEGUM (SO) and SHAH (carriers), and the 60th Escort Group - CAUVERY, (Wentworth-Harvey), GODAVARI, FINDHORN, NADDER and LOSSIE. Commanding the Force was Captain 'Jackie' Broome in BEGUM- an officer of outstanding ability, with the devastating experience of Convoy PQ 27 behind him.

The force was now ready for operations but, alas, Trincomalee had no organisation for dealing with the special requirements of RIN Ships and two days were wasted while CAUVERY and ourselves dashed round to Madras to embark halalled meat. The Force eventually sailed from Trincomalee as soon as we arrived on the 17th June and was joined on the following day by SO60 EG in TAFF, (Commander Ormsby). Ormsby was a highly successful operator from the Atlantic scene; a delightful personality and a pleasure to work with.

Our first sweep was west of the Maldives and Eight and Nine Degree channels and was unproductive. Only GODAVARI had any excitement. In the middle of a foul, pitch black night on the 22nd, we got a firm radar contact which we chased for ten miles. Unfortunately, our R/T was as usual, defective and under the absolute imposition of W/T silence, we were unable to inform our SO what was happening. Ultimately, we fired a star-shell, but saw nothing. The evidence points to the contact having been a 'ghost'. We were recalled, but I regretted not having turned a deaf ear for a little longer. As it was, I had a lot of explaining to do.

The flying weather was frightful and our admiration of the pilots unbounded. Not only did the carriers pitch heavily when steaming into wind and sea, but frequent rain squalls prevented their planes landing at the end of their patrols, with fuel low and daylight fading with tropical suddenness. On the 23rd, one plane was forced to land well after sunset; another came back in trouble and pancaked, while a third Averner misjudged and ditched from the carrier's deck. All the aircrews were rescued by the escorts, thanks to the effectiveness of the planes' dinghies.

Our ability to remain at sea was dependent on refuelling from the carriers. I wrote:

> We fuel every third day, the operation taking three to four hours. The system is known as the "buoyant hose method, without steadying line". The hose is streamed from the carrier, picked up on our forecastle and connected up. Ships steam at ten knots, maintaining a small bight in the hose. Failure to keep within twenty or thirty yards of station means that the hose breaks . . .

And, needless to say, great unpopularity. In bad weather, the operation was a great strain and, though in time the watchkeepers became adept, I never took my eyes off that hose.

On the 28th June, we were detached with HMS FINDHORN to escort

SHAH, which had developed defects, to Colombo. Here we met HMIS NARBADA (Captain M Nott), looking as though she had just come from the Spithead Review. Comparing GODAVARI's rusty topsides, I noted that, while my ship had been in almost continuous bad weather since she was built, NARBADA must have been more fortunate. The truth is, however (as revealed by Captain WJM Teale, RN who was then serving in her), that before entering harbour after a wartime patrol, Nott would heave to, rig stages and paint ship. There was a great spirit of competition between RIN Ships, particularly between CAUVERY and ourselves, but I can't think of any other Captain who would have cared to emulate him to this extent.

Nevertheless, discipline and morale, I noted, 'have been very satisfactory . . . the ship can be considered an efficient A/S unit; however the standard of seamanship is low, particularly in regard to boatwork. This failing appears to be fairly general in HMI Ships, which compare unfavourably with RN vessels in this and, possibly, only this respect'.

Boatwork was not unimportant. On occasions, when at sea, captains were summoned aboard the 'Flag', as in Nelson's day and seaboats were always at readiness to pick up ditched aviators. The use of a boat was also necessary when securing to a buoy, notably in Trincomalee. Here, the escort berths were in a long narrow gut, in which a network of cables precluded anchoring and the wind blew strongly from seaward. If the buoy was not picked up smartly, with their high windage and low power, it was extremely difficult to manoeuvre the sloops back into position again. In the confined space, it was impossible to turn them head to wind without dropping an anchor underfoot, a crime committed more than once as an alternative to being driven on to the rocks.

After a few days in Colombo, SHAH, CAUVERY and GODAVARI proceeded to Cochin to boiler clean. This, together with repairs, took a week – a spell particularly appreciated by those of us whose wives could come down from the Nilgiri Hills.

The Base, which I had helped to lay out some eighteen months previously, was now operational, with Navy Office in the erstwhile hotel on the island. On the night of the 15th July a ship, the SS TANDA, was torpedoed some 150 miles to the northward. The news did not get through until the following day, when CAUVERY was already on her way back to Colombo, so only GODAVARI, delayed by an ER defect, was available in Cochin. She sailed on the 17th and joined SUTLEJ, (John Cornish), in the area the same night. SUTLEJ had carried out two attacks on a confirmed contact a few hours earlier, but we had no luck in our search. Detached to look for survivors, we found the TANDA's second butler afloat on a piece of wooden sun deck. After nearly three days adrift with two lascars, who had given up the ghost during the previous night, he was still able to stand up and wave frantically when we came into sight.

Returning to Cochin, we then escorted SHAH back to Colombo, where Force 66 was again assembled. Another fly-on accident – SHAH's stern rose to a swell and the pilot failed to meet it. A terrible sheet of flame. Miraculously, we picked up two of the aircrew, together with two sailors who had been obliged to jump overboard, in a matter of minutes and relatively unharmed.

On the last day of the month, Force 66 sailed on operations. My Letter of Proceedings for July has the usual bleat about mail delays - no fewer than 170 official communications having accumulated for delivery before sailing. Of more interest, is a remark, under the heading of 'Efficiency':

> The language difficulty remains one of the greatest bars to efficiency. The proportion of officers speaking Hindustani is still small . . Contrary to much wishful thinking, very little English is **understood** by most of the young ratings - for this reason, the utmost care and patience in giving orders is essential. More lash-ups occur through mis-understandings of orders than from any other cause. Only 51% of the ship's company profess to be able to speak English. The proportion who understand it is probably less than half of this.

Almost immediately after leaving Colombo, TAFF got a D/F bearing of a U-boat to the eastward of Chagos Archipelago. Unfortunately, the 'pocket' carriers could not fly off in the windless conditions obtaining and no contact resulted. Force 66 was then ordered to proceed to Killindini for boiler cleaning, prior to operating in the Arabian Sea, where there was a high concentration of shipping to and from the Gulf and the Red Sea. However, on the 6th August, came the news of the sinking of the EMPIRE CITY in the Mozambique Channel. She had managed to get off a distress call before the crew took to the boats, from which they were soon picked up. Sadly, the U-boat, believed to be a large special cargo carrier, took the Chief Officer prisoner. She also, unwisely, made two radio transmissions and was fixed by shore D/F, indicating that she was on a north-westerly course, probably bound for Malaya.

Force 66 reached her 'furtherest-on' position four days after the sinking, when the submarine was sighted about sixty miles ahead and forced to submerge by one of our aircraft. There followed the action described later, when GODAVARI found and held the enemy until FINDHORN sank her by Hedgehog on the 12th August.

On the 18th August, the Force arrived at Killindini for boiler cleaning. Boilers governed our lives - toil and anxiety on the one hand; a rest factor (for some) on the other. GODAVARI had tubes which, by now, were badly worn, a condition aggravated by the rapid speed increases called for when the carriers were operating aircraft. George Watson and his team performed wonders and Alec Briggs, soon to relieve him, Hunt-Pain and Charlton were to continue to keep things going for yet a few months to come. Renewing, or even plugging, tubes at sea was, I gathered, no picnic. At the present juncture, however, boiler cleaning was a welcome break for most of the ship's company. Mombasa was cool and green, the Eastern Fleet had departed and the base staff had little to do except attend to our needs. Spares were short and halalled mutton, as always, a problem, but excellent arrangements were made for leave and recreation.

I was able to spend a few days on a farm some 350 miles up-country little thinking that, within a few years, I would be taking the first steps to develop a holding in these lovely highlands of Kenya.

Apart from boiler tubes, GODAVARI was in good fettle. Jacky Broome visited us and addressed the ship's company in complimentary terms; morale was high; the sick list down to about two a day, (despite the rats, about which more anon), and all hands eager for more action.

On the 28th, we were at sea again, seeking two U-boats known to be busy in the area. Force 65, comprising BATTLER and five escorts, including NARBADA and SUTLEJ, were also looking for them. But, with shore-based VLR aircraft keeping the enemy submerged by day, we had no sightings. On the 5th September, however, some 400 miles south of the Gulf, we encountered wreckage. A major air search for survivors was laid on, but it was our night VLR plane which eventually found the boats, presumably by radar. Ninety-nine persons, including women, were picked up by our advanced screen. They were from the Holt Line TROILUS, sunk no less than six days earlier. Aden's barren hills must have been a welcome sight to them.

From Aden, back to Killindini for, (needless to say), boiler cleaning. And, for GODAVARI, fumigation – for she was infested with rats. Horrible, large animals from British dockyard ports, I imagine. One, at least, had a habit of invading my cabin via a ventilation duct, in order to nibble my toes. The whole ship's company was evacuated for forty-eight hours, mostly to a rest camp.

Next day, the 5th October, Force 66 departed for Colombo, where we arrived on the 13th, after being detached with the endemic boiler trouble. An unusual absence of U-boat activity resulted in GODAVARI being sent round to Madras to sort out leave problems and defects. Royal Navy officers did not always understand the importance of leave to RIN ratings. I noted in my Proceedings that 'the regular grant of annual leave . . . is regarded as almost a necessity of life and I am convinced that the present contented state of the ship's company is due to the fact that all hands have had, or are having, their due leave'. Captain ABCEF was much concerned that a draft of forty ratings who joined the ship at Colombo, to relieve a similar number, would adversely affect efficiency. In fact, most had already served in the ship and soon shook down. (Our leave problem was more acute than most, as GODAVARI had, as yet, had no refit period in India and required a 20% leave reserve).

The draft returning from leave had, in fact, been having a pretty rough time. Owing to the uncertainty of the ship's movements, they had been sent by train from Bombay to Colombo; thence, some days later, by sea back to Bombay, before, once again, being sent by train to Colombo, where, a week later, they were able to rejoin their ship. Throughout, the men had very little money and, while in the train, very little to eat. As a result of this, I made an urgent recommendation to the Drafting Office that all relief drafts should be held in Madras, where accommodation was available and from where they could rapidly be sent to Colombo or Cochin as necessary.

Despite such tribulations, the men were really remarkable. On the

Commander AB Goord, DSC, RIN, on the bridge of HMIS GODAVARI

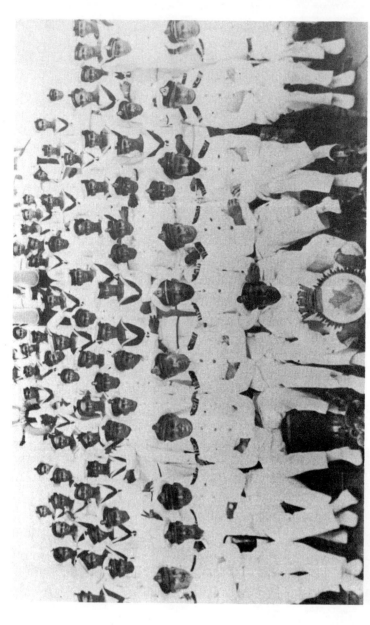

Ship's company of HMIS GODAVARI - 1944

(Front row - left to right) Gunner CSH Smith,RN; Lt JB Akehurst,RIN; Surgn Lt PR Sondhi,RINVR; Lt Bentall,RINR; Lt Cdr(E) A Briggs,RIN; Comdr AB Goord,RIN; Lt JW Craig,RINVR; Lt(E) EG Charlton,RIN; Lt (S) VW Hummerston,RINVR; and Lt PJ Lamb, RINVR

21st October, Navy Day was celebrated in Madras. We had to provide a Guard of Honour for the Governor and the major part of the column for the March Past. Although no drill or field training had been carried out since the ship commissioned, the turn-out was extraordinarily smart and a credit to the RINVR Gunnery Officer, (Craig) who undoubtedly would have felt less nervous in action with the enemy.

On the 26th October, Force 66, less SHAH and CAUVERY, fuelled in Vizagapatam and sailed in search of a submarine reported about ninety miles away. This one should have been in the bag, but the RAF Liberator making the sighting was at the limit of her endurance and had to leave the spot. BEGUM had a defective catapult and there was insufficient wind for flying-off. Another search in early November for a U-boat which sank the SS MARION MOLLER was also unsuccessful. After this, GODAVARI limped round to Cochin on one boiler, together with BEGUM. Cochin and Vizagapatam were now proving their worth as bases, not only for minor vessels, but also for the Force carriers, Moreover, the Escort Force had its own boiler-maker, who proceeded to replace tubes - en masse, in our case. Local leave was given and Bakhri-Id celebrated.

CPO Muhammed Malik described this entertainingly in 'RINLOG':

Recently GODAVARI had a spell of rest, which is not common to this ship. In fact, we were so unused to it that we decided to do something to keep ourselves active.

A 'burra khana', with five courses for Bakhri-Id was the beginning. Appetites not always being too good at sea, food such as 'biriani', roast chicken and pudding, rich in ghee, condiments and spices, was just what was wanted to stoke up with. After the 'khana', our Captain rose to speak. Sometimes he strokes his beard; but, on this occasion, on declaring his enjoyment of the feast, he laid his hand on his stomach. Garlanding of officers was then performed by Yeoman of Signals, Raj Wali and Petty Officer Kaushal Khan, who with witty cross-talk, soon had the whole mess deck in roars of laughter.

The next item was the regatta. The ship's company put up eight whaler crews and, against such skilled oarsmen as the Seamen and veterans like the POs, the Stokers pulled a fine race to beat Communications in the final. The aggressive tactics used by Stoker PO Muhamad Zaman, (we expected to hear the order 'Away Boarders'), may have been the deciding factor.

Then there was an obstacle race. It started with commando stunts, went on to sporting features, had something to do with eating a hot potato from the galley and finished with hoisting flags. Although the Daymen produced, in ship's cook Fateh Khan, the only man who could eat the hot potato straight from the pot, the Torpedomen were the winners. Possibly this was due to the encouragement of their Divisional Officer, Mr Cook, who knows his men and how to spur them on

- or is it possible that he knew a shorter way around the course!

The finale was a race in Carley floats, officers versus POs. The Captain was caught napping at the start and was obliged to take a pierhead jump in the form of a running dive off the jetty in his best number thirteens. We don't know who won the race, but nobody was drowned! Prizes were then presented by four-year old Miss Sandra Briggs, daughter of our Engineer Officer, who, though too young to make a speech, 'shabashed' with gusto each winner who received a prize from her tiny hand. There followed a tea party given by the Captain to all Officers and Chief and Petty Officers. With the Captain moving freely among the ratings, spreading good cheer, everyone enjoyed the tea, cakes and sandwiches and fruit. With three cheers, the party ended. Next day, we started another form of activity - that greater activity which is bound by silence.

After these high jinks, we sailed with BEGUM and R/Vd with an almost completely reconstituted 60th EG off Dondra Head, setting off to catch a Japanese submarine reported to be on a mission to land and pick up agents on the east coast of India. The RAF found him in the middle of the Bay of Bengal and Force 66 followed him across to the vicinity of Coconada, but we never caught him and the Force returned to Vizagapatam. On the 16th we learned that the Jap had landed his agents on the Orissa coast and Force 66 went off to look for him again, but this time, alas, without GODAVARI. Boiler trouble had been continuous and, after an inspection in Vizagapatam, I felt that I had no alternative but to declare the ship unfit for further operations and, indeed, there were doubts about our ability to work our way around to Bombay for refit. However, we managed, though not entirely without incident.

Captain ABCEF inspected us in Colombo and addressed the ship's company in complimentary and encouraging terms, looking forward to our return to the fold.

FINDHORN and ourselves, following up a U-boat report and eager for a double, nearly had a night engagement with a US Air-Sea Rescue Launch. Our last 'action' was off the Basses, where we attacked a most promising contact, which turned out to be a shoal of blackfish. The depth-charge pattern, with a shallowest setting of 150 feet, fired at twelve knots, blew about eight feet off the end of the bilge keel. I decided to do some 'fishing' with some of the really rusty 'cans' on board; a decidedly successful operation which added much to our Christmas dinner. This was celebrated in the wardroom, with several old GODAVARI's, including Captain Jefford and Peter Mahindroo Singh, our sometime Navigator and a fine officer.

Compared with the RN frigates, we were very fortunate to bear such a full cadre of officers and I, myself, lucky to have had a splendid team, including a no-nonsense sawbones in Surgeon Lieutenant Sondhi and an indefatigable Supply Officer in Vic Hummerston, who virtually relieved me of all paperwork. Hamilton, my Number One, was professionally competent and ran the upper deck in a relaxed manner. 'Peter' Mahindroo was succeeded by an equally competent RINR officer in Bentall. The engineer officers, already mentioned, kept the ship going long after she was really operationally fit. All in all, I had a first class team from top to bottom, largely the product of the ship's earlier service since commissioning under Captain Jefford.

As a result, in contradiction to earlier experience, I was able to divorce myself almost completely from the day-to-day running of the ship and to concentrate on operations in progress. My cabin was so near the bridge that it was unnecessary for me to over-burden the OOW with my presence. I was able to keep up with my reading - from Dickens to an excellent monthly review of A/S operations issued by the Admiralty.

Of course, one always looks back through rose-coloured spectacles, but I think we were a happy ship. Wardroom hospitality was generous when in harbour and there was no problem in getting to know the officers. As for the men, I certainly did **not** know them all but, by personally keeping them informed of everything that was going on, I took care that they knew me. There were grievances - leave, mail, personal problems and, of course, lack of halalled mutton - but disciplinary offences were minimal. The whole crew entered into the spirit of the operations and, I truly believe, felt the same exhilaration as I did when steaming out to the chase to the clarion calls of 'A Hunting we will go' or the 'Post Horn Gallop' on the PA system and the rising throb of the turbines below - an unforgettable memory.

Apart from the boiler tubes, our only serious troubles lay with Radar and the R/T. The latter was a 4T battery set, very temperamental and, (I can only assume), operational on one channel. With a force of eight ships, working under active conditions, it was seldom of much use. The principal Radar was a Type 271. Owing to overheating, it would only function for fifty minutes in the hour and required practically the full time of the Warrant Tel. to keep it going. This was a severe handicap as, apart from its search function, it was most essential to night station keeping. In our A & A list for Bombay, I asked for a Type 276/293 Radar, a modern H/F, R/T set and a Radio Mechanic to maintain them. We also completely re-planned the Plot and Bridge lay-out, in the light of operational experience - how it worked out, I was never to know.

By the end of 1944, the end of the war in Europe was in sight, but a long and bitter struggle was expected before Japan could be overcome and GODAVARI was undergoing a major refit to enable her to play her part. Returning from leave in February 1945, I had expected to retain command for at least a few more months - however, it was not to be. After handing over to Lieutenant Commander HMS Choudri, RIN, (later Commander-in-Chief of the Pakistan Navy), I was posted to New Delhi to take up the appointment of Staff Officer, (Operations and Intelligence) at NHQ, following, once more, close on the heels of Joe Jefford, now Captain of AKBAR, the new short-service training establishment. Before leaving Bombay, I witnessed Sunday Divisions there, with some 3,000 officers and men, complete with band, on parade. It was most impressive.

The extent to which the Service had expanded was reflected at NHQ, where over 150 officers, nearly all of them from the Reserves, were engaged in administering the RIN. My own appointment was really that of assistant to the Chief-of-Staff, Commodore John Lawrence and carried with it the function of his deputy.

Within the 'O & I' Branch there were no less than eight Staff Officers; for Bases, Coastal Forces, Landing Craft, Shipping, Movements etc. Each worked more or less independently. What we did **not** deal with were Operations and Intelligence. NHQ was not, of course, an operational authority. However, I don't recall being idle. All the flaps landed on my desk and some, from the NOICs, were, indeed urgent - often concerning the handling of dangerous cargoes.

Although there were two other Commodores at NHQ, both were concerned with administrative duties. One day, it happened that the Admiral was away and the COS sick and, at five minutes notice, I found myself representing FOCRIN at the Commander-in-Chief's meeting in my hitherto forgotten function of DCOS. However, if the 'Auk' was surprised to find a junior Acting-Commander in place of the Admiral, he did not show it. Needless to say, I was unable to contribute much to the triumverate, but it was interesting to have a close professional encounter with this very powerful personality. He was, throughout, at pains courteously to bring me into the conversation - without great effect, as I had no knowledge of what he and the Air Vice-Marshal were talking about.

Some time after this encounter, I was to see more of Auchinleck. With the passing of VJ Day, he decided to set up a committee to report on the detailed form of command to be adopted by the Indian Armed Forces in the post-war era. At this time, it was thought that there would be some ten years in the run-up to independence but there is no doubt that the 'Auk' himself wished to play a major part in the reconstruction - not from personal ambition, but from his devotion to the Indian Army and to India and in the knowledge that he was the best man for the job.

Thus was formed the 'Reorganisation Committee (India)', chaired by a senior Lieutenant-General, (Sir Henry Wilcox) and having as members two Indian Army Brigadiers, an Air Commodore and, (as one might expect), an Acting-Commander from the RIN - myself. After being briefed by the Commander-in-Chief and receiving our terms of reference, we were to make our headquarters in Dehra Dun and get down to work.

'I have reached the conclusion', wrote General Auchinleck, in his directive, 'that, in principle: a) the constitution in India of a Supreme Command and integrated staff and b) the constitution of three separate Service HQs each commanded by an independent Commander-in-Chief, but working under the command of a Supreme Commander, would provide the best future organisation of the higher command of the three Services in India. The Committee was then enjoined to make a detailed examination of the subject, so that the Commander-in-Chief could make definite proposals to the Government of India.'

The idea of several weeks in Dehra Dun was sheer bliss. My wife had been critically ill and a spell in a hill station would do her a world of good. In fact it did, but she had to spend most of the time by herself, as it became apparent immediately upon our arrival early in October 1945 that there was little the Committee could do there. The necessary evidence for its investigations could only be found in New Delhi itself and in London.

So, back it was to the Secretariat, (albeit, in the General's official Cadillac), where we interviewed admirals, generals and air-marshals of varying degrees and in some numbers.

The high spot, however, was a meeting with Lord Louis Mountbatten, his three Commanders-in-Chief and personal staff. The 'Supremo' stage-managed the affair so that we sat at a long table, with his party on one side and the Committee on the other. From the start, he dominated the proceedings and evidently wished to convince us that his own set-up would provide most of the answers to our problem. First, it fitted closely to our directive and, more important, had worked operationally. However, it soon became evident that the system of command whereby Supreme Command and the three Commanders-in-Chief shared the same planning staffs, was creaking badly.

I recall Sir Keith Park complaining that he could get nothing out of the Planners, as they were too busy with the Supremo's work and I had the impression that the Commanders-in-Chief were taking the opportunity to air their views while Lord Louis' overwhelming personality was muted by our alien presence. In the event, the meeting caused us to doubt whether, whatever its merit in an area command, the Supreme Command system was suitable for the overall direction of National Defence.

Next on the agenda was London, flying in a partly-converted Sunderland - over twenty-eight hours - very cold in the air and hot on the ground in the intervals. BOAC very efficient, with lovely hostesses. Karachi - Bahrein - Cairo, (the Houseboat) - Augusta - Poole.

For the next seven weeks, excluding a longish Christmas break, we were busy in Whitehall. First the Army Council, under the DCIGS, Sir Archibald Nye; then the Air Council, with Sir Arthur Tedder - the latter very helpful and unassuming. Sir Rhoderick McGrigor at the Admiralty was not greatly interested, but the Joint Planning and Intelligence Committees had much to offer. Finally, we met Sir Hastings Ismay, Chief-of-Secretariat and Major General Ian Jacob who, between them, finally convinced us that the Joint system of command, (ie, a Chiefs-of-Staff Committee such as was operated in Britain), was infinitely preferable to the system outlined in our terms of reference.

Our report, therefore was something of a fudge, but it did contain conclusions based on facts. Whether or not any use was made of it I do not know. In principle, we found that 'an organisation under which a Supreme Commander can get his advice on matters for which the Commanders-in-Chief are executively responsible, from his staff as well as from the Commanders-in-Chiefs is wrong - the German OKW is an outstanding example. Set up to give advice without executive responsibility - looked upon as one of the most important factors leading to Germany's defeat.'

On the 11th January 1946, we emplaned in a somewhat better

insulated Sunderland which, unfortunately, failed an engine over Biscay. As a result, we alighted at Biscarosse in the Landes of Bordeaux and camped for the night on the floor of the local estaminet - which was **not** insulated. However, the necessary spare reached us in due course and we arrived back in Dehra Dun on the 23rd. Here I found my wife in good health, but completely 'broke', due to our unexpectedly long absence and communication problems.

It did not take long to round off our Report 'The High Command In India'. (Report of a Committee set up by His Excellency the Commander-in-Chief in India, 1946) for which the main credit was due to Brigadier WGS Thompson, Indian Army. Then back to Delhi once more, this time as Staff Officer (Plans), to include post-war planning. But, hardly had my wife and I found digs in The Grand in Old Delhi, when we learned that the Signal School in Bombay had gone 'on strike'. Remoteness in Delhi did not reduce the sense of shock. The affair has been well documented and what occurred is not in doubt. Why it occurred is of more interest. In my Journal, written up some six months later, after close contact with subsequent enquiries and events, I attributed four main causes. They were:-

a. Strong external political influences at a time when the fleet was in a state of inaction and concentration after the war.
b. Inexperience of both officers and petty-officers.
c. Complete inefficiency of the Bombay administration.
d. Lack of contact between senior officers and men.

This last comment needs elaboration. Most of the great commanders during the war and perhaps, indeed, in history, established very close links with the men they led - sometimes by-passing their officers in the process. Mountbatten, Montgomery, Slim and Patton are ready examples. Auchinleck, himself, was known, at least by repute, to every sepoy in the Indian Army, but no such ties existed in the Royal Indian Navy.

Admiral Godfrey was a man of outstanding intellect, but extremely remote. Naturally he had a linguistic problem, but he never appeared to make any attempt to make personal contact with the men. His inspections of ships' companies were, I wrote, 'a scandal. He hardly looked at the men, let alone talked to them'. In fairness, it should be said that Admiral Godfrey's great contribution to the growth of the RIN was the making of it known to the country and particularly to the Indian 'establishment' and to the Army, so that much of his time and effort were projected outwards, rather than towards the Service. This was probably the best use for his great talents. The lack of a strong second-in-command and his own remoteness of bearing, were unfortunate. Rattray, in Bombay, had long lost touch - always looking upwards, (to NHQ), instead of to his own command. I had served with him - a most likeable man, but really living in the past. Lawrence, the Chief-of-Staff, had spent nearly all his RIN service in staff appointments. The only blame that can be attached to him was that the Bombay command was not held by a man of the calibre of Jefford or Nott. He knew of the weaknesses but, whether or not he advised FOCRIN, I don't know. In the upshot, of course, it was Nott who had to sort it all out.

The mutiny lasted three days - there were many more months and reams of paper connected with the aftermath. My first job was to preside over the Board of Enquiry into the events at the Torpedo School at Jamnagar (HMIS VALSURA). It was evident that nothing untoward would have occurred there but for the arrival of a rating from Bombay with stories of 'lorry loads of corpses being carried out of Castle Barracks'. Thence to Bombay, for more Boards of Enquiry, just in time, thankfully, to see my wife embarked for England in the CIRCASSIA.

I now found myself under Captain Nott's orders and daily visiting the camp at Malund, where the ringleaders of the mutiny were being held, in order to supervise the investigations of the various Commanding Officers into the conduct of their men.

The main instigators were now very frightened men, well knowing the penalties that were possible. One morning, I arrived to find the place in a state of uproar. I think Lieutenant Commander 'Queenie' King was in charge and he had wisely decided to have these men removed. Unfortunately, about twenty bad-hats still remained among the 300 men in the camp and these now organised a hunger strike. No one could go inside the wire and the investigations came to a standstill. I was lucky. Next morning, the 'baddies' congregated round the gate, complaining. We opened the gate and they walked straight into the arms of the Mahratta guard. After their removal, we had no more trouble. Warrant Master-at-Arms McArthur was a tower of strength. We both lived within the camp wire and ran the place as an ordinary shore establishment for three months while various enquiries went on. The remaining men, who must have been bored stiff, behaved extraordinarily well and, in the end, few of them were punished.

The mutiny and its political results brought to an end the hitherto rising tide of anti-British feeling. With Independence in the offing, the focus turned to communal problems. So it was that, when the time came, British officers were able to take their leave from the Service in an atmosphere of goodwill, in a sub-continent seething with strife. However, at this time, there were few thoughts of leaving or of the Partition which was to split our Service and all thoughts were directed towards reconstruction.

My own task in the summer of 1946 was to reorganise and plan the expansion of the training establishments and bases at Cochin, Vizagapatam and Karachi. The Cochin plan was particularly comprehensive, covering Communications, Torpedo, A/S and Electrical Branches. The new FOCRIN, Sir Geoffrey Miles, came down to approve the proposals. I was much impressed by his personality and air of integrity.

In September, I flew back to England on leave. Five months later, I found myself back in my old chair as Staff Officer (Plans), facing a very different situation.

My Journal dated 15th June 1947 reads:-

When I left England, Mr Attlee's announcement that Britain intended to transfer power to India by June 1948 had just been made, so it seemed that a limit was now put on our future service. Since then, Mountbatten has become Viceroy and carried the Indian leaders into an agreement giving Dominion status to India and Pakistan by August this year (1947). He has appreciated the need for speed and looks like getting things done at last. It is an unhappy situation . . .

Early in March, I had been appointed, as SO (Plans), to the Armed Forces Reconstruction Committee as naval member. I also sat on the Naval Sub-Committee, (Commodore Jefford, Mansell, Choudri, Soman and others). The prime issue was nationalisation and one of the first steps was the promotion of four Indian officers of Lieutenant Commander rank to acting-Captain. All of them were later to achieve distinction. It was a necessary step, but, of course, no encouragement to more senior British officers to stay on, though the Indians pressed us to do so. For myself, the proposed yearly contract had little appeal and I sadly decided to take premature retirement.

Among my varied tasks was the working out of the proposals for compensation and proportionate pensions. Naturally, the ICS had got their oar in early and, for the Services, it was largely a matter of tagging along. The proposals were generous and sensible. An officer near retirement age got nearly all his pension and small compensation, while a junior, with reasonable prospects of starting a new career, got little pension and some compensation. Those of us in the middle thirties got a fair whack of each - my own pension came out at £300 pa (about one-third of living requirements) and there was a golden bowler of some £6,000, a great deal of money in those days. My final sessions with Mr Jayshanker of the Finance Department were on this problem. In preceding years, I had spent many hours arguing cases with this shrewd able man, who had a remarkable grasp, for a civilian miles from the sea, of what was reasonable and what was not.

My last case was to press for the basic pension of RIN officers to be based on their 20th birthday, the reason being that a majority of those recruited before the war received their training in the Royal and Merchant Navies before joining the RIN, perhaps in their mid-twenties. Jayshanker agreed; Government agreed; but someone in the India Office in London turned it down. It left a lot of us considerably poorer, nevertheless, there is no doubt that British officers taking early retirement were very fairly treated.

On 3rd June fell the bombshell of Partition. This had, of course, been a possibility for some time, but the concept had seemed unreal and there were so many unknowns that contingency planning was almost impossible. Now, the Reconstitution Committees, instead of having a full year to work out comparatively simple nationalisation plans, had just two months in which to divide up the armed forces. It did not simplify the work of the Committees, who had been promised the answers to many key questions, that on this very day, June 3rd, the Commander-in-Chief went on leave. Not only must he have been a very disappointed man, but events were by now probably out of his control.

This was particularly difficult for the Navy, as the distribution of Indian and Pakistani personnel, vis-a-vis the various branches of the Service, was quite unbalanced. Moreover, while ships could be dealt with easily enough, training establishments, having only one set of relatively immobile equipment and being purpose-designed, provided an apparently insoluble problem. However, somehow decisions were reached. There was confusion and frustration at all levels, but the job was done. Much credit was due to the Drafting Office, under Commander Streatfield-James, who on one occasion had to swap bodily the ships' companies of two frigates lying alongside each other.

On the 15th August, the sub-continent was divided into two national units, and with it, the Navy. I myself was in New Delhi on Independence Day, and wrote:

> It was impossible for any Englishman (sic) that day to be unaffected by it. To see one's national flag replaced by another is bound to wound one's pride, but the real pleasure, goodwill and enthusiasm of the vast crowds was such that one could feel nothing but goodwill towards them and their future. On all sides, the past was forgotten . . .

The scene has been described so often that there is no point in repeating it. Suffice to say, it was profoundly moving. Alas, the atmosphere was soon to change.

*   *   *

I had agreed to stay another winter in Delhi, for a number of reasons. A harsh winter in post-war England was not a pleasant prospect; I could clock up another year for pension; the world economic situation might become a little clearer and an offer of passages to anywhere in the world, instead of straightforward repatriation to the United Kingdom, was attractive. The pay was good - in real terms I have 'never had it so good', before or since. And, finally, there was so much clearing up to be done at NHQ that I could not really have left with a clear conscience, (at least, so my Journal says). And so, on the 23rd August, I moved into a bungalow in Lodi Road and made all arrangements for the arrival of my wife and infant son. Wihtin two weeks, I was to cable them to cancel their passages.

Arson, looting and murder broke out on the Lodi Estate on the 4th September. On the 7th, while cycling back from breakfast in the Club, (where I was messing), I encountered a company of armed police, deployed along the road and firing sporadically. On reaching the bungalow, I heard that a party of Sikhs had been to demand the surrender of all Muslims. My Christian cook, a timid little man, had bravely lied and so saved the life of my bearer, Lakhi Zeman, who had been a loyal servant and friend throughout my service. But the situation was deteriorating and it was vital to get him to a place of safety without delay. The previous evening, John Lawrence and his wife had asked me to join their household for my remaining time and, after this incident, I at once accepted and moved, together with my followers, (who now included George Bailey's cook and family), to the Chief-of-Staff's house.

It was clear that an organised massacre of Muslims was being attempted, but it was only by chance that we learned that a 'refuge was being formed for Muslims in the vicinity of the Secretariat'. We drove there and found it was true and a pathetic enough sight it was. The first person to catch our eyes was our erstwhile Deputy Financial Adviser, Mirza Khan, sitting on his luggage with a loaded 12-bore. He was badly shaken, but resolute enough. After seeing people killed all around him, he had more or less fought his way there. He must have had assistance as, apart from his family, he had a mountain of luggage and one of the biggest refrigerators I have ever seen. An hour later, we managed to get all our Muslim servants and their families safely behind the wire and protected by troops and, in due course, they were flown to Pakistan.

During this period, we were completely in the dark as to what was happening. No British troops were deployed and no one knew whether or not the Indian and Pakistani units would hold the line. To their credit, they did - had they not done so, the consequences would have been catastrophic. It was quite evident that a lot of nasty things were happening all around us. Food for the refugees was a great problem. I recall going out in a truck with some other British officers to an area which had been attacked, in order to 'loot' abandoned houses for provisions. It was a very dark night - there were lots of bodies lying around, but we only got one bag of rice.

Following this expedition, I thought it might be advisable to remove my beard - after all, I did not particularly wish to be mistaken for a Sikh, (unlikely), or a Muslim, (quite possible). Being sleepless in the early hours, I decided to do the deed then and there. Unfortuantely, the mirror in my room was extraordinarily high and I had to climb on to a stool to see what I was doing. I slipped and fell with a great crash and, within seconds, John Lawrence, clad in a towel, was in the room fully equipped to 'repel boarders' - he hadn't been able to sleep either!

Slowly, some sort of order was, at length, restored. A huge concourse of Muslims was held in the protection of the Red Fort - a tragic and unforgettable sight. Events overshadowed our work, such as it was, and Partition slowly, almost of its own accord, passed into fact and reality. The Service which I had known and loved was no more and, with nothing more to offer, I left in October 1947.

A few months later, I found myself building a house of mud and grass in the middle of a piece of Africa and entering into a new and absorbing period of my life. I had not applied, like many of my contemporaries, for transfer to the Royal Navy, because I foresaw post-war retrenchment and stagnation. This, too, I thought would occur in India - how wrong I was. I have no regrets about the course I chose, but looking at the great and efficient Indian Navy of today, I cannot but feel that I missed something by not staying on to help build on the foundations which we had laid.

7

In the Royal Indian Navy

H Murray-Clark

In 1935, the RIN (recently promoted again to Navy from Marine), found itself short of officers, in spite of its small size, after earlier parsimony, and advertised in the British Press for RNR officers to apply for commissions as Lieutenant. Shipping was having a slump at that time and there were some 200 applicants. I was fortunate to be the first of four selected - two old Pangbournians; one old Worcester and one old Conway.

HMIS INDUS, (Commander EM Bayfield, RN), a new UK built sloop, modified GRIMSBY class, armed with two 4.7" QF guns, was completed and worked up in time to attend King George V's Jubilee Review at Spithead. Three of us new Lieutenants joined her for watch-keeping duties and she sailed for India on 29th July 1935.

In Aden, we had just finished painting ship, (both hull and upperworks), ready for her first appearance in her Home port, when out of a clear sky, came one of those swishing sand storms with gusts that lifted camels and cars and left the ship looking like a piece of pumice stone. The poor First Lieutenant, (Lieutenant Commander John Hall, later Rear-Admiral), managed to inspire the ship's company to rub down and re-do in the short time available.

There was only one other 'proper' warship in the RIN Squadron, (as it was called); this was another sloop, HINDUSTAN, the remainder being ex-Despatch Vessels or similar. There is an apocryphal story that Admiral Bedford, when FOCRIN, taking some guests from England ashore from their liner, turned even pucer when asked by them whose yachts these were. The total fire power was something under ten 4" QF guns of ancient vintage and INDUS's two 4.7s. Promotion appeared to be automatic and experience was inevitably limited. The whole affair was really top heavy with captains and commanders in these small ships and didn't easily make for enthusiasm. However, the Service had had many ups and downs in its varied history since 1612 and there was a feeling that an 'up' was on the way.

Private Ship Cruises were rewarding and interesting; a fairly typical one when I was Navigating Officer of HMIS LAWRENCE, (Commander HC Beauchamp, RIN), was to investigate beaches and anchorages and to show the Flag at and around Cannonore, Tellicherry, Calicut, Alleppy, Colombo, Cuddalore, Pondicherry, (where, optimistically, we hoped to find French cabaret and dancing girls, but found only a gendarme),

Madras, Bimlipatam, Masulipatam, Vizagapatam, (later to become an important naval base), Pudimadaha, Puri, (good surf for whalers to practice beaching), the Dhamra River - (where the CO, some eighteen stone, fell into the fast flowing waters in sword, medals, full dress white uniform, when returning from his call on the Governor of Orissa; there were crocodiles and an early hoist inboard was essential) - some fifteen visits, many of which had never seen a White Ensign ship. Squadron training was usually carried out based on Trincomalee or Karachi and, occasionally, Aden.

The King's Colour was presented to the RIN in December 1935 by HE the Governor of Bombay on behalf of HM the King at a ceremonial parade - a great honour for the Service. A year later and now Gunnery Officer of HMIS LAWRENCE, I was having breakfast in the wardroom, when I read in the newspaper, with some astonishment, that I was to be the Colour Officer and that the ship was providing an armed guard at a parade ashore in two hours time. The signal ordering this had never been passed - both requirements were, however, just met, rather out of breath.

King George V died in January 1936, a very sad day for everyone and for his Navies in particular. I was in Colombo and commanded the combined Navy and Army guard at the Proclamation of King Edward VIII at the State Council Chambers.

There was an annual inter-ship competition in Parade Ground drill for the Platoon Cup. In September 1936, judged by the Second-in-Command of the Punjab Regiment in Karachi, this was won by HMIS LAWRENCE's platoon, under my command.

The two months' leave a year was sometimes theoretical rather than actual, but gave splendid opportunity to see something of the interior of that great country, if one could afford it, on the small naval pay. Journeys across India by train provided a fantastic panorama and experience. One of the best I had was from Bombay to Kandy, Ceylon, via the ferry across the Palk Strait, with its broomstick channel. Another was from Karachi to Quetta, with the cold mountains and whirligig sand spouts.

In 1938, HMIS INDUS, (Commander CL Turbett, OBE, RIN), was given a rush finish to her refit to enable her to join a Naval Force in the Red Sea, at the time of the Italian attacks on Abyssinia. I was pulled out of HMIS CORNWALLIS and appointed to INDUS as First Lieutenant for a real operation at last. Sadly, it all fizzled out.

Normal service in Indian waters was three years and then UK leave and, usually, courses. Nobody seemed able to decide whether I should specialise in Gunnery or Navigation; it was not one's own choice. I had been Assistant Squadron Gunnery Officer some four months earlier. I remember a visiting Admiral, who had travelled to the UK in the same P & O liner, telling me how appalled he was at the casual way this was dealt with. Actually, my name appeared in the Long (G) course list at about the same time as I was appointed to HMS DRYAD for the long (N) course. I did the latter, which included a training cruise round the UK in HMS ALRESFORD, (Commander I Salter, RN) with a lot of experience in the intricacies of the west coast of Scotland, which were to prove most valuable two years later in the War, when navigational aids were a problem.

After the Long course, I was appointed to HMS SOUTHAMPTON as war broke out - sadly, this appointment was cancelled and I was sent to India to be Senior Officer of a Flotilla of converted coasters as mine - sweepers. Sadly, also, there were no mines and it was never quite clear who might have laid them.

In December 1939, I went searching for a submarine on a camel; first, by RAF Lysander, (four hundred miles), then lorry, (forty miles), camel, (fifteen miles) and footslog in the desert, (two miles), to the vicinity of Pasni, between the entrance to the Persian Gulf and Karachi. This venture was to check up on reports of 'whales with men coming out of them', seen and reported by fishermen. They seemed reasonably authentic and fishermen, as a breed, are reliable and there could conceivably have been an Italian submarine, but I never received any comments on my report.

The first real advance in the RIN was the building of six 'Bird' Class A/S sloops, (later designated Frigates), armed with six 4" HA guns in twin mountings, Radar, fire control, anti-submarine equipment, etc. far more modern than anything previously in the RIN.

I was fortunate to be appointed First Lieutenant of the first of these ships, HMIS SUTLEJ, and in November 1940, I took charge of the naval draft, comprising the Advance parties for the first two ships, taking passage by troopship to the UK. In Durban, I had much pleasure in marching the entire draft of one hundred plus through the streets, laying a wreath on the War Memorial and meeting the Indian community leaders. The NOIC's eyes were on stalks - he had no idea that the sailors were Indian.

HMIS SUTLEJ, (Captain PA Mare, RIN) was commissioned on the Clyde in March 1941, her ship's company of some 205 having been accommodated in a castle on Loch Lomond in the interim. She then worked up from Tobermory and Scapa Flow. The ship made a considerable name for herself and for the Service in the Western Approaches, (Clyde and Irish Sea Escort Forces) and, later, in the South Atlantic Station, Suez Escort Force, Djibouti patrol, China Force and the Arakan. That first ship's company were a splendid body of men.

While in Scapa Flow at about four o'clock one morning, we received a signal from a destroyer nearby 'we are waiting for you to take us to sea' -the first we had heard of any orders for sea and, unbelievably, this was another signal that had not been passed. However, our organisation for emergencies was good and less than half-an-hour later, we led three destroyers and two other escorts out through the Hoxa Gate and into the Western Approaches, to take over a big convoy - in mid-Atlantic from the Tribals, who were whisked away for the SCHARNHORST chase. The RIN became quite well known among the locals in Gourock and Belfast and adjacent bright spots.

In the South Atlantic, after getting to know Sierra Leone and St. Helena, we left with HMS REPULSE and a large military convoy for Simonstown. The dockyard there was too busy to take us and we were sent into East London for boiler cleaning and a week's leave to each watch. Many of us went up country to stay with kind families and places such as King Williamstown, where we learnt the pitfalls of Cape brandy.

While in the Suez Escort Force, we frequently escorted the two Cunard Queens, (operating as troopships); helped put out a fire in the liner GEORGIC and spent a never-to-be-forgotten night in a force ten gale among the coral reefs, (many uncharted), several miles west of the Straits of Jubal, at the southern end of the Gulf of Suez. We were ordered in there to pull a Survey Ship (sic) off a reef on which she had grounded and bent a shaft. We were in the process of pulling this shaft out of the ship, with a maze of wires between us, when the sudden gale struck.

As part of the China Force, SUTLEJ was closely involved with the last stages of the fall of Singapore in February 1942 and the Netherlands East Indies. Our time in this depressing era included escorting the last troop convoy into Singapore Roads, during which the HT EMPRESS OF ASIA was, (not surprisingly), bombed and burnt out. We managed to remove all her depth charges and primers from her after rail and get clear before her mainmast crashed over the side where the rope ladder was. We picked up a number of soldiers and sent them ashore to fight the last battle in Singapore, dressed in such clothing as we could raise from stores, officers' cabins and the scran bag.

In the confusion of those last days, when the Japs were on the Island, it proved impossible to find replenishment 4" HA ammunition and, when we finally left, evacuating the Naval Communication Staff and some very gallant RAF pilots and RN Coastal Forces to Tanjong Priok in Java, we had less than 50% of our outfit - and even less soon after! In one air attack, a swarm of what must have been Japanese bees attacked X mounting's crew, much to their discomfiture, but with no consequent loss of accuracy.

A theoretically impossible radar achievement occurred in the vicinity of Bangka Island. We suddenly started getting blips on the 285 gunner ranging radar set on bearings all round the ship. There were no ships and no aircraft in sight and, not long afterwards, we established that we were in the middle of an enemy minefield, out of which we gently eased our way. Only one surfaced mine was seen.

After refitting in Colombo, SUTLEJ became involved in the continuing depressing retreat up the Burma coast, when the Army showed much gallantry and suffered many losses. Rangoon was captured by the Japs but naval patrols continued just north of this and SUTLEJ oversaw the evacuation of Kyaukpyu. HMIS INDUS was sunk by aircraft while SUTLEJ was trying to obtain oil fuel in Chittagong on a Sunday. A Japanese heavy task force, including aircraft carriers, attacked shipping in the Bay of Bengal.

Among all the setbacks and tragedies of the fall-back operations in Malaya and Burma, there were a few lighter moments. A Burma ML thought she saw a Japanese cruiser entering Ramree Harbour one night and told the rest of her group, up a chaung, (narrow creek) to prepare to scuttle their MLs and escape overland unless this signal was cancelled by a certain time, the code word for which was to be 'Bottle of Whisky'. The

ML then discovered that the Jap cruiser was, in fact, SUTLEJ, but her W/T then broke down and a very worried MLCO came on board. SUTLEJ was able to make the cancellation signal just in time, but the codeword in plain language caused some repercussions with the Commander-in-Chief.

I then had some unwanted period ashore in war, as Commander of RIN Barracks and Depot in Bombay, (during part of which I was still only a substantive Lieutenant), where there were often well over 2,000 men. As a supplementary to this, my specialist (N) qualification was utilised by making me Staff (N) Officer, the main duties being correcting HM Ships' compasses, (which I had always regarded as incomprehensible black magic), and, on one magnificent occasion, going to sea in the Greek Battleship, GEORGIOS AVEROFF, to carry out full power trials, this entailed the sprinkling with holy water by her Greek orthodox 'Chaplain', who walked all round the ship as we went to sea - what a nice custom.

I was next appointed, in 1943, to command another of the new sloops, HMIS JUMNA, the first officer of below substantive Commander's rank to be given one of these new ships - the more junior officer was at last coming into his own in sea command. Among my officers was a certain Sub-Lieutenant Stanley Dawson, RINVR, who has had such an outstanding career and is now (1984), Chief of Naval Staff, India. JUMNA was adopted by the Meerut Division of the United Provinces and a good liaison was established through the Commisssioner, Mr Baynes.

As part of the East Indies Escort Force, JUMNA was first operating as Senior Officer of a Group comprising HM Ships PATHFINDER, PENN and FLAMINGO, escorting troop convoys to Burma in the Bay of Bengal. At a later date, when Senior Officer of another group with HM Ships IPSWICH and LAUNCESTON, a submarine attack on her convoy developed and a Blue Funnel Line ship was hit by torpedoes. Depth charge attacks were carried out by JUMNA and the other escorts and these resulted in the sinking of the submarine, which was later established as the Japanese RO110. I recall carrying out a burial service, (one of the crew of the torpedoed ship), over the starboard quarter while an MTB disembarked wounded over the port quarter and the ship's company remained at Action Stations in case there was still any life in the sunken submarine.

After JUMNA and until the end of the war, (still as an Acting-Commander), I was in Combined Operations, training Army divisions in landing procedures and Naval crews and specialist parties in their functions, and then the operations retaking the Arakan coast in Burma from the Japs, (where I had earlier been when we were retreating).

The RIN Landing Craft Wing, (what a strange word to have chosen - anything less like a bird or an aircraft than a Landing Craft would be difficult to imagine), had to be formed by converting a number of Indian Army battalions to this naval function, basic training being given at Mandapam in South India. These men, mostly Punjabi Muslims, were excellent, of long fighting tradition and proved very adaptable to their entirely new role. I first commanded HMIS HAMLAWAR, a Combined Operations Training Establishment alongside a Commando Unit, (with a splendid CO who was to become one of my best friends), at Marve on the west coast. Some three months later, I took the Flotillas' crews and other teams by special train across India, (route marches and PT on the way), to Coconada on the east coast. Here, I assumed command of HMIS JEHANGIR, an operational work-up base spread around the beaches and the little harbour, where the Naval and Army personnel were to prepare for the re-taking of the Arakan.

At the end of 1944 I moved with all these flotillas and special parties to the Arakan, where they were joined by some Royal Marine Flotillas and operations began. Most of the Flotillas were LCA and LC Ms, with a few LCPL, LCR and LCN. The parties included LC Recovery Units, Beach Signals, Beach Commandos, Engineer repair units etc. My appointment was designated SO Landing Craft Arakan, later changed to SO, LC Bases, Burma.

All sorts of ships and craft were involved, as in Europe, from battleships to dinghies. The small craft were operating in mangrove swamps and many miles up the maze of chaungs. The route taken by landing craft was usually marked at junctions by hanging bumf in the trees on the banks, Army maps were the only charts available and the Army believed that everything that floated, from frigate to dinghy, could go where the map was coloured blue. One of my most frightening moments was finding myself among a vast number of mules in pitch darkness, all lashing out with their hind legs, when I had to walk, (sorry - march) overland from one chaung to another in, I think, Operation Turret.

A full and much wider story of these operations and the gallant part played by so many forces and units and individuals of the Navies, Armies and Air Forces of the Commonwealth and the Allies has been written elsewhere. The main ingredients were probably ingenuity, resolution, a sense of humour and the usual quota of courage. So far as the RINLC Wing was concerned, I have personal letters from the Commander-in-Chief, Allied Land Forces, SE Asia and from the 15th Corps Commander, conveying thanks for the good work and high standards of the RIN Landing Craft crews. There were congratulatory letters and signals from Admiral Mountbatten, General Auchinleck and Army and Corps Commanders to the Flag Officer Commanding, Royal Indian Navy.

Tremendous credit must also be given to the maintenance personnel, particularly the Engineer EOs, a splendid group of men, who somehow kept these elderly and decrepit craft operational, sometimes literally with bits of string. It was always a joy to see the specialist teams, such as the LC Recovery Units, with their huge and ponderous equipment, turn up at a crucial moment.

By April, the Arakan was rid of the Japanese. Meanwhile, the Pacific war was striding on and, later, the atomic bombs brought the end of the war against Japan and VJ Day. On the 1st December 1945, a Navy Day Peace Parade was held in Bombay, which I commanded. Some 500 officers and Ratings from many ships and shore establishments took part. the parade was inspected by Admiral Godfrey, Flag Officer Commanding, Royal Indian Navy and then marched past.

The mutiny was a sad footnote to the advance and achievements during the testing time of war, when the manpower shortcomings in the Service were so well filled by the RINR and RINVR and HO ratings, especially in the 'new functions', such as Coastal Forces and Combined Operations, which were virtually all Reservists and Hostilities Only.

It was, I consider, a mixture between a war casualty, growing pains catching up once the restrictions of operations had ceased and the effects of politics and 'Quit India'. I was President of a number of Boards of Enquiry and, early on in these unhappy events, had an unusual experience. I was sent to Lahore to intercept a special train containing a large Naval draft from Karachi, (a fairly violent centre in the mutiny), which had entrained before the mutiny broke out and whose reactions and sentiments were not known - my orders were to assume them to be hostile and to take action accordingly.

On arrival in Lahore, I called on the senior Army Officer, the Lieutenant Colonel commanding the Suffolks, who could not have been more helpful, and asked for a company of armed soldiers to back me at the railway station, preferably, Indian soldiers. This was arranged and I then asked the Railway Authorities to 'fix' the time of arrival for about 0200, instead of 2200 as scheduled, (man at his lowest ebb).

A Company of the Punjab Regiment with small arms was spread behind me out of sight and it didn't take me long to move down the length of the train, ordering everyone to dress and disembark. Considerable surprise at finding a somewhat brisk Commander in the middle of the night in some strange station in the middle of India was the main reaction. There was a little surliness among a few, which was quickly barked out and the hundred or so ratings were soon fallen in and marching to an Army barracks to spend the rest of the night there. They never knew about the armed soldiers and normal discipline was established, with a route march through Lahore to show all and sundry that this was so.

Now that the war was over and plans for the future were coming into being, an important advance in the Fleet was announced. Three 6" gun Cruisers were to be taken over from the RN. In January 1946, I was very proud to be selected as the Commander of the first of these cruisers, ACHILLES and temporarily appointed to the staff of Naval Headquarters in Delhi for planning this major step and finally, sailed for the UK in May. After visits to various RN ships and establishments, I took command of HMS ACHILLES, with a reduced RN ship's company for her refit in Chatham Dockyard. However, all this was sadly not to be for me. Indianisation of the Navy was now very properly accelerating at this time and about six months later, I was relieved by Commander Katari, RIN. Some years later, he came, as a Rear-Admiral, to the RN Training Establishment which I was commanding in Portsmouth.

With the advent of Independence and Partition in August 1947, the division of the RIN into the two separate Navies of India and Pakistan took place. Each Navy then started a considerable programme of expansion, India, before long, having aspired successfully to a Fleet Air Arm and an aircraft carrier, with appropriate surface support.

This advance from the little squadron of small ships at the beginning of the war, to these new and expanding Navies, making full use of the experience of war, was remarkable and says a great deal for the early training by a small number of dedicated officers and senior rates and for the resolution and inspiration of the Indian officers who took over the reins.

Some regular British officers went back to the RN, some stayed for a while with the new Indian and Pakistani Navies and some retired. I went back to the RN as a substantive Commander and was promoted to Captain in June 1953. In my various appointments at sea and ashore I came across new new Navies, born out of the old and was impressed by their spirit and efficiency. I met a number of old friends and was always made welcome.

8

In the Royal Indian Navy
E M Shaw

In January 1937, having served two years as 3rd Officer in Tankers (Anglo-Saxon Petroleum Co - a subsidiary of Shell) I left the MV ANADARA in Thameshaven and had two month's paid leave. I had a few days at home in Penzance and then went to Cardiff to study for my 1st Mate's Certificate. While there, I received a letter from Harry Sykes of the Nautical College, Pangbourne, advising me that the RIN were advertising for Sub-Lieutenants, RNR (which I was).

I wrote to a friend from Penzance, John Cornish, asking him what he thought about the RIN. On receipt of his reply, I decided to apply. I also thought that, with war clouds on the horizon, I would prefer to be in a ship with guns to being in a tanker. In due course, I went up for an interview, held in the old India Office and was confronted by several senior gentlemen and I hadn't a clue as to who they were - I learnt subsequently that one of them was Vice-Admiral Herbert Fitzherbert - FOCRIN designate.

The one question I remember being asked was why did I want to join the RIN. I thought quickly and wondered should I say honour and glory etc, but decided to tell the truth and replied that I thought it was a good job with good prospects. On that occasion it proved the right answer, because, having waited while others were interviewed, I was told I had been accepted on the spot. I was due to sit the exam for my 1st Mate's ticket the following week and so, for the only time in my life, I knew it did not matter if I passed or failed and, of course, in those circumstances I passed.

I was appointed a Sub-Lieutenant in the RIN on the 17th April 1937, with seniority of 1st July 1935 and received £100 uniform allowance. In May, I joined HMS EXCELLENT with No 2 Supplementary Group - all RNR for Subs courses in Gunnery, Signals and Navigation. As the RIN had no torpedoes, I was not able to do that course, which I think came after Gunnery, so I then joined up with No 1 Supplementary Group. John Cornish was in EXCELLENT doing his Long 'G' course and I met up with John Mansell, who was doing a Long 'S' course.

At the time of the Gunnery course, there were five groups of Sub Lieutenants going through and, on passing-out night, there was quite a party. I think the two supplementary groups, being older and having had responsibility at sea, behaved in a more restrained manner - quite a bit of damage was done by the other groups. There was a blackout because someone had removed all the fuses and an order was issued that no one would go on leave until the fuses were replaced. This proved difficult, because the offender had put them down the recently installed flush lavatories and the fuses were well on the way to Portsmouth Harbour. Someone must have bribed an EA to provide new fuses! The following morning, all the subs groups were paraded and a list of the damage and cost was read out - one item I remember was 'Damage to Captain's cucumber frame - 2/6d'.

Included in the Gunnery course was instruction in a 16" turret on board HMS EREBUS. Once up in the turret, one could not be taken by surprise by a visit from a Staff Officer and, consequently, the Gunners' Mates were more relaxed. In addition to the GM Instructor, (PO Smart) there was the Captain of the Turret. We were being taught the misfire drill and PO Smart said 'should the gun misfire, No 4 with great daring will leap out to the carrier arm'. A voice from the background - the Captain of the Turret - 'I'm . . . if I would!' He knew that if it was not a misfire, but merely a hang up and the gun fired at that moment, No 4 would have had to be scraped off the back wall of the turret.

In the West Battery, there were old 6" guns - the broadside guns of the old Battlewaggons and, when trained out, the end of the barrel was out over the grass. At the order 'Action Stations', everyone leapt to, but the layer and trainer, whose duty it was to remove the tompion from the end of the barrel - he leapt out on to the grass to do this. There was a stentorian roar of 'Still' from the Gunner's Mate and everyone froze. He said; 'Only one man ever walked successfully on water - we all knows as how Peter tried hard - Guns crew correct mistake - carry on!'

One of the star attractions at Whale Island was the Night Action Demonstration. Of course, it was all meant to be taken very seriously. We were ushered into the room, where there were a number of VICTORY ordinary seamen. Some of us noticed that the platform on which we were to stand was connected by wire pennants through blocks to the hands of a very burly Gunner's Mate. We found we were tall enough to see over without standing on it. Each of the Gunner's Mates taking part told us his role - Captain, Gunnery Officer, Star Shell Control Officer etc. Then the room was darkened and we were at sea at night. There was a 'realistic' sound of the sea, made by one of the staff turning a canvas-covered drum and varying the pressure of another piece of canvas held over the drum. Suddenly, the peace of the night was broken by the cry 'Alarm Starboard bearing Green 40'. This was immediately followed by 'Make the Challenge', and a split second later by 'No reply–Open Fire'.

There was a blinding flash and a big bang, which was achieved by one of the staff lifting and dropping the iron lid of a case containing some large wattage lamps. At the same time, the GM gave a hefty jerk on the wires to the platform. This was continued until the order was given 'Cease fire - enemy sunk'. Then we were treated to the sight of the enemy ship sinking and Whale Island's little attempt at humour - Davey Jones sitting on his locker waiting! We were not popular for not having taken it all seriously.

Whilst at the Signal School in VICTORY, after lunch one day we were taken into a special room to have the mysteries of a recognition system shown to us. We noticed that, on the lecturer's platform there was a jelly on a plate, some twelve inch in diameter and one-and-a-half inch thick, with a fork stuck in the side and a matchstick in the middle. We asked the Chief Yeoman what on earth this was. He told us that, during the forenoon, the room had been used by the Senior Officers War Course and the jelly was to show them how radio waves travelled - if you waggled the fork, the matchstick in the middle waggled - we **were** impressed.

When we went to do our Navigation course, we all thought we should do well, all of us having 2nd Mate's or 1st Mate's Tickets and considerable experience of taking sights. Our Instructor was Lieutenant Charles Russell, who informed us that he had sat for and passed the examination for Master Mariner - so that put us all in our place. I saw Charles Russell on many occasions later and I still keep in touch with him - now a retired Captain. When it came to the examination at the end of the course, I was very impressed when Charles told us that we could take into the exam any books we liked, because he regarded it as a practical test and in a practical situation we would have textbooks etc with us. However, he added that if we did not know where to look, we would not have time to start thumbing through volumes. This was the most sensible examination I have ever sat.

While at Whale Island, 'Curly' Evans (he was quite bald) and I jointly purchased a Ford Popular, secondhand for £50. It was a semi-diesel - it did about 37 mpg and 50 to a pint of oil. Every 100 miles, one stopped at a garage and when asked how much petrol you wanted, you said 'none - but a quart of oil, please'.

The car served us well and the joint ownership was a success. I drove home to Penzance for a weekend on more than one occasion. But, being a six volt system, the headlights were inadequate and the windscreen wiper was the infamous Ford suction type - the faster you went, the slower the wipers worked.

After a short leave, I went up to Southampton and was seen off by my Mother and Father and Peggy. The last night we went to the Theatre in Southampton. Then on board the Troopship NEURALIA in November 1937 and we sailed for Bombay. Going down Southampton water, my old friend from Pangbourne days, John Sturges, who had left the Merchant Navy and joined the RAF came over in an Anson aircraft and waggled his wings.

I think there were two or three RN Subs on board as well and in the Bay of Biscay, we more or less had the dining saloon to ourselves. However, by the time we passed Gibraltar, everyone had recovered. I palled up with Bill and Peggy Dankes and family. He was then a Captain, RAMC. I kept in touch with them - Bill died some years ago and Peggy died in June 1984.

On the way out, we had a Fancy Dress Dance. Having got to know some of the ship's officers, I borrowed a palm and needle and a boiler gauge glass and scrounged a piece of rope and with these I made ringlets which I sewed on to a borrowed beret. I borrowed a nightie and some ribbon and went as Shirley Temple - the current child star for Hollywood.

I think one of her songs was 'On the good ship Lollipop' - I won a prize. Before arriving in Bombay, there were a succession of drinks parties, before and after dinner. It became quite hectic and alcoholic.

On arrival in Bombay on the 21st December 1937, I was met by Sub-Lieutenant AF King and found that we were both parsons' sons from Cornwall. My father was then at St Johns, Penzance and Arthur's father was at Lezant. Then an odd coincidence - Arthur's father died and my father went to Lezant in May 1939. I was appointed to HIMS CLIVE with Captain Silas Bayfield. At the time, I thought him a very old man - he may have been over fifty. Now that I am seventy, fifty seems to be young. I think that Bill Mager was No 1 and he and Deidre took pity on me on Christmas Day.

One of my first duties was to get my 'visiting cards' made and then go off in No 10's and call on the Governor, the Chief Justice, FOCRIN and all the senior officers in Bombay. Of course, you never saw anyone. At Government House you signed the book and left cards and at senior officers' residences there were boxes marked 'Mrs So and So, Not at Home' and you dropped your cards in these - all part of the Establishment system of the British Raj.

I was in CLIVE until 28th September 1938. During this time the 'Squadron' went down to Karwar with Admiral Fitzherbert flying his flag in CLIVE. (St JAD Garniss was Flag Lieutenant and Squadron signals Officer). At Karwar, we had moored - ie, two anchors and a swivel. The day came for us to leave and the Squadron were to weigh together. CLIVE had problems with the mooring swivel and there was much wrath.

With the Squadron in Karachi, a Board was constituted to examine Sub-Lieutenants for Lieutenant. The Board were the Commanding Officers of INDUS, HINDUSTAN and LAWRENCE and did **not** include the senior Captain - Captain Bayfield of CLIVE. The Sub-Lieutenants from INDUS, HINDUSTAN and LAWRENCE all passed - those from CLIVE, including myself, all failed. Only in later years did I learn of the great animosity between Captain Bayfield and the other CO's - I wonder if there was a connection between this and our failing?

There were many happy times in Karachi, going up in cutters and whalers for picnics at Manora with the local lasses. I remember one night in the Gymkhana Club - it was late - and I was asked to sign a chit for Rs.5 for a broken glass top on a table. Next day at lunch time, some Americans we had been with the night before came on board for a drink. I said I was surprised at what had happened. It was an old trick of holding a tumbler and hitting a table and the glass does not break. Said the American, 'I don't think it works quite so well with a pewter tankard on a glass top table!' - he was right.

It must have been in August 1938 that Fitzherbert took the Squadron up to the Persian Gulf and off Bahrein he decided that there was a need for up-to-date information on the turning circles of the ships. This information was acquired by an officer sitting in a whaler, with a sextant, taking angles while the ship steamed round. Those of us who had to sit in the whalers thought it was an over-rated form of sport, in that in that heat our knees got very sun-burnt. Although the ship was not air-

81

conditioned, the Admiral was able to sit in the comparative cool of his cabin and drink his gin and tonic before lunch.

The Squadron was in Karachi at the time of the Munich crisis and great activity ensued. All hands set to and the yellow funnel and white upperworks and ship's side were soon covered with Admiralty grey. The RIN sloops would never look the same again.

We all returned to Bombay and, on the 29th September 1938, I joined HMIS LAWRENCE as Navigator and Signals Officer. HMS Choudri was First Lieutenant. I was only there three months and on the 1st January 1939, I took up the appointment of Executive Officer, Barracks. This caused some problems because there were other officers in the Depot who were senior to me; but I was the Executive Officer. However, I think everything went smoothly, with goodwill on all sides.

On the 3rd May 1939, I joined HMIS HINDUSTAN as First Lieutenant (the Captain was Philip Mare - a great Victorian gentleman). HGP Taylor was the Engineer Officer; John Gibbs was Navigator and Roland Williams was GO. Philip Mare was a great and memorable character, always most courteous. At dinner parties on board, the guests would be offered a glass of sherry, then wine at dinner and, after dinner, Philip would suggest playing Hohenzollern - a complicated card game, which took some time to explain to the uninitiated. Then time for one game and Philip would explain that, while he didn't wish to hurry anyone, we all had to be up early in the morning and that was that.

We visited Port Blair in the Andaman Islands - a penal settlement. I was told that a new British Resident who visited the barber and was being shaved with a cut-throat razor, learned afterwards that the barber was serving a sentence for having murdered somebody by cutting his throat. While there, I purchased a nest of six little tables, each made of a different local wood, for £1. They are still in daily use.

We went on to the Mergui Archipelago. There was a special confidential chart of this area, as it was a protected Fleet anchorage. We tried seine net fishing there, but without much success. One of the residents was an original beachcomber - a Britisher who had taken unto himself and wed a local lady who had borne him two beautiful daughters. Mother professed to speak no English, but we quickly found she understood most of what we said. They had got married a few years before and we were told that the daughters, who must then have been in their late teens, did not see the humour in being bridesmaids.

We had a nasty accident there. We were hoisting the motor cutter when the hand on the after fall let it slip off the drum of the winch and the boat was left suspended by the forward fall with gratings etc falling into the sea and a strong tidal stream running. Fortunately, the coxswain in the boat managed to grab the forward fall and hold on.

We went on and visited Penang before returning to Trincomalee to join up with the other ships of the Squadron. I can't remember what I did or what someone else had done, but for some reason known or unknown, NHQ decided that I was to leave HINDUSTAN as No 1 and join INDUS on 23rd July 1939 as Navigator and Signals Officer - a demotion. As it transpired, this did not last long.

The crisis was getting nearer. After lunch one day, there was a signal for all Commanding Officers to repair on board CLIVE forthwith. On their return, we learned that we were to sail for Bombay 'with despatch'. HMS LIVERPOOL was at Trincomalee and Charles Russell was her Navigator. He was to have come to lunch the next day. We sailed and that evening we decyphered a signal ordering LIVERPOOL to sail forthwith with all despatch for Masirah. The next afternoon, we were south of Ceylon when LIVERPOOL hove in sight. What a sight - doing about thirty knots. Her 10" SP started flashing. It was a signal for me from Charles Russell: 'Sorry I am late for lunch. May I come to tea?'

Steaming up the west coast of India, we sighted a German merchant ship, but war had not been declared so we could do nothing. She went into the Portuguese port of Goa and was there for the duration. We arrived in Bombay on the 30th August 1939 and on the 31st August, I joined CLIVE as First Lieutenant, with Captain Hughes-Hallet in command. War was declared on the 3rd September 1939. We heard the declaration over the radio and all wondered what the future would hold for us. We sailed from Bombay, straight out into the south west monsoon and, when I went up on to the bridge to take over the watch, I seemed to be the only one not affected by seasickness and I prayed that we would not have to go into action that night.

We had a few problems with darkening ship and, as can be imagined, with no air-conditioning, the atmosphere in the messdecks was pretty stuffy, to put it mildly. We were bound for Masirah Island, (which we nicknamed 'Base Q'). If Italy had come into the war immediately, this was to have been our NCSO base.

Our first task on arrival was to dan buoy a swept channel. I think we carried two proper dan buoys, so we had to use our imagination and made up an oddly assorted lot. We had been warned that the natives on the island might not be friendly and could not be relied on, so, when we landed recreational parties, Verey pistols were carried, but in the event never had to be used.

After a fairly short spell there, during which a tanker was diverted to refuel us, we left and went up to Khor Kwai, to patrol the Straits of Ormuz. This proved fairly monotonous. However, I was fascinated when boarding a dhow from Zanzibar to see their lack of navigational facilities. We relied on the BI slow Gulf boats, (the 'B' class), to bring us supplies and mail from Bombay and we used to divert a tanker into Elphinstone Inlet for refuelling. This is alleged to be the hottest place on earth, it being like a Norwegian fjord and the sun beating down and being reflected from the sides. At one time there had been a cable station there and the story goes that one of the operators went mad in the heat and murdered the other operator.

Our Navigator was Jacques Bayliss and he drew pilotage money for taking the tankers in. However, under CNA regulations, he could only draw this for six trips, so when it came to the seventh time, I went, and on boarding the Shell tanker, found the Chief Officer was the man who had relieved me when I left Shell in January 1937. I asked the Captain whether he wished to entrust his vessel to me, or did he prefer to take her in himself. He wisely decided on the latter course, but I was still able to draw my pilotage money.

I rejoined CLIVE in Aden and we must at some stage have gone back to Khor Kwai, because we were suddenly ordered to 'proceed forthwith' to Aden and, as the BI was due the next day, we were low on food. So the Chief Bosun was sent ashore to buy goats from the Headman on Khor Kwai. These were brought back on board, with a supply of fodder and slaughtered as required on our way to Aden. Months later, we received an objection statement from the Controller of Naval Accounts, taking us to account for the price we had paid compared with the market price in Bombay. In Aden, we met up with CORNWALLIS, HINDUSTAN and INDUS at different times.

We went on the Perim Patrol, steaming up and down day and night and identifying every ship that passed. As Hughes-Hallett's First Lieutenant, I had a permanent middle watch. He would not trust anyone junior and didn't trust me very much. I did have one alarming experience. At about 0030, we were steaming south - darkened ship and showing no navigation lights. I had two vessels in sight, one on each bow. The one on the port bow was, I thought, much closer than the one coming up on the starboard side and the signalman called up the one on the port bow. I was watching for her reply when I glanced to starboard and suddenly realised that, whilst the vessel to port had full navigation lights on, the one to starboard had dimmed navigation lights and was very close. I switched on our navigation lights full and held my breath. The shaded stern light of the ship to port illuminated our ship's side as she passed. By the time Hughes-Hallett appeared, we were clear and I was breathing again, although my knees were still shaking. A post-mortem was held and he retired to his cabin. By 0330, I was beginning to recover my self-composure, when he re-appeared on the bridge again and we had a second post-mortem. It must have been after that that we returned to Bombay for boiler cleaning and docking and Hughes-Hallett left and Dick Inigo-Jones came in command. I got on well with him and life became much easier.

HMIS HINDUSTAN was in at the capture of Massawah, (Geoffrey Beamish in command and JE Gibbs was either No 1 or Navigator) and we were there later in CLIVE on mine clearance. Initially, INDUS was sweeping and we were dan-laying and sinking swept mines. The local Indians thought we were mad. They said, 'we never work in July and August - we always go to Asmara, to the hills'. The fact that there was war on and that we were clearing a channel for troopships taking the 4th Indian Division from Massawah to the Middle East failed to impress them.

We used to start at 0600 and at first the breeze we made by steaming was pleasant, but not for long. We went on all day until 1800 and as soon as we had anchored there was no breeze at all. If one turned in sober one lay in a bath of perspiration and could not sleep; if one turned in drunk one felt awful next morning, so one had to get the quantity of alcohol just right to ensure a night's sleep.

One day, we were joined by RATNAGIRI, (Karmarkar in command) so both INDUS and CLIVE were sweeping in formation and RATNAGIRI was dan-laying, Both Inigo and I thought RATNAGIRI was laying the dans outside our sweep, but perhaps it was an optical illusion. However, next day RATNAGIRI having departed, we were picking up her dan buoys. I was up forward just ready to lift a dan on the port bow when Ronnie Edwards shouted from the bridge and pointed to the starboard bow. We just had way on and, as I glanced over the starboard bow, there was a nice horned mine about six feet away. We all moved aft at a very high speed, with the engines going full astern. When we re-swept the area, up came three mines and the dan buoy.

On another occasion, we left Massawah to sweep ahead of, I think, the BI KENYA, loaded with troops. Having got to the sweep out, all seemed well. However, by the time I had got up to the bridge, Inigo said, 'where is the float?'

I went aft quickly and found the sweep wire twanging like a harp. We slowed down and started to winch in the sweep, with everyone standing well clear of the wire. The winch was groaning and one could see movement on the holding down bolts. Then the water looked as if it were boiling and there was something black under the water. What we had swept up was a Blenheim Bomber which had crashed into the sea and was upside down, with the undercarriage down. We hauled this close up under the stern and could see that the sweep wire was jammed between the axle and the undercarriage. So we had to rig a slip wire and take the weight on that, in order to release the sweep wire. Not something one could do hurriedly and Inigo was pressing me to be quick because we had to get the troopship out through the swept channel before dark. I wonder how many tons weight was on that sweep wire when we were hauling in.

After the Perim Patrol and long before the Massawah minesweeping, we went from Aden over to Djibouti, shortly before its fall. Three-pounder guns had been taken out of some ships and sent over for use as anti-tank weapons. We carried over an assortment of small arms ammunition. Some of the boxes fell apart and we were amazed to find that they contained not one size of ammunition, but a complete mixture. We also loaded on the quarter-deck some drums about ten feet long and two feet in diameter and had no idea of their contents. In Djibouti, the easiest way to unload them was to take down the guard rails on the quarter-deck and place long planks from the ship down to the jetty and roll them off. In the meantime, there was an Italian reconnaissance plane flying overhead. As one of these cylinders hit the ground, the end came off, revealing that each contained some 48 kilo incendiary bombs. While all this was going on, we had sent Jacques Bayliss, who spoke French fluently, ashore with the mess wine funds. He returned with some cases of pink champagne, for which he had paid I think Rs. 3 (4/6d) a bottle. This we decided to keep until there was a suitable occasion to celebrate.

On our return to Aden, we were told we were to proceed to Suez, taking with us aviation spirit in cans on the quarter-deck, to be put ashore on the island of Kamaran, where there was a small airstrip; Rs. 20,000 for the Levee at Jeddah, who were threatening to mutiny because they had not been paid and the documents from the captured Italian submarine GALLILEO GALLINI, for GHQ Cairo.

I was much happier when we got rid of the aviation spirit. We duly handed over the cash, which had been stowed in one of the magazines, at Jeddah and so on to Suez. We decided our safe arrival there was a suitable occasion for a celebration, so we opened up the pink champagne. Inigo-Jones had gone ashore to report to NOIC. He came back and joined the party and told us that an officer had to take the documents to GHQ Cairo. An official car would be provided and whoever went could either come straight back in the car, or spend the night in Cairo and pay his own way back next day. We diced to see who should go and to my amazement, I was the lucky one. By the time I left, I must have drunk the best part of a bottle of champagne. I went up to Navy Office after lunch and found they were not ready for me, so went into the French Club to wait and, while there, I met Captain Williams, MN of the NCSO, who said he would come with me. So, off to Cairo with the documents. (I did not have to sign for them; we found GHQ and I did demand a receipt.)

I knew that a very old friend of mine, Maureen Meredith, was in Cairo. Her husband was in the 22 Rajputs. I didn't know her address. I asked if the Regiment was in Cairo. A pongo (nautical term for soldier) went away to make enquiries and came back and said that they were not in Cairo - all I wanted to know - and then went on to tell me exactly where they were in the Western Desert - so much for security. Williams and I went to Sheppards Hotel and, later in the evening after dinner, I suddenly spotted Maureen sitting at a nearby table. Her military escort was quite surprised at our reunion.

Williams and I returned to Suez the next day and HMIS CLIVE became half of the northern Red Sea Escort Force, the other half being HMS GRIMSBY - a very chummy ship. We used to take a convoy half way down the Red Sea and rendezvous with the northbound convoy and the much larger escort from the South. About seven days out and seven in Suez. We had some good lunch time sessions in GRIMSBY. The Officers' Steward - I think called Petty Officer Parker - had done his twelve months as a seaman and been re-engaged as an Officers' Steward. We used to have 'Loader Drill' - a deck mop being used as the combined sponge and rammer, a loaf of bread as the projectile and Parker operating the pantry hatch as the breach of the gun. Quite a high rate of firing was achieved. Ferdie Brown was the CO - no sense of humour or imagination. On one occasion, we realised he was watching our antics through the skylight.

The instructions on air raids were that the Navy should not open fire, but leave the defence of Suez to the AA batteries. After one air raid, some snyde remarks were made by the bright young things in the French Club about the Navy not having fired. Of course, CLIVE only had close range weapons, but GRIMSBY had her 4" HA/LA guns and took these remarks to heart. GRIMSBY was lying stern on to the wall when the next raid occurred at about 0530 one morning. She fired seventy-eight rounds per gun and shattered all the glass in the end window of the Port Trust Workshop. The 'Doc' of GRIMSBY was a great character and had been ashore, returning on board at about 0400. He came into the wardroom for breakfast about 0930 and eventually it dawned on him that the others were talking about an air raid and he innocently asked 'What air raid?' He had slept through the whole raid in his cabin down below 'X' turret.

Early in the month, we would go ashore in the evenings to the Casino, which was a wooden structure on piers out over the water. We never thought it would be hit, but some time after we left, we heard it suffered a near miss and the whole thing collapsed like a pack of cards. On several occasions, at the end of the evening when one called for the bill, there was a shortage of cash. so one sent for the Manager and signed an IOU. This was all right until the end of the month came.

On other evenings, Inigo would come down to the wardroom about 1800 to listen to the news on the radio. When that was finished, Inigo would ask around if anyone was going ashore and when it was found we were all staying on board, we would settle down, having dinner later. Once, we had dinner on the wrong day (most unfair on the wardroom Stewards).

There were two squadrons of Wellington Bombers based at Ismalia and we got to know many of their crews. One squadron was commanded by Squadron Leader Jimmy Wilde - wild by name and wild by nature. He gave a marvellous impression of Hitler addressing the Reichstag. One evening, I had been with him in the Hotel Misr in Suez. On the steps were big brass bowls containing aspidistras and as we left, Jimmy ordered me to pick up one of these and take it into the taxi. On arrival at the dock gates, Jimmy decided that it was unseemly for me to carry it back to the ship and told the 'boy' with the driver to carry it. However, the policeman objected to the boy entering the Dock area. After some discussion, a compromise was reached. I led the procession, followed by Jimmy; followed by the 'boy' carrying the aspidistra, followed by the policeman - the gate must have been left unattended while this was going on.

These Wellingtons used to go out and bomb Bengazhi and other targets when there was no moon. At first, during periods of moonlight, the crews used to go on leave to Cairo, but the novelty soon wore off and it was expensive. So we started 'Strength through Joy' cruises. We would take four or five officers on our trip down the Red Sea and back. One of the officers gave a talk to the ship's company, who were thrilled and astounded to find that this man had actually bombed Berlin.

In return for our 'Strength through Joy' cruises, they took us for flights in the Wellingtons. I went up one day with Inigo-Jones and George William Forrest. Inigo said he would like to see Suez Bay, which was crowded with ships, from 8,000 feet and it was surprising how much open water there was between the ships. Having done that, the pilot then took us down the Suez Canal, (without a Canal Pilot), at about twenty to thirty feet - most interesting.

The Rear Gunners in these Wellingtons were quite remote from the rest of the crew and sitting on a bicycle saddle for an eight-hour trip was monotonous. We were told that some of them took empty beer bottles with them, which they threw out over their target in Germany because they made a nice whistling sound going down.

The mental strain on these Rear Gunners can be imagined. One of them, who was a lawyer in peace time, was in the Ismalia Club one evening and had had a few when he fell off his stool. The rather pompous and officious Naval Provost Marshal witnessed this and the unfortunate man was court-martialled for 'conduct unbecoming'. He arranged for another lawyer in the squadron to be the accused's friend. Many of the rest had a bacon and egg party before attending the Court-Martial. When the Provost Marshall gave evidence, he said the accused had fallen off his stool. 'Yes', said the accused's friend, 'but how?' There were many ways of falling off a stool and he insisted that the Provost Marshall gave a demonstration of exactly what had happened - much to the amusement of all the other officers. I think the Rear Gunner was reprimanded.

In Suez, we went into dry dock for a quick bottom clean. George Watson, (EO) and I both had beards and both wore white boiler suits. This caused confusion with the Egyptians and I was frequently addressed as 'Mr Chief'. When we were first in Suez, Inigo also had a beard, but he decided that the grey flecks in it were bad for his image.

On one occasion, after the Golf Club dance, at which I had had an argument with the Adjutant of the 3rd Rajputs, the Colonel came down on the Sunday morning, saying I had insulted the Regiment - utter nonsense - and Inigo had upset one of the senior ladies (who had a bit of a pash on him), by not having turned up at her cocktail party, which, she said, she had given in his honour. So both sat down to write our respective apologies and Inigo summoned his Steward, Mascarenhas, and said 'Do arsemi lao', (two Horses Necks) to assist us.

After we left Suez, we went back to Massawah. At about this time, Inigo Jones left us and Rob Caws came in command. In passing, when I got my 2nd Mate's ticket, I joined the SS PALUDINA, (anglo-saxon part of Shell), and the Master was Gerry Caws - Rob was his brother. Prior to the war, Rob had spent some years seconded from the RIN to the Port Trust at Karachi. On his return to the Service, it was evident that he had lost none of his skill - he was a most magnificent seaman.

We were off Massawah and the ship had a very foul bottom; we were down to little more than seven knots at full power and, one day, we were getting under way and Rob ordered 'Half ahead starboard; half astern port'. The Bosun's Mate 'repeated' this as 'Half ahead port; half astern starboard'. Rob, in his laconic way said 'Have it your own way, Fred - it doesn't matter - it's like trying to navigate a half tide rock'.

I got near to heat exhaustion, but after spending a night in the air-conditioned hospital in Massawah, I was able to rejoin CLIVE and return to Aden. Here we were briefed for the assault on Assab. The flag-ship was a cruiser - AJAX, I believe. She had been bombed in the Mediterranean and A and B turret had been struck and one of the guns was sticking up in the air. Prior to the assault, we went up to Kamaran and liased with the RAF there, who were flying Wapitis, (open cockpit). Their crews came on board and had a drink and said they would see us next day at Assab.

We sailed from Kamaran and rendezvoused with the rest of the assault force and went in at dawn. I think HINDUSTAN,(or INDUS) was sweeping and we in CLIVE were dan-laying. Just as we were trying to lay a dan buoy, our RAF friends came over at mast-top height, taking off their Bombay Bowlers and waving to us. The ship's company were more interested in this than in laying the dan buoy.

Before the assault, the latest intelligence report was that the garrison was not more than 100 strong. Before sunset that day, the Army were celebrating having captured their 1,000th prisoner.

On one of our visits to Aden, we found HMS ANSON there, making every effort to let everyone know that she was HMS ANSON. In fact, she was the old radio-controlled HMS CENTURION, which had been mocked up to look like ANSON, which was still building. Conditions on board were very spartan and she only carried a skeleton crew. The inhabitants of Aden had a great surprise when one of her 14" gun-barrels went over the side and floated.

Another episode in which CLIVE was involved was the capture of Cape Guardafui and the restoration of the lighthouse, while Inigo-Jones was in command. We started off by sailing south to a port north of Mogadishu. And, having anchored, Inigo went ashore with an armed guard to negotiate with the Port Commandant. Inigo was in his office, telling him that a large force was approaching inland and a naval force was on the way and suggested that they should surrender. At that moment, three ancient bi-planes, on their last few hours of flying time, came down low overhead, but invisible to the Port Commandant. That clinched the matter - he surrendered.

The force coming from inland duly arrived, (MUSCOL) - a very mixed bag of Africans, Arabs etc, under the command of Major Musgrave, who in peacetime had been in Burma in oil. They embarked in HMS KING GRUFYD - a 'Q' Ship, (merchant ship with guns under cover). A meeting took place on board CLIVE to discuss the Guardafui operation. I was away dealing with some matters ashore and when I returned I found I had been detailed off as Forward Observation Officer to land with MUSCOL. The Navigator, Jacques Bayliss, had said obviously he couldn't go and George Forrest as Gunnery Officer couldn't and Jonathan Dixon, as a junior VR officer couldn't - so it had to be me.

On our way back, we pored over the charts and went through the Admiralty Pilot and noted a landing place marked on the charts. We arrived off the nearest fishing village to Guardafui during the night and closed in just as dawn was breaking. I was in charge of the landing operation and was in CLIVE's motor cutter, towing our two whalers full of troops, followed by the boats from KING GRUFYD. When I was very close to the recommended landing place, a cove at the eastern end of the beach, I suddenly saw a pinnacle rock in the middle so we withdrew hurriedly and eventually the locals co-operated with their boats and took us all ashore through the surf. I had a Leading Signalman from CLIVE with me - sadly, I can't remember his name. Having got everyone ashore, we then started the climb up some 800 feet through soft sand to reach the plateau. Of course, all in MUSCOL were very fit and used to this sort of thing, but for me, having lived a comfortable life on board, it was extremely testing. We had made the top by mid-day - it was extremely hot and the only vegetation were giant thorn bushes. Fortunately, no bombardment was necessary, so I did not have to act as FOO.

The Italians were down below in a ravine and Musgrave said it would have taken a Brigade to flush them out. However, the old Italian colonel had lost interest in the war and decided on an honourable surrender. While this was going on, Flight Lieutenant Cox, who was unfit for flying duties, went off with a few men and got the lighthouse in action again. Unfortunately, at about 1400 I succumbed to heat exhaustion and Musgrave said that my Leading Signalman and I were to make our way back independently to the beach and CLIVE. In the early evening, we came across a Bedouin encampment, who saluted and said 'Viva Il Duce'. We tried to explain that that was now all over. They gave us some goats' milk and, in the circumstances, it tasted like nectar. I think it was the most welcome drink I have ever had in my life. As night came, it was dangerous to be down in the sand - eventually we got back on board.

The Italian POW's were embarked in KING GRUFYD and we had a few officers on board for the passage back to Aden. We explained that we did not have a lot of food on board and they would have to share what there was with us. In due course, we received an objection statement from the Controller of Naval Accounts, asking under what authority and on what ration scale we had fed the Italian officers. To my astonishment, we received the following signal:-

SECRET. OPERATIONS DANTE, GUARDAFUI.
From: Senior Officer, Red Sea Force.
Date: 24 July 1941.
To: Commanding Officer HMIS CLIVE (R) C in CEI

The Commander-in-Chief, East Indies Station has requested that an expression of his commendation may be conveyed to Lieutenant EM Shaw RIN for the part he played in the operations leading to the capture of Guardafui lighthouse and the clearing up of the north east corner of Italian Somaliland.

R N C Hallifax
Rear Admiral

I felt a bit of a fraud and did not think I deserved it.

On the 9th July 1941, I received a signal informing me that I had been selected for the Long 'S' course in January 1942. On the 31st July, this was amended to April 1942. CLIVE returned to Bombay in November 1941 and I went ashore to the Signal School, awaiting passage. I sailed from Bombay in the WINDSOR CASTLE on the 6th January 1942.

We called at Capetown and Trinidad to refuel. During a run ashore, we were in a taxi and passing a hockey match in progress. I produced my whistle from my pocket and blew it. The hockey match stopped - the players looked at the referee and the referee looked bewildered - we continued our tour in the taxi.

We then sailed unescorted for the Clyde. While on passage, the other naval officers of Lieutenant rank did duty as extra watchkeepers. Captain John Lawrence was also taking passage and we had a draft of RIN ratings on board. We arrived in the Clyde on a bitterly cold morning and the RIN ratings were first of all kept hanging about on deck and then aboard the tender and, by the time we got them ashore, many were on the verge of hypothermia. I proceeded on leave; had my tonsils out and then got married on the 21st March 1942, just before starting my Long 'S' course at HMS MERCURY, at Leydene, near Petersfield.

At Leydene, the standing instructions were that, in the event of an unexpected air raid, all were to scatter into the woods, (there were males and females under training). One lovely summer's afternoon, we had been shown the mysteries of a loud-hailer and this had been left in our classroom on the first floor, overlooking the parade ground in front of the building. During the afternoon stand-easy at about 1515 the temptation proved too much for O'Brien, who switched on the loud-hailer and gave a most realistic vocal display of a dive bomber attack. The effect was wonderful - everyone obeyed instructions and scattered into the woods - many not getting back until after 'Secure' had been piped!

On completion of my Long course, instead of being sent to destroyers or convoy escorts, (sloops, frigates etc.), NHQ New Delhi said they wanted me to have cruiser experience - heaven only knows why. Admiralty said 'Sorry - all cruisers are full', so I was sent to the mighty battleship HMS ANSON, additional, on the staff of VA2, Vice-Admiral Sir Bruce Fraser (later Lord Fraser of North Cape), and joined her in Scapa Flow. We spent Christmas in Akereri, Iceland, surrounded by snow and ice and, on the messdecks, they were singing 'I'm dreaming of a white Christmas'. We were up inside the Arctic Circle and the sun had not risen for three days - I made Admiral Fraser smile when I told him that I was drawing Indian allowance.

We sailed later from Scapa Flow, with a destroyer escort, to give cover to a Russian convoy. Because of W/T silence, we did not know that the convoy had been delayed. The weather was shocking - ANSON was covered in ice and our escorting destroyers had no hot food for three days. Eventually, we went into Seidesfjord in Iceland, to refuel the destroyers and, as we did so, we heard that Captain Sherbrook and his flotilla of destroyers were engaging the HIPPER - he was awarded the Victoria Cross.

Later in Rosyth, I met Commander Austin, who was in command of one of the destroyers. He told me that he was on the bridge and had just received the signal 'Enemy in Sight - one Hipper class battleship bearing Green 40', when the Doc arrived on the bridge with a signal which he had deciphered which read: 'ANSON entered Seidesfjord'. He said 'I knew we were safe then'. Never having been in action, I asked Commander Austin what it was like. 'Oh', he said 'a wonderful experience, but I'm buggered if I want one like it again!'

While in ANSON in Scapa Flow, I received a signal saying that my wife had given birth to our first child, Beatrice on the 6th January 1943. Shortly after I left ANSON and went for a spell in the Headquarters at Rosyth, I managed to get down to London to Queen Charlotte's Hospital to see Peggy and Beatrice and I was given VIP treatment by the Matron.

*　　　　　*　　　　　*

Later, I joined Joe Jefford at Stamshaw Camp, Portsmouth, standing by GODAVARI. Our ratings and some of the officers were doing various courses. The Captain's Secretary, a 2-striper VR was an amusing character and had an infallible filing system. He kept two files - one 'IN' and one 'OUT' and, whenever Joe couldn't find what he wanted in a file, the Secretary would say 'Oh well, sir, it must be in the other file'. Then, as GODAVARI progressed, we moved to Woolston and established an office at Thorneycrofts. George Watson was the Engineer Officer and Joe Wright the Second Engineer. James Craig was Gunnery Officer and Sober Lamb was A/S officer, while Peter Mahindroo Singh was Navigating Officer. It must have been around this time that Stuart Young joined as Paymaster.

Finally, the great day came and on the 22nd June 1943, the ship that had just been a number was commissioned and became HMIS GODAVARI. Dorothy Jefford, Pat Wright and Peggy were there for the ceremony and Beatrice slept peacefully throughout in her carry-cot in the Captain's cabin. The next two days were spent ammunitioning ship and then we started trials. I see, from the War Diary, that on the 10th July, whilst carrying out a practice shoot, a 4" fused shell jammed in No 2 hoist and also, due to gunfire, we had superficial damage. We had to go back to North Corner Jetty to remedy defects.

On the 14th July, we sailed from Cowes Roads and joined a west-bound convoy as 'additional escort'. I was very apprehensive. German E-boat attacks on coastal convoys were common and here we were, in a new ship, just commissioned. However, we were lucky and the trip down Channel and round Lands End was uneventful. I note from the War Diary that, on the 14th July, we parted company with the convoy off Lundy Island and proceeded independently for Scapa at fifteen knots. 'Weather fresh with rain and wind squalls during day, causing large incidence of sea-sickness in a very new and green ship's company'.

The only excitement we had was sinking a floating mine off Milford Haven. We sank another off Cape Wrath on the 17th and at 1230 that day, arrived in Scapa Flow to start our working up. On the eighteenth day of our work-up, the 5th August at 1100, RA (D), Home Fleet Destroyers (Rear Admiral IG Glenuve, CB) returned the CO's call and was introduced to the officers and, at 1545, the First Lord of the Admiralty (Mr AV Alexander) accompanied by the Commander-in-Chief Home Fleet (Admiral Sir Bruce Fraser, KCB, KBE) inspected the ship and addressed the ship's company. We cheered ship on the departure of the First Lord - I don't know how much of his address was understood by the majority of the ship's company.

I see from the diary that on Sunday 8th August GODAVARI played HMS DUKE OF YORK at hockey and lost 2-0, the ship's first defeat. (On this subject, Lieutenant Commander Wright writes: "As far as I can recall, GODAVARI couldn't get a decent hockey match, so the challenge was to the Home Fleet - so how many of the team were really DUKE OF YORK I don't know - but anything went then.) On Thursday 12th August, having been at sea carrying out a full calibre shoot at night and patrolling the

92

Pentland Firth, we returned to harbour at 1230 and anchored near the Fleet Flagship, HMS DUKE OF YORK, on duty as AA Guard Ship during the Visit of HM KIng George VI to Scapa Flow. From the time that His Majesty arrived in HMS ONSLOW at 1600 and transferred to the DUKE OF YORK, we were at cruising stations, with all close-range weapons manned during daylight hours.

On Friday the 13th, Day 26 of our work up, the weather was foul - raining and windy. His Majesty visited various ships. The Fleet Signal Officer was Commander Dickie Courage, whom I had first met doing Sub's courses in 1937 and again when I was doing my Long Signals Course. Prior to the visit of His Majesty to GODAVARI, Dickie sent over a signalman with a Royal Standard, which, on Commander in Chief Home Fleet's directions, we were to wear while His Majesty was aboard. We were the only ship in the Fleet, except, of course, DUKE OF YORK, to do so. The signalman was also instructed to take over our V/S watch, so that all our signalmen could go down to see His Majesty.

At 1645, the Royal Barge came alongside and HM the King, accompanied by the Commander-in-Chief Home Fleet, Admiral Sir Bruce Fraser, came aboard and was received by Joe Jefford and I, as First Lieutenant, was presented. The weather was so bad that we could not have the ship's company on the upper deck, so they were all down in the mess decks.

Joe led off, going up the starboard side, while I stayed at the top of the gangway, receiving the remainder of the 'accompanying party'. When it got down to 'Movietone News', I decided that they could follow the others and I steamed up the starboard side. Just before reaching the forward end, I came up with a tall 'pongo' - Major, (then), Piers-Leigh, personal stooge to the Monarch, who said 'Are you anything to do with this ship?'. 'Yes', I replied, 'I am the First Lieutenant'. 'Well', he said, 'tell me what is this GODAVĀRĪ - is it a bird or something?' I replied, 'Actually, it's pronounced Godāvari and is the second largest river in India, rising near Bombay and reaching the sea north of Madras'. 'Good God', said the Major, 'do you know that I was in India for eighteen years and never heard of it'.

We went round the forward end of the mess decks and started down the port side, following the procession, who all genuflected as they went under the thwartship pipes which did a bend under fore and aft pipes in the deck head. Not so the Major, who remained erect and gave his head a nasty crack. To the delight of George Watson and the whole engineroom department, His Majesty went down and inspected the engineroom, where everything shone and gleamed. George lent the King a pair of gloves, not that he needed them and, afterwards George kept one and Joe Wright the other.

The day before the King's visit, Joe Wright called the Chief Mechanic and the Chief Stoker to the office and told them about it and that the King may well go below. They stared in disbelief, then muttered to themselves, then asked for extra cleaning gear. 'Carry on, Chiefs', Joe said and left them to it. Next day, the King did go below, sliding down the ladders in the proper manner and, later, Joe marked up the glove with his remark to George - 'the finest engine room I have ever seen'. No holding our lads then - bursting with pride.

After the engineroom, His Majesty suggested going into the wardroom until the Barge came alongside. Of course, everyone remained standing - except Major Piers-Leigh, who flung himself into the nearest armchair. On the mantelpiece was the ship's badge, which had only just arrived and we had not had time to fit it to the forepart of the bridge. It consisted of India in white, surrounded by the Indian Ocean and the Bay of Bengal in blue and the Godavari River picked out in black.

His Majesty noticed it and Joe said 'Yes, this is the ship's badge' and pointed out the Godavari River. The King said 'What did you say?' and Joe repeated 'Godavari River'. Whereupon, His Majesty turned on Piers-Leigh and said 'I asked you last night how to pronounce the name and you told me Godavāri and I don't suppose you even knew it was a bloody river!' Of course, at that moment, I was the only one who knew that this was true. It was most noticeable that, in the wardroom in a relaxed atmosphere, His Majesty had no impediment in his speech whatsoever.

When His Majesty and the Commander-in-Chief had departed, we found the wardroom full of hangers on - 'Movietone News' etc, all with their tongues hanging out. I noticed, among this motley crew, a Commander wearing an Observer's badge and guessed, correctly, that this was in fact Commander Anthony Kimmins and I invested three double gins in him. We had a handsome dividend, for, in the postscript to the 9 o'clock News, Anthony Kimmins broadcast the following:-

> His Majesty had brought 'King's Weather' with him and now, as ONSLOW steamed close up to the Fleet Flagship, DUKE OF YORK, the great ships lying at anchor in the soft northern light could not have looked more magnificent. As bugles sounded the 'Alert' and bosuns' pipes shrilled, the King ran up the starboard gangway of the DUKE OF YORK. As he reached the quarter-deck, the Royal Marines Guard of Honour presented arms and the massed bands broke into the National Anthem. With the men stiffly to attention and the officers at the salute, there wasn't a movement - not the flicker of an eyelid. And then, as the last notes died away, the King stepped forward and, smiling broadly, grasped the hand of the Commander-in-Chief, Admiral Sir Bruce Fraser. A royal visit - a happy reunion of friends.
>
> It was the same everywhere he went. No matter what the ship, whether the MALAYA, one of the battleships in which he had served in the last war, our own Fleet destroyers, the Greek destroyer THEMISTOCLES, the HURON, manned by lusty Canadians, a submarine or the Indian sloop GODAVARI - wherever he went the King always seemed to be finding old friends - friends he had met on his travels overseas; old shipmates; men with ribbons on their chests whom he had decorated at Buckingham Palace; youngsters whom he had last met at his Duke of York camps.

94

The Royal Standard at the masthead in HMIS GODAVARI – 13 Aug. 1943

HM King George VI aboard HMIS GODAVARI – 13 August 1943

96

Australians, Canadians, South Africans and men from all over the world had come thousands of miles to serve in the Home Fleet, but perhaps the scene in the Royal Indian Navy sloop GODAVARI brought this home more than anywhere else. Somehow, those dark glistening faces and the Sikhs in their white turbans looked grander than ever up there in those cold northern waters. Their ship was spotless. When they had first heard the news of who was coming aboard, they had just not believed it. They had set to and spent the whole night cleaning and polishing. By the time the King arrived, their ship, from the shining brasswork down to the ship's cat, with a blue ribbon around her neck, was a picture.

I felt that I must stop and hear them cheer at close quarters. When His Majesty left, I purposely remained on board. 'Three Cheers for the King Emperor' - there was something in that cheer I can't describe. As the Royal Barge steamed away, the 'Disperse' was sounded, but those men didn't leave the rails - they watched until the Barge had gone alongside the Flagship - until their King Emperor had gone inboard and for a long time after he had disappeared from view. Sometime later, I was talking to the Indian Yeoman of Signals who had broken the Royal Standard at the masthead - his hands were still trembling with excitement.

Next day, when His Majesty took his Fleet to sea, that small sloop was given the proud privilege of being the leading ship - the Guide of the Fleet - as we steamed out of harbour. As we reached the open sea, she hauled out on the starboard beam. At her yardarm fluttered the signal 'Long live the King Emperor'. Down her side, those men from all over India stood cheering themselves hoarse. The King Emperor jumped on to a steel chest and saluted until they were well astern. And then, just as they had watched him disappear the night before, stood very still watching them disappearing out of sight.

That day, when His Majesty took his Fleet to sea, was a very historic one. It was historic because it was the first time for nearly six hundred years that a reigning Sovereign had taken his Fleet to sea in wartime. It was historic because every possible modern development of naval warfare was exercised and there were great proud moments - great battleships, the finest in the world, steaming at full speed with their bow waves streaming over their fo'c'sles; Coastal Command aircraft roaring past to demonstrate low-level bombing; the Fleet Air Arm diving down with sleeve targets and being met with a curtain of tracers racing up. Others suddenly appearing through the clouds to carry out torpedo attacks. Gunnery practices of all kinds, culminating in deafening broadsides from the assembled battleships.

Shortly after His Majesty had left, the mail arrived and in it was a letter saying that Joe Jefford had been promoted to Captain and we were all set to celebrate, but a sudden squall deferred it. We were dragging our anchor and did not have time even to hoist the gangway before getting under way. However, we settled down again and were all able to express our delight at Joe's promotion. The following morning, Saturday 14th August, I sent a signal to the Fleet Signal Officer, Dickie Courage, 'The end of a perfect day - heard last evening that Jefford promoted to Captain'.

At 0930, we weighed and proceeded - leading the Battlefleet out of harbour - HMS DUKE OF YORK wearing the Royal Standard, HMS ANSON wearing the Flag of FA2 HMS RENOWN. We were doing twelve knots and, as soon as we cleared Hoxe brow, we hauled over to starboard and the Battlefleet increased speed to twenty-four knots. In the middle of this, hoisting 'Long live the King Emperor' and cheering ship, DUKE OF YORK called us up on the signal projector 'Personal to Captain Jefford - congratulations on your promotion - HM'. There was Joe conning the ship, when I read the signal to him. He said 'How do I reply to that Number One?' 'I haven't a clue' was my reply - this was not a situation covered in my Long course. However, Joe was equal to the occasion and made a correct and suitable reply.

I heard later from Dickie Courage that he was on the Admiral's bridge of the DUKE OF YORK with Commander-in-Chief and His Majesty and he showed my signal to the Commander-in-Chief who told him to show it to His Majesty. When we returned to Sulter Sound and secured to No 19 buoy, we found we had a problem. The Press had got to hear of Joe Jefford's promotion and were all set to publish a story that he had been promoted personally, 'in the field' by His Majesty. That story took quite a lot of stopping. So, after all the excitement, we continued our work up.

An interesting note in the War Diary, which probably only the Captain knew : '21 August 1426 Returned to harbour and secured to No 19 buoy. Signal received from Admiralty directing ship to boiler clean at Londonderry due to sabotage in NARBADA which was assumed to be caused by anti-British influences in the Clyde area. Admiralty contacted by secraphone from Tyne and arrangements made to boiler clean at Greenock, as delay would have been caused if modifications to feed pumps, which were of necessity to be carried out by Messrs. Weirs at Greenock, were not carried out concurrently with boiler clean. Admiralty were advised that ship was most unlikely to react favourably to subversive influences. Completed with ammunition.'

Next day, Sunday 22nd August, the ship was inspected by RA(D), who addressed the ship's company. RA(D) complimented the ship on a very satisfactory work-up in which results, well above average, had been obtained. On the evening of the 23rd we sailed for the Clyde and 'cleaned boilers' from the 25th to the 31st, during which time seventy-two hours' leave was granted to each watch in turn. From the Clyde we went to Londonderry and came under the orders of Commodore (D), Western Approaches and spent a week on harbour drills. On the 14th September, we weighed and proceeded to an exercise area with C2 Group and, after various exercises and manoeuvres, arrived back in Morville at midnight.

Then on the 16th we went to sea with C2 Group and joined Convoy ON 202 as additional escort until 0100 on the 17th, when we were detached and returned to Morville.

A digression - during our visits to Londonderry, we heard of many people going over the border into the Free State in plain clothes - especially on a Sunday - and coming back with things you could not get in Northern Ireland, or 'other purchases' at a much cheaper price. The best person to go with was the Chief Constable of Londonderry because the boot of his car was never opened by the Customs Officers at the border on the return journey.

Later on, we were in Londonderry for a boiler clean and leave was granted to the ship's company. I remember being very surprised at the destinations to which we issued Rail Warrants - it seemed that our ratings had made friends all over the UK. 'Absent over Leave' was an all too common offence in the RN. I was very proud when all our ratings except one were back on time and that one had a chit saying that, through no fault of his own, he had been put on the wrong train.

I remember Joe Jefford asking if we could escort a North Atlantic convoy all the way - I think that he and the Senior Officer of the escort had done the long A/S course together - but this was turned down by the powers that be who said that the North Atlantic was very quiet at the time and, instead, we would be escorting a Gibraltar one on which we stood more chance of seeing some action.

On the way to Gibraltar, we did sight a Focker Wulff and opened fire at extreme range. I was by X gun and found that, through habit, they were passing up practice projectiles from the magazine. It took a few moments to get the message home that this was the real thing. I think the Pilot got frightened, because he had no idea where the next burst from our guns would be and he decided to go away. Incidentally, that was the only time I ever saw guns fired in anger during the war. Later, we heard that things in the North Atlantic were no longer quiet. The convoy we would have been with was the first to be attacked by U-boats using homing torpedoes - how lucky we were.

We found that, in a seaway, GODAVARI's stern 'flexed'. This was duly reported and eventually a member of the Royal Corps of Naval Constructors came to sea with us, just off Londonderry, to see what actually happened. Later, it amused me to read the official report which said 'Although there is no structural weakness, some additional stiffening is considered desirable.' The original plans for GODAVARI had been stamped and approved by the RCNC, so there could not be any structural weakness.

Joe Wright recalls the 'flexing' as follows:

> Yes, the stern did flex -right from the word go. George complained in Woolston to the Overseer that the plummer blocks were moving in circles and got the answer "do the shafts go round -yes - then off to sea with you". But the point of "flexing" was my aft cabin bulkhead - all the detonators were just there. It got even worse and the bulkhead banged

away like nobody's business, after we had tried out, in heavy weather, some deep depth charges, set to 900 feet, after it had been discovered that the U-boats were diving below the normal 300 feet setting.

Normally, it would have been all right but, in heavy weather, it was bad, as Y turret, plus stiffening, had been removed to accommodate Oropesa, Double-L sweeps and a load of extra depth-charges - all dead weight and no compensation. That was put right eventually, but could we get those main engines lined up? - no, so we had to keep pouring water over the plummer blocks to prevent a seize-up. They were corrected at last in Bombay - $3/8$" one way and $5/8$" the other.

We were in Devonport from the 1st to the 11th December 1943, having this additional stiffening fitted. My wife Peggy and our daughter Beatrice were at that time living with my mother in Launceston. Most Captains took advantage of a spell like this to have some leave and would leave the First Lieutenant in charge. Not so Joe Jefford. Dorothy was staying in the Grand Hotel in Plymouth and Joe insisted that we did alternate nights on board - a very generous gesture. It was during this time in Devonport that we had the festival of Ramadan. I should mention that a large number of Muslim ratings on board had said that they wished to observe the fast for the month preceding. It was explained to them that a dispensation had been given and that at sea, we would have to continue in three watches at Cruising Stations, with Action Stations at dawn and sunset and no special concessions. Nevertheless, they were resolute and earned our admiration.

So, back to Devonport and a live sheep was requested for the feast. I said I could not promise anything, but would do my best. I went and saw the NSO and stressed the religious importance of this to the ship's company and the live sheep was delivered. I don't remember this, but Joe Wright swears that around this time our Paybob somehow managed to extract six bottles of Drambuie from Saccone and Speed for the wardroom mess. He (Joe), went ashore for the night and was looking forward to having a tot of the precious liqueur when he returned on board, but not a single bottle remained - must have been quite a party.

On the 17th December we sailed from Devonport to rendezvous with convoy 0562/KMS36. The following morning, just after 0400, when I had just come on watch, without any challenge or exchange of recognition signals we were suddenly illuminated by a magnesium flare dropped from a Coastal Command aircraft. I felt very naked and exposed. We then received orders from Commander-in-Chief, Plymouth to chase and capture a reported blockade runner. Owing to a strong south-westerly gale our maximum possible speed without causing damage was only ten knots and at 2359 on the 19th, we were ordered to abandon the search and proceed to rendezvous with the convoy, which we did on the 22nd and the SO of the convoy allocated us position 'S' in the rear of the convoy -all right in fine weather and in good visibility, but somewhat hazardous in adverse conditions. By the end of that afternoon, a strong north-westerly gale was blowing and this continued throughout the night. The convoy became disorganised and several ships were unable to maintain steerageway. I turned in at about 2100 and GODAVARI was doing everything - corkscrewing. At about 2145, I felt a violent lurch and thought 'that must have been a big sea'. Moments later the Chief OA dashed into my cabin and said 'Sahib, sahib, we have been torpedoed. It came in one side and went out the other'. I went forward to the mess decks and realised something was wrong because there was a strong smell of fresh air. Joe Wright and I assessed the damage and found the CPO's mess and No 2 magazine were flooded. We reported to Joe Jefford and set about emergency measures. Everyone was safely out of the CPO's mess and the hatch secured. From somewhere, a pot of black paint appeared and spilt on the deck and in this I stepped, leaving a permanent reminder on the grey flannel trousers I was wearing. There was large gash in the starboard side and this we blocked up with hammocks and timber shores. By 2300 the situation was under control and I heard from Joe Jefford what happened.

Visibility had been reduced to a few yards and Joe had been trying to maintain steerageway and found himself between two columns of the convoy. He then tried to turn GODAVARI round to starboard. In the middle of this manoeuvre, a ship in the starboard column, (believed to be a 'Manchester Liner'), suddenly altered course to port. Just before the moment of impact, Joe with incredible presence of mind, went full ahead, so that we were only struck a glancing blow. For some unknown reason, the other vessel had her port anchor down to the waterline and this is what did most of the damage. It swung in and ripped out part of our ship's side. She struck us a further glancing blow further aft, damaging the motor boat. I went on watch at 0400 on the 23rd. Joe was still on the bridge, covered in salt and his eyes all red. It must have been a hell of a night for him.

The Flower Class Corvette, HMS CLOVER was allocated to escort us and Commander-in-Chief, Western Approaches ordered us to return to the UK. The weather started to improve and we were making six knots. On the 24th, there was a further improvement in the weather and we were able to make ten knots. During the forenoon, we decided to try and rig the collision mat over the hole in the starboard side. This necessitated splicing on two wire pennants. The Chief Bosun's Mate did one splice and I did the other - to my joy, I finished first. However, having got it into position, it only lasted twelve hours before carrying away. Our troubles were not over. On Christmas Day the reserve feed tanks started showing signs of salinity and the density was rising in the boilers. Eventually, our speed was reduced to five knots, but we made Lisahally Gilties under our own power during the forenoon of Boxing Day. In the afternoon of the 29th, we were towed to No 5 berth in Londonderry and commenced temporary repairs the next day.

We all thought that we had much to be thankful for. So, arrangements were made for services to be held. The Muslims and Hindus held their services on board and Protestant and Catholic services were held ashore. So everyone was able to thank their God/Gods for a safe return. On 31st December 1943, we heard that we were to go to Newcastle for repairs. However, much to my joy this was changed and we went back to Devonport and I was able to get to Launceston. In October 1944, our second daughter, Frances was born. Before leaving Londonderry, I bought some tweed from a Mr Kelly who could supply most things and was not worried about coupons. I took the tweed ashore in Devonport with a load of Confidential Books. Later, my wife made it up and it lasted for years. On another commodity, however, Mr Kelly let me down. I asked him if he could get me a ham to take home. His reply was 'You've as much chance of finding Holy Water in the Orange Lodge!"

I can't remember how long the repairs to GODAVARI took, but eventually, they were completed and we sailed. I do recall that we escorted a fast convoy to Oran and then proceeded independently through the Mediterranean and, when passing Malta, it was during the month of May and we had a snow storm. In Port Said, George Watson and I went ashore one evening for a meal. In the restaurant/cafe, we were offered bacon and eggs and asked how many eggs - three or four or more. I believe George had sixteen, but they were all very small. Nevertheless, after wartime England it was a surprise. We stopped in Aden and it was there we heard news of the explosion in Bombay Docks which did such enormous damage.

Then to Bombay and the end of an era. Joe Jefford was relieved by Brian Goord and I was relieved by Ham Hamilton and there were major changes in the ship's company. I was sorry to leave GODAVARI, but I would have found it difficult to serve under another Commanding Officer after having had the privilege of being Joe Jefford's First Lieutenant. Joe Jefford was a gentleman, an outstanding seaman and a wonderful Commanding Officer.

I came ashore in Bombay from HMIS GODAVARI on the 27th May 1944 and quickly became aware of the devastation and extent of the damage caused by the explosion that had taken place in the Docks. I was granted leave and had planned to go up to Kashmir, but that had to be deferred because I went down with dengue fever, which led to infective hepatitis and I went into the RIN Hospital. In the same ward was Commander Hemming, recovering from a severe gash in his leg, sustained in the Dock explosion. Eventually, I got out of hospital and went off on sick leave to Kashmir and Rawalpindi, (from where I was given the opportunity of visiting the Khyber Pass). On my return from leave towards the end of July 1944, I took up my appointment as Staff Officer, (Signals), Bombay.

The Central Communications Office was at that time in the 'dungeons' of Castle Barracks and a new CCO was being built. On the 24th August 1944, my title was changed to Staff Communications Officer, Bombay. I see that I have kept a copy of a signal to Admiralty from FOCRIN, reading:- 'Controller of Naval Accounts requires confirmation that CO and all personnel of HMIS GODAVARI were absolved from all blame for accident to GODAVARI when escorting 0S62/KMS36 on 22nd December 1943. Request you will confirm.' Presumably, the Admiralty did, otherwise I suppose that CNA would have wanted Joe Jefford to pay for the cost of repairs.

In November 1944, I went up to NHQ (1) in Delhi for a couple of days, discussing the manning of the new combined RNRIN Central Communications Office. The Combined CCO was quite a challenge. We had RIN ratings, RN ratings, WRINS officers and TWA's, (Temporary Women Assistants), who had been recruited and trained by the RN in Bombay and had civilian status.

Many of the WRINS officers were the wives of officers who were senior to me and some did not take kindly to my decision to put 2/O Pam Gorton-Walker, WRNS in charge. But it did work out - Pam was a most efficient officer and was a great help to me.

In January 1945, Trevor Cole took over from me as SCO and I went to HMIS TALWAR, which was the combined RN and RIN FarEastern Signal Training School and took over from George Bailey as Commanding Officer and I moved into the CO's bungalow. The total number in TALWAR was about 1,000 and, as in the CCO, I had RN and RIN ratings and WRINS officers and ratings.

One day Second Officer Lilly, who was in charge of the WRINS detachment, told me that one of the trainee WRINS ratings had kicked over the traces. She was an Anglo-Indian girl and was brought before me as a 'defaulter'. I listened to the case and quickly realised she was a spirited young lady who, I thought, had potential. I said to her, 'Do you know what I would like to do to you?' 'No', she replied, in a very cocky manner. I said. 'I would like to clear the lower deck and have everyone out on the parade ground and take you out in the middle and put you across my knee and smack your bottom'. For a moment, while she thought I might do it, she looked very frightened. I told her to behave in future - I knew she was due to complete her training in a few days. I contacted Zena Bailey, who was First Officer, WRINS in Bombay and told her about this girl and said I thought she was a natural leader, who needed to be given responsibility. I was proved right and she did very well indeed.

Field Marshal Sir Claude Auchinleck, Commander-in-Chief, India, visited TALWAR and he expressed interest in some particular exhibit. Subsequently, I sent off some photos of this to his ADC and a few days later, received a personal letter, thanking me for the photos and saying how much he had enjoyed the visit. It was only when I got to the end that I found that it was signed, not by the ADC, but by 'Auchinleck, FM'. The fact that a man in his position could find time to write a personal letter of thanks, made a deep impression on me.

In April 1945, Peggy, Beatrice, and Frances, (five-and-a-half months), arrived in Bombay on board the STRATHAIRD. We all settled down in the CO's bungalow in TALWAR and the dachshund Wendy accepted them completely. Beatrice quickly became concerned about the ghari horses and the way they were treated. We had been down to Crawford Market one day and got into a ghari for the return journey and the driver started to whip the horse. To our astonishment and the amusement of the onlookers, Beatrice, in a loud voice, said 'Ghari wallah - mat maro!'

103

Signal Bosun Bahadur Suleman Sahib was a wonderful man, (he was Yeoman of Signals in CLIVE when I first joined). He assumed personal responsibility for Peggy and the family when I was away. The Captain's Steward was Leading Steward Mascarenas, (he had also served with me in CLIVE). Two stories about him. I used to nip over to the bungalow sometimes for a cup of tea and Peggy told Mascarenas to make some sandwiches. He asked what kind and Peggy said, 'Oh, some egg and some jam'. Yes - you have guessed - I took a mouthful of bread and a mixture of scrambled egg and apricot jam.

The other story was that I had been over to Calcutta and, in the evening, Mascarenas was late and eventually turned up drunk. Suleman Sahib, who had a bad stutter, had a lot to say to him, but Peggy had the winning shot. She told Mascarenas that if he didn't behave in future, she would have to tell me about his drunkenness - she never had any more trouble from him.

Of course, the 8th May 1945 was VE Day. A parade and march through Bombay and a service in the Cathedral. And then, the 14th August was VJ Day. Another parade and march and I think it was then that I had to lead the RIN contingent. Why a Communicator and not a Gunnery Officer, I don't know. When we got to the Cathedral, we found the same service sheet as for VE Day - amended - 'for VE Day read VJ Day; for Europe or Germany, read Japan.' It did seem a bit mean.

On the 25th September 1945, NHQ decided on another of its strange moves. Trevor Cole, who was SCO, was appointed CO of TALWAR and I was go to back as SCO and take over from Tom Sheppard, who was to go to Delhi as Flags to Admiral Godfrey. So, we had to move out of the CO's bungalow and, as a temporary measure, we went and stayed with Ann and Arthur King, which was most kind of them. After a while, we moved in to the ground floor of 'Sealands', a lovely flat facing the sea. We took in 'lodgers' - at one time we had staying with us Tom Sheppard, Dick Charlton and Harry Bird. On Christmas Eve 1945, I received a signal from NHQ which shattered me. Commander FW (Freddie) King, RIN was appointed to TALWAR and I was to go back there as Executive Officer, having previously and recently been there in Command. Trevor Cole, who was to be relieved by Freddie King, was appointed to Calcutta.

It must have been at about this time that Trevor Cole had reported to the Flag Officer, Bombay that there was unrest in TALWAR and he thought that something serious might develop. It is sad to relate that his report was not taken seriously - in fact, he was considered to be ill and he was subsequently invalided out of the Service. Kohli was supposed to relieve me as SCO and Durnford was to leave Calcutta, when relieved by Cole and come to Bombay as SCO (T). I did all I could to avoid going to TALWAR as Executive Officer.

On the 15th January, Kohli was granted twenty-four days' leave, so he could not take over from me. So Durnford was appointed to relieve me on the 15th January. On the 18th January, FOB sent a signal to NHQ, saying he intended granting me twenty-eight days' war leave from the 15th February. The reply to that was that I could not be spared. In the middle of all this, Singapore had been re-taken and, at Bombay Fort W/T

Station, we noticed that Admiralty, (Whitehall W/T), were having great difficulty in establishing regular W/T communication.

Bert Spence, who was the Warrant Telegraphist in charge of the transmitting station at Mahul, suggested that Bombay Fort could help and, therefore, assistance was offered to Admiralty. For a time, Bombay Fort was receiving and re-transmitting all traffic to and from Admiralty and Singapore. On the 2nd February, the following signal was received:-

FO BOMBAY (R) FOCRIN CINCEIS from ADMIRALTY
The recent prompt action by Bombay W/T in providing a W/T line to Singapore to clear congestion on Service 6 was most effective and much appreciated. 311121.

On Friday, 8th February - I was still SCO - things started which were to have sad and serious consequences. The following extracts from my personal diary illustrate the turn of events:-

Friday 8th February 1946

At about 0930, I received a telephone call from Commander King, Commanding Officer, HMIS TALWAR. He informed me that, whilst TALWAR ratings and WRINS were at Divisions at 0845, some CCO ratings, who were in their barracks adjacent to the parade ground, made 'cat-calls' to the WRINS on parade. When he walked into the barracks to reprimand them, he said no one took any notice of him and he said, in a loud voice, 'Stand up'.

He further stated that if CCO RCO ratings were accommodated in TALWAR, he considered that at least they should conform to TALWAR's routine for Divisions. I explained that CCO RCO ratings were watch keepers and that it was difficult for them to conform to the routine of a training establishment. I made enquiries and six V/S ratings were brought before me as having been in the barracks at the time stated by Commander King. I said I expected my ratings to set an example in TALWAR and that I did not want to hear of any more reports like the one I had just received.

I subsequently visited TALWAR at about 1230 with Mr Ashirwadan, Warrant Telephonist in charge of the RCO, to discuss with Commander King the question of CCO RCO ratings attending Divisions. It is worth noting that, during this conversation, at which Lieutenant Nanda was also present, Commander King referred to the ratings as 'sons of bitches' and 'buggers'.

Saturday 9th February 1946

Lieutenant Filby, Officer-in-Charge, Bombay Fort, informed me at about 1220 that fourteen ratings wished to see me as Requestmen to state a complaint. I said I would see them at once. I think I saw eight and, as the others were off duty, I arranged to see them at 0930 on Sunday.

Sunday 10th February 1946

I saw the remainder of the Requestmen at 0930. I was most careful to explain to all fourteen ratings the Regulations regarding stating complaints. I saw each man individually and, having heard what he had to say, I told him to state his complaint. I also appointed Lieutenant Filby to assist the complainants.

Having seen all the Requestmen, I typed out a letter to the Commanding Officer, HMIS TALWAR, with a copy to the Chief Staff Officer to the Flag Officer, Bombay, informing him that these ratings wished to see him; stating briefly the nature of their complaint - ie, that they alleged that Commander King had called them, singly or collectively, 'jungli Indians', 'coolie buggers/bastards', and asked that I might be informed when it would be convenient for him to see them.

The latter was delivered to TALWAR, marked 'Important and Confidential', at about noon on Sunday 10th February. As far as I know, Commander King did not open this letter until Monday morning.

Monday 11th February 1946

Commander King telephoned me and said that he would see them at 1030 on Saturday, which was his normal time for seeing Requestmen. I visited Commander King and discussed the matter with him. He stated that the whole thing was a frame-up and said he would see the ratings and inform them that, in accordance with the Regulations, they could, after twenty-four hours, if they so desired, state their complaint in writing.

I suggested to him that, in view of the nature of the complaint and that, in my opinion, the ratings' feelings on the matter were very strong, it might be advisable to see these Requestment before Saturday. After some consideration he declined to accept my suggestion.

Saturday 16th February 1946

I went to TALWAR at 1030 and was present when Commander King saw the fourteen Requestmen. He heard each man and informed each of them that it was a serious offence to make a complaint which the rating knew to be untrue, but that, in accordance with Regulations, he would give them twenty-four hours in which to think it over and, if at the end of that time they so desired, they could state their complaint in writing. Lieutenant Filby would assist them.

(Note: I cannot now remember if the ratings did, in fact state their complaint in writing. I think they probably did, with Lieutenant Filby's assistance.)

Monday 18th February 1946

At about 0930, I received information that all the ratings in TALWAR, including the CCO RCO ratings had 'gone on strike'. The

Forenoon Watch were on duty and were carrying on normally. I reported to the Flag Officer, Bombay, who asked me how this affected the CCO and what I intended to do. I said I wanted to make two signals immediately - one, 'Minimise' and the other closing down certain services.

I was told not to make them, but to wait and see what happened. In the meantime, Lieutenant Durnford had been finding out what Royal Navy Communications personnel were available in Bombay.

Mr Ashirwadan visited TALWAR and tried to find out what was the matter. All the ratings appeared to be in a very excited state, but he did obtain a list of certain things the 'strikers' were demanding.

At about 1145, I again visited the Admiral's office and met Admiral Rattray - on the stairs - he then being on his way to TALWAR. I asked him what I was to say to the ratings who were then on duty at the CCO and who were due off watch at 1230.

He said, 'Well, you will have to tell them the truth - tell them what has happened'. To this I replied, 'Tell them that TALWAR has mutinied, Sir?', to which Admiral Rattray replied, 'Good God, no, Shaw - what a dreadful thing to say - no, tell them that the ratings in TALWAR refused duty.'

On return to the CCO, I made the signal 'Minimise' and 'Most Immediate', saying that, due to trouble with Communications Ratings, only certain services would be worked at hand speed. By this time, Lieutenant Durnford had arranged for a watch of RN ratings to be ready to come on duty at 1230.

I sent Mr Ashirwadan round all operators at 1225, to tell them to proceed to the Message Checking Room. I also arranged for all V/S ratings to proceed there as well. When all the RIN ratings had assembled there, I told them that a very serious situation had arisen; that all ratings in TALWAR had refused duty. I told them that, in the Service, there was a correct way of stating complaints and that, if anyone wished to make a complaint, I would see him afterwards. I pointed out to them that the name of the RIN, as far as communications were concerned, was vested in Bombay Fort; that the name of Bombay Fort had always stood high and that it would be the greatest tragedy if that name were brought in disrepute.

Ordinary Telegraphist, No 33121 P Bannerjee interrupted and said that the pride of the RIN meant nothing to him. I told him that, if he wished to state a complaint, I would see him afterwards.

I then said: 'All ratings who are going to carry on working are to go on to the RCO. Those who wish to go back to TALWAR are to turn right along the passage and proceed outside, where transport is waiting.'

Most of the ratings turned right down the passage. I saw a few go into the RCO and was hopeful, but I subsequently found out that they had only gone in to collect their caps. The Chiefs and PO's remained on duty and one Leading Hand, Mohamad Sadiq, also remained on duty.

The RN ratings arrived and took over essential services at 1245. I then went with Lieutenant Filby to Colaba, where I told all the ratings who were awake what had happened. I explained that I had come down personally to tell them the truth, as I did not want them to hear wild rumours and not know what was happening. I explained the seriousness of the offence committed by the ratings in TALWAR and said that I hoped they would have the good sense to remain on duty and to represent any grievances they had in the proper Service manner. I then returned to the CCO at about 1420.

At about 1500, Mr Bawoo, Signal Bosun, rang up and informed me that the ratings at the Breakwater Signal Station were talking among themselves about striking in sympathy with TALWAR ratings. I reached the BSS at about 1530 and addressed all the ratings on similar lines to those I had used at Colaba and said that I would see any rating who had a complaint then.

As will be seen from these personal notes, RN ratings took over essential services at 1245 on Monday 18th February. Things did become a little hectic. I do remember that I got about twelve hours sleep in one hundred and ten hours.

There were civil riots in Bombay. Road blocks were set up, screened by the crowds and vehicles set on fire. One incident amazed me. TALWAR was the HQ of the mutineers and I had to go there for some reason, on my official conveyance - a motor cycle and sidecar. On approaching TALWAR, I saw a column of mutineers from other establishments marching in, with one TALWAR rating holding up the traffic and directing them. When he saw me, he halted the column, waved me in and saluted me.

One of the nastiest incidents with which I was involved was late one evening, when we had word that a party, led by an armed Indian Officer from HMIS HAMLA, was approaching the CCO and Castle Barracks. An old Commander from HMS BRAGANZA, armed with a .45 revolver, was on the scene to meet them and they were in an ugly mood. The Commander had a severe speech impediment, but, nevertheless, he called them to a halt and said that the CCO was now a Royal Navy establishment and warned them, that if anyone took as much as one pace forward, he would shoot. By the tone of his voice he meant it and the message got across and, to the relief of all of us, the party retreated.

I did have to go to the Yacht Club and get hold of the boss of Cable and Wireless, to get him to have their transmitter switched on out of normal schedule, so that I could put through an immediate phone call to the Duty Signal Officer in Whitehall, warning him that all codes and cyphers on board the RIN ships **could** have been compromised. This was a precautionary measure.

I am not certain when, but probably at the end of the three-day mutiny, Commander King was relieved of his command in TALWAR and Commander SG Karmarkar, RINR was appointed in his place. There can be no doubt that he had a lot to do with the ending of the mutiny. He was in touch with the leaders of the Indian political parties.

When it was all over, I had a lot to do with him and found him extremely co-operative and helpful - he was able to obtain information which I never could have done. On February 23rd, Saturday, the mutiny ended with all ships flying black flags to indicate surrender.

Then followed the rounding up of all the suspected ring-leaders and their interrogation and Boards of Enquiry in all the ships and in every shore establishment.

On the 7th March, Harry Bird was appointed CO TALWAR, vice Karmarkar. Ken Teare was to relieve me as SCO and I was to go to TALWAR as Executive Officer. By this time, Cole and Durnford were 'sick' and NHQ (I) were asking C in CEI and Admiralty for the loan of a Staff Communications Officer. I reported in TALWAR on the 14th March, so I had 'stalled' going from 24th December to 14th March and I had avoided serving under Freddie King.

By this time, I was thoroughly unsettled and so was India. I was uncertain as to how things would go, so I decided it would be best if Peggy and the family go home - so they sailed in the NEA HELLIS in April 1946.

As an aside - the W/T Transmitting Station was at Mahul - quite a way out of Bombay and in quite a remote area. Living there were Warrant Telegraphist-in-Charge, Bert Spence - a big, heavy man and his little wife, Mona, who was very skinny, and a detachment of RIN ratings. During the mutiny, the diminutive Mona was sweeping the steps outside her bungalow when she saw two junior ratings, carrying a Congress flag approaching the flag staff, from which the White Ensign flew. When she asked them what they intended doing, they said they were going to replace the White Ensign with the Congress flag. Mona waved her broom and told the two ratings that as long as she were there, the White Ensign would continue to fly and they could bugger off. The White Ensign continued to fly throughout.

After the mutiny, I think morale was low, not only among ratings, but also with the officers and, in particular, British Officers. There was talk of a large number of officers being seconded to the RIN and at the same time a lack of information on the future for British Officers in the RIN. Then the official enquiry into the RIN mutiny was held. The members of the Board of Enquiry were three Indian judges, Major General Rees and Rear-Admiral Patterson.

I gave my evidence and said what I believed to be the truth. I and many others were astounded when the findings were published, for they said that there was no political background to the mutiny. Many years later, when Admiral Sir Geoffrey Miles was Guest of Honour at a RIN Association Reunion lunch, I was more than interested to hear him say that he had been astounded at the findings too. On the 10th May, I wrote regarding the original complaints made by my ratings and, as far as I can recall, no action was ever taken, to my great regret. A copy of my letter reveals that I withheld this information from the Enquiry.

On the 22nd May, I heard that Mumtaz and I had been selected for the next Staff course at Greenwich. I think Mumtaz did go to the UK by sea. I was relieved by Johnny Durnford as Executive Officer of TALWAR on the 31st May and was appointed to FEROZE additional, but my departure for the UK was delayed because I had to stay in Bombay until after Commander King's Court Martial. Freddie King's Court Martial duly took place. I don't recall who sat on the Court, but I do remember that Captain MHStL Nott was the accused's friend and did a very fine job defending Freddie King. Nott cross-questioned me at length on my evidence and even asked me what my political views were, but the Court would not allow that one.

Once away from the Court Martial, I flew up to Karachi and then home in a 'York'. We left Karachi just before sunset and I was in a seat on the port side in line with the wing. When it became dark, I was perturbed to see a ring of fire round the engine, but nothing disastrous happened and I realised it must be the exhaust. We landed shortly after midnight in Sharjah, where we were offered hot roast beef. Then on to Cairo and Sidi Barrani for an over-night stay. It was there that I saw the cage in which Rommel had kept his eagle. From there, we flew non-stop to Lyneham, near Swindon and I had a few days at home before going to Greenwich on the 22nd July to start the Staff Course. Before leaving India, I had been told that, on completion of the Staff Course, I was to go on and do the Joint Services Staff Course and, on completion of that, I would take my long leave - a very pleasant prospect. Just before the Staff Course finished in December 1946, I heard that I was **not** going on to the Joint Services Staff Course.

I bought a Singer sports car for £100 from a Wing Commander on the Staff at Greenwich and applied for some petrol to get the car down to Cornwall, (ten gallons, I think). I went along in uniform and finally got in to see the 'official' who controlled the issue of coupons. He suggested I should send the car down by rail. I pointed out that at the time we were asked to keep all but essential traffic off the railways. I told him that while I had served in tankers, I had seen more than this go over the side and that during the war I had been involved in escorting millions of gallons and, finally, that while in his waiting room, I had been told how to get black market coupons. Next morning, in the post was a letter from a friend of my younger sister - a person I had never met - saying he had heard I wanted some petrol and enclosing coupons for fifty gallons.

I enjoyed the Staff Course immensely and learnt a lot from it, much of which stood me in good stead in later years. I left Greenwich a few days before Christmas 1946, in the Singer Le Mans and drove west, in convoy with my cousin Peggy. It was a foul drive. Black ice and freezing fog and I remember I slid into the back of Peggy's car, doing more damage to her than to me. I did have Christmas at home and then the India Office in London phoned and said I had to be flown back to India for a Combined Operations Exercise, arriving 8th January - I was livid.

So, I was to go back and not have my leave. I remember that Peggy and I had been invited to go to the Hunt Ball in Launceston Town Hall on the 3rd January. I said we would go and we did. Whisky was still in fairly short supply, but rum was plentiful. That evening, I drank a lot of rum and ginger ale, but such was my state of mind, that I remained quite sober.

I left Launceston, by train, on the morning of Wednesday, 8th January 1947 and, having reported to BOAC, went in a coach to the train in Victoria Station, where compartments were reserved for those flying on Service 13Q94, most luxurious travel and VIP treatment. We arrived at Harbour Heights Hotel, Sandbanks in time for dinner and, next morning, after an excellent breakfast, we went by launch out to the converted Sunderland flying boat. We took off at about 1000 and had lunch flying over France at about 13,000 feet and landed at Marseilles about 1600, where we were taken to a hotel for the night. BOAC were most apologetic about our having to be called at 0530 the next day. We landed at Augusta in Sicily for lunch and then on to Cairo for another overnight stay.

Saturday, 11th, Cairo to Basra for lunch and then on to Bahrein for another night stop. Sunday, 12th January we took off from Bahrein for the long hop to Karachi and arrived there in the afternoon and I flew on down to Bombay by Tata's Air India.

I then started to make enquiries about this Combined Operations Exercise that had necessitated my being flown back from the UK. Incidentally, I had had nothing to do with Combined Operations, and there were other officers who had. I did fly down to Colombo for a meeting and, in Bombay, had a lot to do with a Group Captain, RAF, ex-Battle of Britain, Duncan Smith - quite a character. It ended up with my writing one-and-a-half pages of communications orders for the exercise and that was that.

While all this was going on, I had a letter from Chippy Samson, (on the 29th January 1947), who was then SO Naval Appointments in NHQ, New Delhi, saying that he was sorry he could not get me Staff rates of pay for this appointment, but that, when the exercise was over, I was to go up to Delhi as Staff Officer in the Inter-Services Cypher Security Directorate in General Headquarters - on consolidated rates of pay, with the possibility of home leave towards the end of the year. That sounded a most interesting job - however, it did not materialise.

On the 8th April, I was appointed to AKBAR as Officer-in-Charge, Cruiser Drafts. I believe this was an idea to get me home so that I could have long leave, but it did not materialise either. On the 18th April, the sailing of the Cruiser Drafts was deferred until further orders and, on the 24th April, my appointment was changed to Training Commander in AKBAR.

For a short time, I was there with Joe Jefford as Commanding Officer and then he was relieved by Jumbo Paine. The Executive Officer was Commander Wentworth-Harvey and he and I had adjoining quarters. It became an established routine that, at about 1800 Wentworth's bearer would knock on the door and say 'Commander Sahib salaam do'. I would go into Wentworth's quarters and the bearer would produce two chota pegs, which would be drunk in silence. Normally, during the second drink, Wentworth would say, in a very solemn voice 'I can't understand those buggahs in Delhi - why can't they see their way clear to promote me?' The bone of contention was that Jumbo Paine, now a Captain, had originally been junior to Wentworth. We did not often dine in the wardroom, preferring to eat in our own quarters.

I did try again to get my long leave, but to no avail. However, another matter had now raised its ugly head. I had still not passed my Lower Standard Urdu examination and, unless I did, I would not be confirmed as Lieutenant Commander. So, on the 24th June, I took ten days casual leave and swotted hard and took the Lower Standard Exam on the 8th July and passed by **one** mark. How vital that one mark was.

AKBAR was some twenty miles outside Bombay – the New Entry Training Establishment, built on a site cleared from the jungle, but still pretty wild. 'Willie' Williams was staying there one night and, in the morning, shook his slipper before putting his foot in and out fell a scorpion. Captain Jefford went into his dining room one lunch time and his dog barked and barked. Before sitting down, he looked under his chair and there was a krait. The ceilings in all the buildings were cloth. When there was a wardroom party and some guests 'hung-on', the easiest way to speed their departure was to start speaking about snakes and then point to an indentation in the 'ceiling' and prod it with a broom handle. The snake would slither away and the guests would depart.

Well, Wavell was gone – he was not prepared to accept responsibility for what he saw as the inevitable bloodshed. Mountbatten had taken over as Viceroy and was pushing ahead at full speed with Partition, which was to take place on the 15th August 1947. I think that we were all concerned with what our futures would be. In July, I went up to Delhi for three weeks temporary duty and, on Partition Day, I was appointed Staff Officer, Naval Appointments. The situation in Delhi was ghastly – rioting and shooting in the old city. There were no trains in or out of Delhi; the airport was closed and the roads out were locked. Very nasty indeed.

I did some work organising 'Certificates of Service' for British Officers and then set about organising my own relief – this was achieved on the 10th September 1947. While in Delhi, I was going from one lot of offices to another, when I was stopped by a sentry, who said 'Pass, Sahib'. I pointed to my shoulder tabs and said, in Urdu, 'What are these?'

He replied, 'I know, Sahib, but must see Pass'. So I took out my wallet and showed him a ticket in the Cambridgeshire Sweepstake, which had a picture of a female on it. He looked at it and said 'Thik hai, (OK), Sahib' and let me through.

I heard one day that there was going to be a train from Delhi to Bombay and I went down to the station – but no train – only stinking dead bodies, victims of riots, piled up on the station tracks. A few days later, a train did arrive in Delhi, having come down from Rawalpindi – full of British troops, wives and children. Three armed soldiers riding on the front of the engine and others, armed, riding in the cab. I had been issued with a revolver and was one of those who went down with the driver to the sidings to pick up coaches to accommodate those joining in Delhi. Finally, we left and later halted and each of us went along to the 'restaurant car', manned by the Army, and got some food which we took back to the compartments. We were warned that we were most liable to be attacked during the first night out of Delhi, but nothing transpired. The normal journey time from Delhi to Bombay is twenty-four hours – our train took seventy-two hours.

Then, farewells in Bombay and the voyage home and the start of twelve months leave on pay, pending retirement. I arrived in Launceston in October 1947 and gave myself until the 1st January 1948 before starting to look for another job. What followed, is another story.

In the ship in which I came home, was a Commander RN, who gave art lessons which paid his bar bill. Before arriving at Southampton, he had let it be known that he knew how to deal with Customs Officers. We arrived and the few Naval Officers were allowed ashore before the Army families and we were in the Customs shed about 0815. I had a list of items and prices and paid £2 or £3 duty and caught the train to London. I saw the Customs Officer with the Commander before I left. I went to London and reported to India Office and was back at Waterloo at lunch time to catch my train to Launceston, when the first boat train with the Army and families arrived. I was told that, when they left Southampton, the Commander was still there and the Customs officer was going through every piece of his luggage – he knew how to deal with Customs Officers!

9

A Volunteer Officer in the RIN
H M Darbyshire

At the outbreak of war in 1939, I was employed in the Tea Industry in Calcutta and had, since 1933, been a member of the Calcutta Light Horse and in the Army in India Reserve of Officers. The RIN had decided to recruit some executive officers, (there were a number of reserve paymasters on the strength at the time). I applied to join the RIN because I thought my early education at the Nautical College, Pangbourne made me more suitable for the Navy rather than the Army. The change of Service proved a difficult problem and one had the usual streamers of red tape to surmount.

However, in February 1940, I was appointed a Temporary Sub-Lieutenant, RINVR and despatched to Bombay to go through the separate shore courses required before being appointed to, what I hoped would be a sea-going ship and not a stone frigate, as shore establishments were termed. The RIN at that time had few ships, but I was one of the lucky ones in my course. In May 1940, I was appointed Junior Watch-Keeping Officer in HMIS LAWRENCE, due to join the Standing Patrol in the Persian Gulf. Despite the boring nature of our commission and the devastating heat of the Gulf in summer - 170 degrees in the Engine room at times - I enjoyed the experience. I was helped by some very pleasant shipmates, all being regulars except the doctor; Trevor Cole, (1st Lieutenant), Tom Sheppard, (Navigator), Midshipman Kohli, (later to become Chief-of-the-Naval Staff, Indian Navy), Carl Wykman, (Chief), Bhandari, (Senior Engineer), Bhusan, (3rd). Not least, Mr Coates, (Gunner), seconded from the RN, to whom I was appointed 'tanky' or assistant; a superb product of Whale Island.

We were in the Gulf some six months, going into Bahrain for boiler cleaning once, otherwise we patrolled at sea continuously, In Bahrain, I met St. John Philby, great Arabist, father of the notorious Kim, the MI6 spy, the former a convert to the Muslim religion. Philby was a very interesting and courteous chap - he always seemed immaculately dressed and wore a dinner jacket every evening.

Whilst we were in Bahrain, the Italians made a daring air raid, (flying from the Dodecanese Islands in the Mediterranean), on the adjacent oil fields on the mainland at Daharan. It was thought that some of their airmen had made forced landings in the desert. Philby organised a party in which two of us from LAWRENCE took part. Mounted on camels, we set off on a most uncomfortable journey into the hinterland in

114

search of the airmen. After thirty-six hours, my colleague and I could take no more and we persuaded Philby to return to Bahrain. On our return to India, we had Philby on board, occupying my cabin, because the powers that be adjudged that he was carrying on subversive activities and deemed he should be imprisoned in Karachi.

I spent the winter of 1940-41 in Bombay, doing refresher courses and, thereafter, rejoined LAWRENCE for a further spell in the Gulf. 1941 was memorable, for firstly, LAWRENCE took the boy-King of Iraq and the Regent to safety from Basra to Kuwait - a port in those days with a few shanty dwellings, camels and donkeys. We entered Kuwait in a sandstorm and our august passengers proceeded on by air to Transjordan. Later that same year, the decision was made to invade Persia and a force sailed under the overall command of Captain Nott, RIN, consisting, inter alia, of the Australian AMV KANIMBLA and the sloop YARRA, (later sunk in the battle of the Java Sea).

The force assembled in the Shatt-el-Arab and I was appointed for a short time to YARRA, as part of the invasion force to land troops at Khorramshah. After YARRA and before the attack, I was re-appointed to KANIMBLA which, with LAWRENCE, were to lead the attack on Bandar Shapur, in which port a large number of Axis merchant ships were anchored, some Italian, but including four or five vessels of the Ferman Hansa Line fleet. These ships had taken refuge there in 1939 at the outbreak of war. The boarding parties embarked in tugs lent by the Anglo-Iranian Oil Company and I was one of the party selected the pride of the Hansa Line, the MV HOHENFELS, (10,000 tons) on her maiden voyage. The attack was not a total success, since at least three of the ships successfully set themselves on fire or scuttled. The Germans blew the scuttling charges as soon as I boarded HOHENFELS and a ventilator descending from a great height flattened me and I woke up in the sick bay of KANIMBLA.

The overall invasion achieved its object and I was detailed with a number of other officers - Indian, British and Australian - to steam STURMFELS, (about 8,000 tons), not scuttled, to Karachi. After so long swinging round her anchor, the ship, especially her engines, proved a headache. However, we got there eventually and proudly entered harbour flying the White Ensign over the German equivalent. Docking had its problems because one anchor, the one called for by the Harbour Master, had its cable so rusted that, even with a sledge hammer, I was unable to veer it. The flare of our bow struck a large crane, which fell through the roof of a cargo shed. This effort, coupled with the further damage described later on in the part concerning Paddle Steamers, was not very popular with NOIC.

On or about 12th December 1941, I and other Volunteer Officers were detailed to man paddle steamers in Calcutta, normally used to carry tea and jute on the inland waterways of Bengal and Assam, with the ultimate object of delivering them to Basra, at the head of the Arabian Gulf. I was extremely proud of my first command, PS CALICUT. The boats were, of course, reinforced to increase the freeboard because of the increased stress of navigating at sea.

December 17th was the date of the Japanese attack on Pearl Harbour and, consequently, all lights in the river Hooghly were dimmed. Four boats, including CHAKDINA, (SO), CALICUT, (Self) and CHUNAR left Diamond Harbour, the leading boat, (I cannot remember her name), commanded by a regular naval officer and in charge of a river pilot. Unfortunately, disaster occurred when our leader went between what he, or the river pilot, thought were the lights of two fishing vessels at anchor. This turned out to be a big Norwegian tanker with dimmed anchor lights showing. The resultant collision was disastrous - the boat sank - fortunately the crew were picked up. Incidentally, the operation was started some three days earlier but, regrettably, all three first-away boats ran ashore somewhere north of Madras. These boats were flat-bottomed and therefore vulnerable to wind, also, strong currents as were met in coastal parts of the Bay of Bengal. This problem, as I will tell later, made navigation somewhat hazardous.

The remainder of us, three officers to each boat, with CHAKDINA in the lead, followed by CALICUT and CHUNAR, in that order, managed somehow to navigate the rest of the river without a pilot and finally arrived at the Pilot Vessel at the mouth of the Hooghly, some 120 miles south of Calcutta. Soon after sailing, I discovered that I had twenty degrees of error on my compass, although it had been checked before leaving Calcutta by NOIC's staff.

The boats were mainly crewed by Inland Waterways staff, including a Serang, domestic and engine room personnel, Signalmen, (No W/T), being provided by the RIN shortly afterwards, we sailed for Vizagapatam, our first port of call. All went well and we duly arrived there some three days later. At Vizagapatam I was able to have my compass calibrated and, having taken on food, fuel and water, we sailed for Madras. It was then that structural trouble occurred - the paddle on the port side, (they had also been reinforced), became loose and the blades splintered. This caused a tragedy insofar as the cookhouse, being abaft the paddle, was destroyed. Two cooks were killed and our feeding arrangements considerably disrupted. I asked permission of my senior officer to stop and conduct a simple funeral for the dead, (both Muslims) and to effect what repairs I could. An hour or so later I continued the journey, but found from shore bearings that we were making no headway at all, due to a strong northerly set and shortly afterwards the senior officer, having the same problem, appeared steering back to Vizagapatam. We all returned there since the conditions made it impossible to reach Madras with the fuel reserves we had. Considerable assistance was obtained from the NOIC and his staff and, some two or three days later, we were able to continue our journey. Sad to say, we did not receive the help to be expected in Madras. I later had my revenge over this Port Authority by indenting for an Oxometer and a can of Pissolene, which 'foxed' the NSO. In the end, I had to explain that an Oxometer was an instrument for measuring bullshit and Pissolene was necessary for oiling an Oxometer. No joke was seen.

We were glad to leave on the next part of our voyage which involved navigating the Palk Straits between India and Ceylon and thereafter proceeding west and north around Cape Comorin. We, in CALICUT, were forced to undergo engine repairs in Mandapam on the Indian side of the Palk Straits, where we celebrated Christmas, thanks to the hospitality of the Resident Engineer of the Madras and S Indian Railway, whose daughter, aged about eighteen, seemed to be somewhat attracted to my First Lieutenant. I suspect that this was reciprocated.

Early in the New Year 1942, we took our leave of our friends in Mandapam and proceeded along to Cochin, where we rejoined CHAKDINA and CHUNAR. The three of us, once more in company, sailed on for Karachi. A severe storm, however, caused considerable damage to CHAKDINA, who was compelled to seek shelter in Diu, a port in Portuguese India. Accompanied by CHUNAR, both very much the worse for wear, I arrived safely in Karachi in mid-January. CHAKDINA joined us some days later.

Once storm damage had been repaired, we were left bored and frustrated for several weeks in Karachi because the weather reports ahead were consistently bad. It was vital that we had good weather for the haul from Karachi to the Gulf entrance via the Gulf of Oman and through the Straits of Ormuz. The stretch to be navigated now involved much open sea, ie, steering away from land at night and closer to the coast in day time. There were virtually no terrestrial navigational aids – being wartime, most of the beacons and shore lights, such as they were, were turned off. Up till now, round the Indian coast, we had been able easily to navigate by shore fixes. Early in February, an improvement in the weather forecast, (which subsequently turned out to be totally inaccurate), made it possible for us to leave Karachi. I disgraced myself when departing by colliding with the oil jetty. It should be mentioned here, though not as an excuse, that these boats' paddles would either go ahead or astern, ie, you could not manoeuvre like a twin-screw ship by putting one ahead and the other astern, so assisting the turn in a small area. It would seem that I did more damage to the harbour than to myself, because on clearing the entrance, I received an urgent signal on a morse lamp from the Port War Signal Station to return. I therefore signalled the Senior Officer in CHAKDINA, enquiring as to the procedure following the knocking down of an oil jetty in a major port. His reply was terse and said 'Slip away into the night and say nothing about it'. I therefore replied to the PWSS with a series of 'W's, meaning 'Your light is not trained and cannot be read'. My ship mishandling, coupled with the damage caused earlier in STURMFELS, was to catch up with me when next I visited Karachi. NOIC had a long memory and too little to do, I suspect.

The next part of our voyage took us to Gwadar, a small port on the coast of Baluchistan, where we fuelled and took on food for the, to us, long haul to the entrance of the Gulf, (Khor Kwai). In Gwadar we learned the sad news of the fall of Singapore to the Japanese. We safely navigated the Gulf of Oman and entered the Arabian Gulf, where we met strong headwinds and finally encountered a 'shamal' - a strong sand-ridden wind known to navigators - harmless to most steamers but to us, with a high freeboard, something of a menace. We were using a lot of fuel fighting this headwind and, with a maximum   speed of six knots flat out, CALICUT was in danger of needing a tow. CHAKDINA and CHUNAR had by then lost touch.   A reference to the publication 'Persian Gulf Pilot' indicated a small port sheltered from the 'shamal' on the Persian side called appropriately Dairyir, (pronounced 'diarrhoea'), - I was getting quite scared by this time. We made this anchorage with no fuel to speak of and began to break up the furniture and any wood we could strip off without reducing our freeboard. Food was the next problem - we, that is to say, my two officers and I, had used up our supplies and we were eating the Muslim fare which, with no meat available, was surprisingly good.   I decided to send the First Lieutenant ashore, (the Port had last been visited by HMS CROCUS in 1924), to rustle up what he could bargain for. Some two hours later, I was horrified to hear two volleys of musketry -'My God', I thought, 'They have been executed'. It must be remembered that this was a very wild coast but, as it turned out, there was in residence a Wali, a junior sort of Sheikh.   The rifle fire was, it subsequently transpired, a sort of salute - cum - welcome and some hours later I was delighted to see some scruffy ruffians rowing a boat, towing our lifeboat, in which were several hundredweight sacks of rice and a whole sheep on the hoof, not to mention the First Lieutenant in person.

We left Dairyir the next day and the moment we left the lee of the land the weather became progressively worse and it was touch and go as to whether our improvised fuel supplies would last out as far as the Shatt-el-Arab, (the confluence of the Tigris and Euphrates rivers). We decided that the rest of the so-called wardroom furniture and anything ignitable must be sacrificed, including the reinforced planking fitted, even if this affected the freeboard.

After a traumatic few days, leaking like a sieve, we arrived at the entrance to the Shatt-el-Arab, where we found it difficult to anchor because of the very strong ebb tide and the depth of water, having regard to the length of our cable.   At this point we could still expect no assistance from the shore authorities; there were none and it was another week before we were able to navigate up to our destination Basra, arriving on the 5th March, very exhausted indeed.

At this point, I pay tribute to the humble Indian sailors, on deck and in the engine room, accustomed to a peaceful life carrying jute and tea by river in Bengal and Assam, for their courage in leaving their families to go to sea in a far from seaworthy craft. These paddlers were later put to use in Persia to augment the urgent supply route via the back door to Russia. So far as I recall, thirty-seven paddle boats set out from Calcutta and over thirty reached Basra safely.

Having handed over PS CALICUT to the local Inland Water Transport Authorities in Basra, I was detailed, with one or two other unfortunates, to take another paddle boat, owned by Gray, Mackenzie & Company, (an offshoot of P & O, I believe), up the Tigris with stores for the garrison at Kut-al-Amara - a dead and alive place which had become notorious in World War I. The only incident on this occasion was the fact that we were able to rescue some unfortunate RAF men, who had been captured by rebels involved with one Rashid Ali - an Iraqi firebrand who

118

had taken this opportunity to throw in his lot with the Germans. The latter had, by this time, reached Baghdad in small parties. The RAF men were lucky in so far as, instead of being killed or mutilated in true Arab fashion, they had been hung up by their wrists or thumbs and would have died of thirst. Thereafter, most of us were repatriated, if that is the right word, to India, where I took certain refresher courses in Bombay and was able to have a badly needed rest.

Towards the end of March or early April 1942, I was drafted to Colombo to join HMS DORSETSHIRE, (Captain A Agar, VC, RN), to enable me to do the required time to obtain my Major War Vessel Watch-Keeping Certificate. I hardly had time to stow my kit when we sailed, with CORNWALL in company, and immediately encountered the Japanese Naval Air Force. As history relates, both of us were sunk as a result, I recall, of the only incursion during the war made by the Japanese Fleet into the Indian Ocean.

I spent an uncomfortable thirty-six hours in the water, before being rescued by the Australian destroyer PALADIN. I can remember a sailor hauling me inboard, stark naked, (I had been taking a shower when Action Stations were sounded) and weak from a large intake of fuel oil, calling to his mates enquiring whether this was the Loch Ness Monster! After some survivor's leave, I returned to Bombay, where my next appointment was as First Lieutenant and Navigating Officer in HMIS BOMBAY, (Lieutenant Commander GP Frazier, RIN) a new ship of the Bathurst Class in which I spent a very happy commission, escorting convoys in the Indian Ocean, Persian Gulf and Red Sea. I had, by this time, been awarded a Major War Vessels' Watch-Keeping Certificate and, in December 1942, I obtained the coveted 'Qualified Officer Status', enabling me to rank with regular officers of the same rank.

After spending some months in Bombay as CO elect of a Basset Trawler, being built, (for minesweeping duties) in the docks, I realised that the war might end while I was stagnating with no, or very little, building work in progress. I persuaded the powers that be to draft me to Coastal Forces. A number of MTBs were being built in the Annapolis yard in America for service in the Far East. They were powered by three super-charged Packard engines and two Ford V8 engines, (for silent running), and operated on 100 octane fuel. I had the good fortune to be given command of MTB 278, (16th Flotilla), commissioned in Calcutta in April 1943. Tragedy struck immediately, when an explosion took place, whilst I was ashore and two sailors, a Chief Motor Mechanic and a Stoker died of burns as a result. There were strict rules to be observed because of the highly inflammable nature of the fuel and, as a result of the Enquiry, the deceased were adjudged to have been at fault. I, as CO, received a reprimand, which was a bit unfair as I was nowhere near the vessel at the time of the accident. At least I had my life - so why complain?

The MTBs turned out to be something of a white elephant since their range was limited and, compared with the narrow seas of the Channel where they had operated successfully, there was no way such craft could operate in the Bay of Bengal. In September, I was promoted to Lieutenant

Commander and transferred as CO of the 55th ML Flotilla. These boats were less fast, had a longer range and were more heavily armed than their counterparts elsewhere in the Mediterranean and the Channel. Between November and March, we carried out offensive operations and landed agents on the coast of Burma. We carried out the raid on the Arakan Coast from a forward base called Tek Naaf, our main base being Chittagong.

On one of these forays, the bombardment of the Japanese-held island of Ramree, the Japs reacted savagely and I, with three other MLs in company, were heavily bombed on our return journey. The first attack was with light bombs and a strafing by fighters. I signalled for Air assistance, the only result being repeated warning signals from Chittagong W/T that enemy aircraft were approaching - a fact I knew only too well when the second wave of aircraft attacked with heavy bombs, about 500 lbs, I would guess. One near miss caused a blast which blew me off the bridge and I landed aft with the wireless aerials wrapped around me. At this point, I ordered a signal in plain language to be sent to Chittagong, asking them 'for Christ's sake, to do something'. A calm reply indicated 'RAF fighters are over you now'. I could see nothing but vapour trails overhead. In fact, the RAF (224 Group) had a field day shooting down a number of Jap aircraft. My coxswain received superficial wounds in the neck, my Motor Mechanic was gassed, though not seriously, through an escape of carbon monoxide caused by blast. My Coxswain, Allyar Khan, was decorated with the DSM. It seemed that the Commander-in-Chief Eastern Fleet had intercepted my panic signal to Chittagong and, later on, I received a personal signal from this very senior officer, referring me to a passage in the Bible which, in effect, told me 'not to blaspheme in times of dire distress'. A nice touch and a well deserved rebuke.

In March 1944, in a detached operation with the Army, in a landing craft, I was again sunk - this time by cannon fire from a lone Jap aircraft off Tek Naaf. Having swum ashore, I was nearly shot by a party of Indian soldiers, (Garwhalis), who thought I was a Japanese airman. Thereafter, I avoided Army games and remained with my MLs - far less hazardous. In passing, it should be related that, when this cannon shell punctured the hull of the landing craft, I, having the biggest 'arse', was told to sit in the hole. After some time and a very cold bottom, I realised that my companions, unknown to me, had abandoned ship and I was left sitting alone in my hole!

By April 1944, the onset of the cyclone season in the Bay of Bengal put an end temporarily to Coastal Forces activity. I remained with MLs until June 1944, when I was posted to the staff of FOCRIN in Delhi - a new appointment as Staff Officer, Coastal Forces. In theory, this was a good idea to try to get the men of the 'little ships' represented in higher places. In practice, it proved another white elephant because FOCRIN and other Indian Navy and Army officers sitting in Delhi were not interested in coastal forces. In fact, although I was supposed to be rated a Staff Officer, I never ever met the Admiral except once in a urinal (heads) - the only act we seem to have had in common.

I soon began to realise that one was bashing one's head against a brick wall and, having been in the East since my last return from leave in 1939, plus the 'hard-lying', as the Navy called it, in Coastal Forces, I had something of a nervous breakdown and made a thorough nuisance of myself. So many of those in Delhi, not all, had made a very comfortable niche for themselves far from the war. One can understand this as a possible reason why Mountbatten transferred his HQ to Kandy in Ceylon.

I was granted leave in the UK in August 1944 and, allowing for the wartime conditions in the UK, which made **me** anyway aware of the relative comforts of those living in India at the time, I felt the change to be beneficial, despite the discomforts, such as rationing and V1 flying bombs. In the UK, I was not allowed to get away scot free from the Navy, because plans were afoot to instal Radar in Coastal Forces boats in India. Although I underwent some training in the use of radar in the Channel, nothing ultimately came of this idea, which was overridden by the end of hostilities in 1945.*

My short leave in the UK having ended, I returned to India in December 1944 and, on arrival in Bombay, I found that my misdemeanours in Delhi had caught up with me and I was assigned to the Anti-Submarine School in Bombay, (Captain Sanders, RN), as First Lieutenant. A rather humble and downgraded appointment which I found frustrating, to say the least. I remained there until May 1945, (VE Day) when, with the help of certain Coastal Forces friends, I obtained a transfer to HMIS BARRACUDA, (Commander LG Bingham, RNR). This ship, formerly the HEINRICH JESSEN, was fitted out as a Depot Ship for Coastal Forces craft, carrying all the stores, spare engines etc, required to replenish the boats. It must be remembered that, because of the huge distances involved, unlike the English Channel, a floating mobile base was essential. We spent many weeks waiting, so common in wartime, off the Nicobar Islands, though, from time to time, called at Rangoon, now liberated, where I collected a useful sum in pilotage for navigating the river.

At long last, in August the Japanese surrendered and BARRACUDA, along with units of the Royal Navy, arrived in Singapore, where we collected and helped to feed some of the inmates of Changi Gaol, including the later Bishop of Birmingham. How grateful they were - although I do remember one RN ship serving rice pudding.

We remained some time in Singapore and I was fortunate to be selected to form part of the bodyguard escorting the Japanese military contingent, headed by General Igitaki, who surrended in a brief ceremony to Admiral Mountbatten.

We sailed for Batavia to collect and bring to Singapore a number of Japanese personnel, both military and the infamous 'Kempei Tei', stranded on the various Indonesian Islands. BARRACUDA finally sailed for Calcutta to decommission and the war for me had ended. I obtained my demobilisation papers and returned to my civilian job in Calcutta, where I remained until 1955.

* Editor's Note: The author is incorrect in this statement - several MLs were, in fact, fitted with radar before the war ended.

121

HMIS CAUVERY in Hong Kong

10

HMIS CAUVERY

R Williams

HMIS CAUVERY, known to the Royal Navy as 'Covery', was one of the ships and establishments unaffected by the RIN mutiny and the story may be of interest, since I do not think that it has been told generally.

CAUVERY had the odd distinction of never serving under the direct operational control of NHQ (I) until well after the mutiny. She had three Commanding Officers - Bones Beeton, Wentworth Harvey and Bill Moger and, during her war time and immediate post-war service, only two First Lieutenants, Queenie King and myself. (I believe my own appointment as Number One to be, probably, an RIN record at thirty-four months).

After service with the 60th Escort Group, (and the redoubtable Captain Broome of Force 66), up-river bombardment in the chaungs, the invasion of Malaya, we joined the British Pacific Fleet Escort Group and took part in the occupation of Japan. At this stage, Bill Moger had the difficult task, (and in retrospect, I concede that it must have been a considerable task), of converting us back from war to peace, which he did with a degree of tact worthy of Solomon himself.

At the time of the mutiny, CAUVERY was on detached service in the Inland Sea of Japan, off Shikoku, at Mitsuyama, the port of Mitsuhama. One cold spring morning - and it could be chilly in the Inland Sea - having turned the hands to, I retired to the wardroom in search of some hot coffee. Listening idly to the radio, I was somewhat shaken to learn from the BBC News that Bombay, in particular and the Service in general was in a state of mutiny - so was the goggle-eyed steward!

The Captain was equally surprised, on being called, by this 'stirring news', (a BBC headline). The tactics subsequently adopted were based on that superb and little read BR, 'Mutiny in the Royal Navy', which lays down clearly certain principles to be adopted. It had been studied because, for some time, there had been a feeling in CAUVERY that disaffection in the Service, irrespective of political issues, must cause trouble and, previously, we had received a severe reprimand from Admiral Godfrey for reporting this feeling in a Morale and Security Report. It was considered, in the wording of the reprimand, that an official report had been used 'to express, through this channel, private opinions of a highly objectionable nature'. At 0900 lower-deck was cleared and the news was given to the ship's company, as far as it was known. An Immediate signal, in plain language, was made to the Commander-in-Chief BPF, (R) BPF Escort Force and NH1 (I), reporting that we 'understood the Service to have mutinied and asking, **as absolute priority,** for official facts to confound rumours,' ('Mutiny in the Royal Navy'). We also guaranteed the loyalty of the ship's company of CAUVERY, out of hand.

I lost a file several years ago or I could have quoted these signals in original - they were really quite dramatic. This signal, without comment, was posted on all ship's company notice boards immediately. With great celerity, we received a reply from Commander-in-Chief, BPF, 'Personal from Admiral Fraser', which said, in essence, 'Good show', followed shortly by a terse signal to NHQ (I), demanding facts to be signalled forthwith (R) forthwith. It remained quite unanswered - for ever. There was considered to be one 'potential' mutineer in the ship's company and a ballot between the Chief Buffer, the Chief Mechanic and the Chief Stoker, (all of them with long service in CAUVERY,), with a deciding vote from Number One, produced exactly the same name - Krishnamurty.

The three senior ratings mentioned were all first class men and were instructed to watch one Radar Operator like hawks and, in the event of any incitement, to act first, as brutally as possible and ask afterwards. At 'Clear lower-deck', the point was made that the Bombay action would cause CAUVERY acute embarrassment and that we would all be classed in the BPF as 'bloody mutineers', (Admiralty manual - 'Pour scorn' etc).

We all went ashore for the week-end, leaving CAUVERY, detached, fuelled and victualled, in the charge of junior officers and implicitly trusted senior ratings. To our relief, she was perfectly under control when we came back, after which we were, in one sense, 'adopted' by Lord Fraser of North Cape, who treated us with much charm and consideration, in consequence, on the station.

*   *   *

The end of the story appeared in 'Blitz'. On CAUVERY's eventual return to Bombay - still very untidy from the aftermath of the mutiny -we were berthed, not in the Dockyard, but in the Bombay Docks, as a special case. Our first act was to land some forty ratings, all grossly overdue for discharge, as we were invaded by the local Press, to whose discomfort our time-expired men gave three cheers for the King-Emperor; three cheers for the Captain and three cheers and a 'Tiger' for CAUVERY. 'Blitz' cited it as a 'clear signal of British repression'.

Later, we were berthed alongside KISTNA in the Dockyard. Bill Moger was re-appointed and I finished my days Acting-in-Command of CAUVERY - a nice end to three very happy years. Most of the ship's company spoke excellent English and, in the Pacific, had acquired some regrettable Australian expressions, due to mixing with HMAS SYDNEY. After the Chief Stoker had told one untidy-looking rating in the Dockyards to 'Take that . . . fag out of your gob, you scruffy bastard', I was summoned by the Flag Officer, Bombay and ordered to control the ship's company, as he did not want any more trouble on his hands. Further, to report officially that there would be no such incidents of this nature in the yard in future. He said it, as always, with a delightful twinkle in his eye, as only Jack Rattray could.

Alas, in the lost signal file, is that superb document according the 'ex-post-facto sanction of the Governor General in Council to the issue of a rum ration to the ship's company of H MIS CAUVERY on the occasion of VJ Day', also, the whole of the correspondence with the Controller of Naval Accounts, concurring the rebate of all income tax paid by officers and ratings of CAUVERY whilst outside Indian territorial waters and, thus, out of the jurisdiction of the Government of India, so very brilliantly conceived and executed by the peculiar mind of 'Chockers' Nott, (on whom be peace). Memories, occasionally, can be fun.

11

HMIS NARBADA, the Andamans, 1943

W J M Teale

At about 0930 on September 26th, 1945, the Officer of the Watch sighted two small boats about five miles ahead of us. They were identified as a Japanese motor launch and a landing craft. At once all was pandemonium on board as we rushed around preparing to greet the envoys from Port Blair.

A guard was fallen-in on the quarter-deck under the command of the Gunner's Mate; a piping party blew furtively into their pipes to make sure that there were no obstructions therein; three or four officers with cameras draped themselves on various vantage points; the RPO rushed around hunting people away from scuttles through which they were peering; the Captain and I placed ourselves at the head of the gangway and all was ready.

As the motor launch got closer we were able to discern the figures of five Naval officers, a Marine bugler, a Marine standard bearer with a white flag and two civilians wearing marine caps. With a mighty crash, followed by a splintering of wood, the craft struck the gangway - the shipwright had taken over a month to repair it. I called down a variety of curses on the heads of the Japanese.

Then, amidst a twittering of pipes, a diminutive Lieutenant Commander appeared at the head of the gangway; he turned aft and saluted the ensign - cameras clicked furiously - then he turned and saluted us and walked on board. The remainder followed and repeated his actions. The Captain then led the way to his cabin - Lieutenant ES Joshua RIN and I, wearing revolvers, followed astern.

On arrival in the Commanding Officer's cabin, the Japanese arrayed themselves in front of the table and the CO Lieutenant Commander AA Lawson, RINVR, SO(I) Designate, Port Blair and two Civil Affairs Officers seated themselves on the other side. The two officer guards placed themselves at either entrance and stood by in case anyone should decide to commit 'harakiri'. I gather that our duties were to remove intending suicides to a place where the mess did not matter. A series of questions were then put to the Japanese regarding minefields, anchorages etc. All this was done through the medium of an interpreter, who bowed and hissed repeatedly. After the requisite information had been gained, we proceeded towards Port Blair and anchored off Ross Island.

The envoys were given a list of questions and told to bring the answers back by noon the day following. Then came the big moment - the

Lieutenant Commander bowed very low and said that he had been instructed by the Vice-Admiral commanding the Andamans to enquire when it would be convenient for him to call on the Commanding Officer, HMIS NARBADA, to thank him personally for bringing supplies to the prisoners of war and local population. The Captain appeared to give this matter his consideration and graciously gave his consent to the Admiral's request – I am certain that he relished the thought of the Admiral begging permission to call on a Lieutenant Commander RIN. The envoys then left the ship.

During the afternoon, we went around in the ship's boat to all the landing jetties, with a view to deciding which would be the most suitable for landing the supplies. Wherever we went, parties of Japanese were fallen-in to salute as we passed. At times this could be most disconcerting, as they always remained at the salute during the whole time we were in their vicinity.

After inspecting the jetties, it was decided to visit the prisoners of war. In all, there were 143 Indians in Aberdeen and one Englishman on Ross Island. The Indian prisoners seemed to be in very good shape, considering the scarcity of medical supplies and the resultant high incidence of disease. It would appear that International Law had been followed. This is probably due to the fact that the island was controlled by Japanese Naval Forces, of whom there were over 3,000 in and around Port Blair. Spread about on the islands there were also some 5,000 Army troops.

I visited the Englishman. He was a DEMS rating who had been torpedoed between Java and Christmas Island. He and six others, (two of whom had died), sailed for eighty-nine days in an open boat before they reached the Andamans. His few remaining companions, who were officers, were sent to Singapore. He was kept on the island and employed as an MT driver. He did not seem to be particularly excited at seeing us and stated that, after over three years on the island, he had grown to like it and had little desire to go away. He had made friends with some of the Japanese seamen, who had been very good to him. In all, they had paid him Rs.800 during his stay. We gave him some supplies and told him that he would be taken off when the main force arrived.

Promptly at 1000 on the 27th, the Admiral arrived. He was met with a guard and piped on board. He was accompanied by the Major General in charge of the Army forces ashore – various staff officers of both services accompanied their respective chiefs.

They were all led forward to the Captain's cabin. On arrival, they presented their cards, accompanied with profound bows – after about five minutes of this, everybody was bowing to everybody else. I expected that any moment we would take our partners for a minuet! For the next half hour, through the medium of an interpreter, compliments were exchanged. The Admiral went on to tell us of the conditions ashore and the methods of administration which he had employed. He told us that anything we required they would give us – provided it was available.

Previous to their arrival, I had suggested to the Captain that we should ask for the services of some local carpenters for repair work and then, once they were aboard, I would be able to augment our shipwright's party. The Captain explained to the Admiral the disaster which had befallen our gangway. The Admiral expressed his profound apologies and said that the officer concerned (a Lieutenant Commander), would be dealt with. We were both a bit taken aback by this, as we rather expected a formal presentation on the quarter-deck of one head - Japanese Lieutenant Commander for the use of.

The Captain hastened to assure the Admiral that no blame could be attached to this officer and that it was merely the fault of the swell running at the time. The Admiral stated that the matter would be attended to immediately on his return ashore. The conversation proceeded most amicably from then on. The General hardly spoke at all. Whenever he was spoken to, he rose and bowed low to the Captain before replying. Before the party left the ship, the Admiral said that he would be honoured if the Captain would condescend to return his call. That afternoon, a craft arrived alongside bearing the Lieutenant Commander, who still appeared to be all in one piece. They removed the gangway and bore it ashore, where it was repaired and returned to us the following morning.

At 1030 on the 28th, the Captain and I, wearing our last remaining suits of No 10's and with clanking swords, set off to return the call of the Admiral. We were met at the jetty by a Lieutenant Commander, who led us to an enormous car waiting for us. A saluting Petty Officer held the door open for us and we seated ourselves. The Japanese got in front and we drove off past a guard at the 'Present'. The drive that followed was reminiscent of a royal procession - every fifty yards or so along the route were parties of police and sailors at the salute; also, the local population were out in force and they 'salaamed' as we went past. It was terrific.

The arrival at the Japanese Headquarters afforded us the pièce-de-résistance of the whole day. There was, of course, the usual guard, but, in addition, were the two Commanders-in-Chief, with their respective staffs, lined up in a row. As we stepped out of the car, as one man they all bowed low before us. We were led upstairs to a large room where all the senior staff were presented which, of course, was accompanied by a lot of bowing and hissing. They then left the room and we were left with the Admiral, the General and an interpreter. We were offered cigarettes, which were very good; one was provided for me by the Major General, who bowed low and then lit it for me. As we were seated by this time, the Captain and I acknowledged the bows with regal inclinations of our heads.

Half-an-hour or so of compliments followed and then, to our very great surprise, the Admiral asked the General to leave. When the door had closed, he said that we could then talk as between Naval Officers. He gave us a most interesting insight into the views held by the Japanese Navy. It was obvious that there was a great enmity between their Army and Navy. He regretted that the Navy was unable to avert both the spreading of the 'China Incident' and the present war, but he said that, once the policy of the Government had been formulated, it was the bounden duty of every Japanese to put aside his own opinions and fight. He told us of his very high opinion of the bravery and discipline of the

British Navy, of which he had had personal experience. He had visited England on three occasions. The conversation lasted two-and-a-quarter hours and then we had a repeat performance of our triumphal drive to our ship. We found that the officers were a bit apprehensive for our safety and were considering coming ashore to see if we were still alive.

When the Japanese in the Andaman and Nicobar Islands signed the Instrument of Surrender at a ceremonial parade at Port Blair, the RIN was represented by a guard detailed from the ship's company of HMIS NARBADA, which had assisted our forces in the re-occupation of the islands. Forming part of the guard mounted jointly with men of the Royal Navy and the Royal Marines, the RIN contingent was led by Lieutenant R K Raisenghani RINVR, of Karachi.

Fresh from vital patrol work in these waters before the main force arrived, officers and men of NARBADA came in large numbers to witness the ceremony, held on the tennis court of the Gymkhana Club, facing Sesostris Bay. The Union Jack flew from a tall flag staff and round it the Naval and Military guards formed a hollow square. Brigadier J A Salomans, commanding our forces, read out the Instrument of Surrender, the white-gloved Japs listening intently. The documents were then handed over for signature. Vice-Admiral Teizo Hara signed and fixed his seal first and Lieutenant Commander Tazawa, Major General Tamenore, his Staff Officer and Captain Shimazaki followed suit. For us, the documents were signed by Brigadier Salomans, Captain JH Blair RNR, the Naval Force Commander and Mr NK Patterson, the Chief Commissioner Designate.

Immediately afterwards, the Japanese handed over their swords. Their gloved hands fumbled with their belts as Vice-Admiral Teizo Hara led them to the table opposite, where they deposited their weapons, saluted in turn and marched off towards their cars. They were driven away to the accompaniment of cat-calls from the large crowd of islanders who, in witnessing the ceremony, had shown extreme delight at the end of Japanese occupation.

12
Letters to a Father

1. On Pay

November 22nd 1935

Today the Admiral and COS arrived back from Delhi . . . the scheme is that a somewhat absurd and unfair system of allowances should go and a general rise in pay come in. At present, one officer may be earning twice as much as another of the same rank - and possibly have an easier job. And when he goes on leave he takes his allowances with him, and for two months his successor only gets his pay. So, there are some grounds for reform.

December 20th 1935

The Old Man (Cooper) is grand. He does nothing on the bridge except a word of advice here and there. He is giving me half the pilotage (allowance) - which will be quite a lot of money. Of course, seeing that he never even looks at a chart, it is only fair in a way - but his is the chief responsibility, and not all skippers do it.

December 26th 1936

. . . the pay is out. The signal came just as we had finished our Xmas dinner - so it seems that the Government of India is sometimes quite human. Briefly, it consists of an Indian allowance, a marriage allowance . . . so that everything except our basic pay is the same as the Army. So I shall be getting Rs.450 a month instead of 300 . . . . Incidentally, marriage allowance is only to officers over thirty.

2. On Ceremony

November 29th 1935

On Thursday, the RIN paraded a Guard of Honour for the arriving Commander-in-Chief, India. The Guards, one Naval and one Army, were drawn up on the landward side of the Gateway of India - ours having the privilege of the right, on account of British custom and of being the oldest

Service in India - bar none. And, in spite of the Durham Light Infantry band playing them on at 140 instead of 120, our troops ran the soldiers (Punjabis), very close - which is really very creditable . . . for it's just a sideline for us, whereas heaven knows what else the soldiers do out here. The same show was repeated for the departure of Sir Philip Chetwode yesterday.

April 17th 1936

Today the new Viceroy arrived, (Linlithgow) . . . I was appointed Captain of the State Barge and so had the honour of bringing their Excellencies ashore. Tomorrow, the Willingdons go - unfortunately - and again I shall have the job of taking them off. Linlithgow doesn't look the man that Willingdon is, but is perhaps brainier. His lady looked very beautiful . . . .

June 10th 1936 - HMIS HINDUSTAN at Trincomalee

While at Colombo, we learnt to our disgust that we are to return there for a King's Birthday Parade. These parades seem to be the limit of this Admiral's ideas - charming man though he is, he's becoming very unpopular. Here we are, 400 miles from Colombo, and getting on with training nicely - then we pack it all up and go back for a week. 'Sheer waste of time', vide Percy, our Captain.

Everything is going well with the new Captain - in spite of his reputation, he is a most lovable man in many ways and very human . . . we have been out all day firing . . . he thinks up tactical situations and dumps them suddenly on one . . . .

July 7th 1936

It seems pretty definite that I shall go to CLIVE in a month's time, (CLIVE is Flagship). Fortunately, our Captain is going as well and there's no one I'd rather serve under.

3. On Exercises

March 21st 1936

. . . As I was ten hours on the bridge both yesterday and the day before without a break.

The efficiency test was great fun. The Admiral and Staff, together with the Governor of Bombay came on board with a packet of envelopes. One by one they were given to the Captain and according to the content we had to act - open fire on a submarine; close capture by boarding; cope with fires etc. The Captain was very glad to be 'killed' very early in the proceedings.

I thought the Governor, (Lord Brabourne) was a Press man until I spoke to him. He was very tickled - the Yeoman had ticked him off for

overlooking a confidential signal book   (A charming personality).
Yesterday, we had a full calibre shoot and all ships at sea making smoke
screens and manoeuvering . . .

4. On the Prospect of War

February 12th 1936

I'm afraid we all share your apprehensions about the world in general
- especially about Germany. I think we've got Italy well taped as regards
any direct aggression. The Abyssinian war was then in progress. But, if
that attack on our fleet had materialised when it was perhaps intended, it
might have been a different matter and there is good reason, (which
cannot be committed to paper), for believing that it was not the rather
undignified scare that the public thought - it was more than likely a bold
stroke that by pure chance failed to come off. Now, of course, it would
be hopeless. I don't think there's a single precaution that we haven't taken
. . . . But what about later - a powerful starving Germany - a weak
exhausted Italy - how I'd hate to be a Frenchman . . . .

5. On Trincomalee

Have just returned from Sober Island - reserved for the use of
wardroom officers. It is a glorious spot, with a grand bathing beach.
There is a 'Wardroom' and a caretaker - one can have beer or tea - and a
tennis court . . . we sailed out there and tea'd, tennised and swam . . . the
'wardroom' overlooks the whole harbour - the Squadron lying away in the
background puts the finishing touch on a perfect picture. Really, the
island of Ceylon is one of God's own spots - perhaps that's why it comes in
Hymns such a lot.

March 1st 1936 - HMIS HINDUSTAN

This week has been fairly eventful . . . I played tennis with the
Admiral and Mrs - they play even worse than I do. They are a charming
pair . . . . He fell into the drink a couple of times during the evening -once
trying to catch his dog and once trying to tie up his comic little boat -
about seven feet long, which he actually sails.
On Wednesday, there were five pulling races . . . the enthusiasm had
to be seen to be believed. Afterwards, Mrs Bedford gave the prizes.
Last evening, Jimmy and I sailed the skiff down to Sober Island and
bathed. It was lovely just drifting along in the evening breeze, listening
to the birds and watching the fish leaping.
Last night, there was a local defence exercise . . . . Our Sub who had
our half platoon, sank in his canoe with a couple of men - you should have
heard what Number One had to say when he reported two rifles at the
bottom of the harbour at 0430 this morning. Nothing loath, he and the
Sub lowered the cutter with the diving gear . . . and get them they did by
0730 and came back very pleased with themselves. Neither of them had a

wink of sleep, but at 1100 we were At Home to the Admiral in celebration of our Regatta Victory, (this had been a series of pulling races spread over several days).

Tomorrow, we are going to carry out an indirect bombardment over a ridge. We do a full calibre shoot on Tuesday and Thursday, thank goodness, a whole day's holiday - a whole day to spend on Sober Island.

13

The Anti-Submarine Branch

REMINISCENCES OF CW PARKINSON

As a newly-commissioned Sub-Lieutenant, RINVR, I was posted to class 'C' in July 1940. We were mostly ex-box-wallahs with varying degrees of ignorance of naval matters, but there was a sprinkling of young Indian officers and some NR officers. Successively, we had short three-week courses in Seamanship, A/S, Signals, Gunnery and Navigation. The short A/S course was in what I imagine was a very new A/S School high on the ramparts at the south-east corner of Bombay Fort, looking out over the harbour with the Naval Dockyard to the south and the Commercial Docks to the north.

In charge of the School and instructing was Lieutenant Brian Goord who had recently, I believe, completed his long A/S course at HMS OSPREY. Equipment was short and whilst we had a complete Asdic to train on, there was no way of simulating echoes other than by Brian Goord's famous mandolin. Enthusiasm and imagination in instruction triumphed over material deficiencies so far as this short A/S course was concerned - and, indeed, the same applies to the other courses - with the result that a stream of Reserve Officers, enthusiastic and, within obvious limitations, well trained, was turned out.

On completion of these short courses, some twelve or fifteen Reserve Officers chosen from the first four or five short courses were posted to a long Signals and A/S course. Sadly, most of the names escape me, but certainly this first long Signals and A/S course in the RIN included Lieutenant RD Katari, AJ Braund, George Armstrong, Jack Dickins, Nair and Nick Rashleigh. A theoretical course in Magnetism and Electricity was followed by about two months in each of the Signals and A/S Schools, totalling some five months from November 1940 to April 1941. At the end of the course, some members were sent to A/S posts and some to Signals posts. Whether combining the two specialisations was wise is debatable. The A/S specialists were mainly given Port A/S Officers' jobs around the various Indian ports. For myself, I was to remain at the A/S School as an Instructor under Brian Goord.

By this time, the School was running continuous SD courses, occasional HSD courses and successive three-week Reserve Officer classes. The first three or four courses consisted, predominantly, of newly-commissioned VR officers, but the emphasis was changing and more and more RINR Officers, who had been serving afloat, were being relieved by the newly trained VRs and brought ashore for these short courses.

They were much older men with mercantile marine experience; some with Master's tickets; and they had had their own commands. Some did not take too kindly to being brought back to 'School'. Fortunately, this attitude did not seem to apply to A/S work and I found the instructing most exhilarating.

Around the middle of 1941, Brian Goord was transferred, (to a Staff job) and I was appointed Officer-in-Charge of the A/S School. He had built the school up to a high standard, (as I found when I was seconded, temporarily to the RN the following year), and taking over was pretty straightforward.

Running the HSD classes we had a Punjabi SDI Petty Officer whose name, regretfully, I forget. His family had a long history of service in the Indian Army and he combined a fatherly protectiveness towards the young recruits with firm discipline. A threat to 'write to his father' would bring any recalcitrant rating to order immediately. Instructing the SDs was, I believe, Leading-Seaman Abdul Hamid who later served with me in KONKAN. During the closing months of 1941, we ran the second long A/S course. Again, it was combined with the Signals and was very much on the lines of the first course. The second course finished by the end of 1941. I was posted to the UK for the commissioning of the Bangor Class minesweepers and Lieutenant TJ Hudson, RINVR took over the A/S School.

On my return to India, late in 1942, in HMIS KONKAN, I was posted back to the A/S School and found myself instructing the third long A/S course. By this time, MACHLIMAR was being built at Versova and this course was the last in the old A/S School. The transfer to MACHLIMAR was completed by about March 1943 and, instead of moving to MACHLIMAR, I was appointed A/S Training Officer, Bombay on NOIC's staff and housed again in the old A/S School on the familiar ramparts of the Fort, complete with the original School equipment.

In Spring 1943, I was appointed A/S Training Officer, Bombay, inheriting the old A/S School buildings in Bombay Fort. The original equipment, now complete with an A/S Tactical Table, remained, together with a number of classrooms. The purpose was the training of ship's A/S teams while they were in harbour. Initially, as I recall, the staff consisted of myself and an SDI. The ships' teams would usually consist of the CO, the A/S Officer and SD ratings. At this time, the emphasis of Naval operations was moving eastwards and the number of ships using our facilities increased rapidly. Apart from RIN vessels we trained many RN ships up to sloops and destroyers, Australian corvettes and Bathursts and at least one Dutch destroyer.

However, my attachment to HMS WESTERN ISLES, the small ship working up base off Tobermory, had taught me the necessity of integrating depth-charge drill into the total A/S picture and on-board depth-charge drill and working-up sea trials became equally important. Another innovation was the convoy 'game' which we would organise whenever there were sufficient escorts in port. These would last the best part of a day, involving five or six escort 'teams', U-boat packs and some air attacks to liven things up. How useful these 'games' were I don't know but they were certainly enjoyed by all who took part.

The work-load and the staff of the centre continued to rise until mid-1944 when the War had moved further east and, due in part at least, to the immobilising of Bombay Port by the explosion, the number of escort vessels visiting Bombay dropped precipitately - so much so that by the end of the year I had been transferred to the escort group under Captain RR (Bob) Caws.

Only isolated memories of this period remain. Depth-charge drill alongside was always a worry. Fortunately, we never dropped a charge in the mud, but the thought of such an accident was always present. The memory of HINDUSTAN undergoing sea-trials after many months in dock when we dropped a pattern of charges, still remains. The second charge exploded as it hit the surface - the stern rose three or four feet and we limped back to port with every engineer on board rushing every this way and that as the propellor glands leaked. But, perhaps, best of all, was a charming letter from Captain Murray-Clark saying that JUMNA had bagged a U-boat and thanking the centre for training which had contributed to the success.

"THE LONGEST CHASE" by AB GOORD

On 6th August 1944, the British merchant ship EMPIRE CITY was sunk by a U-boat in the Mozambique Channel. The crew took to the boats, but not before the radio officer had transmitted a sighting report. At this moment, Force 66, comprising the carriers BEGUM, (SO Captain 'Jackie' Broome, DSC), and SHAH, with six escort vessels including HMI ships CAUVERY and GODAVARI, was some 2,000 miles distant, in the vicinity of the Chagos Archipelago.

Immediately on receipt of the report, the Force altered course, to start what seemed likely to be yet another fruitless chase of an undersea enemy half an ocean away. However, with Force 66 already making best speed westwards, the U-boat commander rashly transmitted reports of the sinking. As a result, she was 'fixed' twice by shore D/F, giving a clear indication that she was proceeding in a north-easterly direction, probably towards Japanese-held Malaya.

By the 10th, four days after the sinking, the Force had reached the submarine's furthest-on position. The carriers put up an air search and, sure enough, at about 1400, the U-boat was spotted some sixty miles to westward. The aircraft attacked unsuccessfully and the enemy dived. By the time the escort group arrived in the area it was nearly dark and an Asdic/Radar search during the night failed to find her.

At daylight, acting on the assumption that she would have made off on the surface at high speed during darkness, Captain Broome decided to move the Force north-eastwards at ten knots. The 11th August drew a blank, but at about 1000 on the 12th, an aircraft from SHAH found the enemy on the surface. An accurate bombing attack caused him to porpoise, circle and stop. A few bursts were exchanged, after which the U-boat trimmed down and proceeded south-eastwards before finally diving. This action took place some fifty miles ahead of our advanced screen and seventy miles ahead of the carriers, close screened by CAUVERY and GODAVARI, (the RIN sloops were usually chosen for this duty as they were not fitted with the forward firing multi-bomb 'Hedgehog' and suffered from chronic boiler tube trouble).

CAUVERY was released almost immediately to join the search, but it was not until 1410, when FALMOUTH and GENISTA fortuitously joined, that GODAVARI got off the leash. Three hours and thirteen minutes later, in the seemingly empty expanse of ocean, she got an unmistakeable submarine contact.

Not being fitted with 'Hedgehog', a 'silent' attack was denied her. Thus, in accordance with general policy, she sat patiently on the U-boat's tail, moving at about three knots, for three-quarters of an hour, until the first of the Group, FINDHORN, closely followed by PARROT, came steaming up. Nothing patient about them; with GODAVARI as directing vessel, FINDHORN sailed straight in and, with a shower of 'Hedgehog', scored two hits. Within five minutes, loud explosions were heard on Asdic - it was the end.

In so far as GODAVARI was concerned, the action was a text-book one. It is not improbable that the unfortunate U-boat, by reason of damage from the air attack, or because of GODAVARI's position practically in her wake, was unaware that she was being stalked. Nevertheless, she was deep and, with wake interference, the contact had been far from easy to hold and John Akehurst and his team rightly received great credit for maintaining it for the best part of an hour.

Less obviously, it may be said that the ship would not have been there at all but for the unending efforts of her Engineer Officers, past and present, (Watson, Wright, Briggs, Hunt-Pain, Charlton and others), in replacing boiler tubes at sea. For the crews of the six 4" guns the finish was, of course, sheer anti-climax - if only we had brought up the U-boat with depth charges. FINDHORN's attack, with the U-boat at an estimated three hundred feet, was astonishingly accurate. Her captain later complained of a lack of information, in which there was an element of truth, as the R/T was jammed by indiscriminate use by other ships not even engaged. In fact, under ideal conditions, old fashioned flags proved adequate, as the signal logs and the outcome proved.

However, all was forgotten when the ships were cheered round the Escort Group. Many the mutual congratulatory messages, with some from the heights. But the greatest personal credit was, in the writer's view, due to that untiringly tough tactician, Jackie Broome, who had directed a submarine hunt which, in terms of distance, time and variety, must have been something of a classic. The chief recollection of the writer, however, is of simple astonishment at receiving a 'ping', loud and clear, in the seemingly empty space of the wide blue ocean.

I transferred to the Navy from the Indian Army on the 3rd June 1943. I had expected to be drafted to Combined Operations, as I was a fully trained Infantry Officer, but, after the manner of the Services, I was told to report to Lieutenant AK Chatterjee, RIN, at that time Staff Officer, Anti-Submarine Warfare and Lieutenant Appleby RNVR, his technical adviser.

In 'civvy street', I had been manager of the General Electric Company's Radio Department and perhaps this influenced the decision to divert me from Combined Ops. For a few weeks, until the other officers arrived, I was under instruction from Lieutenant Appleby, subsequently supplemented by a short course at HMIS MACHLIMAR in Versova. While all this was going on, a detail of one Royal Navy Petty-Officer and four Leading Hands had arrived from the UK and were busy installing the instruments we were to use. They were to remain with us until the end of the war.

Here I shall digress for a moment to explain the functions of the A/S Fixed Defences, which were primarily to protect the Harbour from submarine attack, with the assistance of HDML's. In addition, we were provided with a powerful W/T set, which enabled us to keep in touch with the XDO and other harbour defence installations. In Colaba, for instance, we were sited just below the local coastal battery in which, incidentally, my brother was a serving officer. It was part of our job to establish contact with these odd bods every morning and with the Guard Ship.

The equipment we had for detection of both undersea and surface vessels was strictly classified and I am unsure whether I am free to describe it. Suffice to say the systems, (we had two), were quite capable of detecting the movement of any, even the smallest, underwater or surface craft. Sometimes this was a disadvantage, as even shoals of fish could cause a minor alarm. However, our HDO's, (Harbour Defence Operators), soon became quite skilled at sorting out the wheat from the chaff.

After a few teething troubles, Colaba A/S FD Station was fully operational. The ship's company consisted of the CO Lieutenant 'Willy' Cuffe, RINVR, the First Lieutenant (me), three Watch-Keeping Officers, a Chief Petty-Officer, four Killicks and thirty odd AB's and OD's. In addition, at that time, we carried four or five other junior officers under training for subsequent appointment to other stations when they were commissioned. We also had two cooks, two stewards and a civilian dogs-body to look after the heads.

There were two messes - RN and RIN. The OOD had his food provided by the RN cook and ate it in the wardroom. Rations were provided by the RIASC and were collected each morning by one of the Leading Hands of the duty watch. The CO and the other officers were able to return home for lunch - you wouldn't think there was a war on. Early in October, I went back to MACHLIMAR for further Asdic training of an advanced nature. About this time, too, we had a change in command, Lieutenant Cuffe being replaced by Lieutenant Girling, RNVR.

On the 14th January 1944, a signal from Navy Office summoned me to SOA/S's office. On arrival, I was told to report to HMIS ADYAR, Madras, where the next ASFD Station was to be opened. A place on an IAF flight had been booked for me. This unexpected development took me by surprise, as it would mean leavng my wife behind in Bombay, where we had few friends; moreover, my wife was expecting our first baby. Lieutenant Chatterjee was sympathetic, but unable to help.

Desperate situations called for desperate measures; I asked for and received permission to see Commodore Rattray, COMBAY. An additional problem was that Madras was a front line base and married officers were not ordinarily permitted to have their wives there. I can never speak too highly enough of that great man, Commodore Rattray. After enquiring about my wife and wishing us well, he agreed to allow me to take my wife with me and instructed his secretary to contact Lieutenant Chatterjee, to arrange rail transport for me the next day. And so it was we bid Bombay a temporary farewell and set forth, for us, to the unknown south.

We were met at Madras Central by Lieutenant 'Jimmy' Braund, PASO, Madras. I can still remember the look of horror on his face when confronted by not only me, but accompanied by wife, dog, servant and a mountain of luggage. Of course, no one had thought it necessary to warn Madras of the change in plan and James had booked me in to a cabin in the mess. However, Jimmy Braund was of the salt of the earth and soon had things organised. A phone call to Spencer's Hotel, which was practically a Naval Hostel, booked us a cottage in the grounds of the hotel and very comfortable it proved to be.

I reported to Captain Hughes-Hallett, Naval Officer-in-Charge, Madras, who briefly enlightened me of the situation relevant to the ASFD - which was that I represented all that there was of the ASFD in Madras. He instructed me to team up with Braund, pending the arrival of our equipment. Working with Jimmy was interesting, in that I had the opportunity to familiarise myself with Asdic sets for ships, as distinct from those we used. Of more interest was helping with the assembly and setting up of the Attack Trainer, which Jimmy had recently acquired. Once completed, this provided not only Base staff, but visiting Trawlers, ML's and other craft with excellent practice in the art of submarine spotting and chasing and, hopefully, sinking.

In early March, I think it was, we received a signal from Bombay that a Lieutenant Akroyd, RNVR was en route to take over command of the Station. This was a blow to all of us, as it had been clearly implied that I was to be CO. However, as things worked out, I was well enough content; Maurice Akroyd was a most congenial type and we got on well together.

The question of siting the station was difficult. The apparent best choice had already been snaffled by the RNAS, who were even then preparing to move into Burma. The problem was that the building had to be relatively close to the sea; our under-water cables had to be brought ashore at a conveniently isolated spot. In the end, the Garrison Engineers' Department found a two-storied house within easy reach of the shore; also, the owner had left when Madras was bombed a short while before and the building was lying vacant.

Certain alterations had to be done, of course. The drawing room became the instrument room. The two bedrooms on either side became the Killick's living accommodation and mess. The CPO had his own room and a small adjoining room was his mess. The RIN ratings were accommodated in barracks at the Base and each watch was transported to the station by truck. Upstairs, the three resident officers were comfortably accommodated - I, of course, was still living in the hotel.

All this took time and, meanwhile, the submarine cable we were to use had arrived and I was given the job of clearing it and storing it. I had the help of an Indian Pioneer Company, under a subaltern, but the offloading had to be supervised by either Lieutenant Akroyd or myself. Maurice Akroyd, assisted by two Leading Hands, took the day shift, while the CPO and the two remaining Leading Seamen stood watch with me. It was a wearying and boring job, but it had to be done. The cable was too valuable to be left to the tender mercies of the Pioneers. The coil had to be meticulously arranged so as to avoid kinking. Finally, the job was done, but, even then, we still had to maintain a guard on it for fear of sabotage. We were armed and I still remember the weight of the Service .45 slapping against my thigh.

In Bombay, a new intake of young officers and seamen had been vetted and were now training in MACHLIMAR, while the station at Colaba was functioning like clockwork. It still puzzles me why it was thought necessary to protect the harbour with an expensive anti-submarine system. First, there was a boom defence; then the Colaba battery and, lastly, the enormous 15" naval guns sited on Elephanta and protecting the harbour entrance, while, further out to sea, there were several dhows and trawlers on patrol. There must have been a good reason.

Reference to the 15" guns, might well serve to revive old memories. It appears that an American cruiser, when seeking to enter harbour, was requested to make his number for identification. This he flatly refused to do and it was not until a warning shot was fired across his bows that her captain ordered 'full astern' and the ship was halted. When he was taken subsequently, on a guided tour of the harbour defences, the guns were shown to him and he was somewhat taken aback. This story, while nice to believe, is not authenticated and may well be just a story.

Back in Madras, things had been happening. We had the cable, now we had to lay it. A cable ship had been requested, but she was busy in

Trincomalee, so Akroyd decided to go it alone. We borrowed the BEO's motor boat and handled a coil of cable into it and started paying out the cable over a fairlead. It was heavy going for the little boat and, after burning out the clutch several times, BEO decided enough was enough and grabbed his boat back. He was very annoyed.

Finally, the long awaited cable ship arrived. I went aboard to see the Captain. My arrival was most impressive. I was met at the gangway by the OOW and the Quartermaster and ushered into the Captain's cabin - it was very small, just allowing two people to stand or sit comfortably. On a map of the harbour, I indicated what we thought was a suitable site and, accompanied by his First Lieutenant, we recced the proposed site. Finally, the business of laying the cable started the following day - this took some days, as we were constantly employed in chasing away fishermen, whose favourite fishing ground we had invaded. However, it was done at last and we took the cable ends ashore. Our task was easier, because we used a ready-made pathway, in which the cable was bedded in a trench.

The RN party, all skilled men, had meanwhile installed and got working the recorders and other gear, so the station was soon operational. Lieutenant Akroyd was recalled to the UK and Lieutenant Harman RNVR took his place. It was made clear to me that, while the RN were in nominal charge, the RIN were in effective control; that is to say, Harman dealt with administration, while I had executive charge. We were now joined by two Sub-Lieutenants, one a Scot and the other a Parsi - all proved to be excellent shipmates. Indeed, my relationship was better with Harman than it had been with Akroyd.

I shared the watchkeeping with the subbies. I was mainly concerned with discipline and such other duties would fall to a First Lieutenant aboard ship. The two Subbies looked after stores, maintenance and censorship. It was a humdrum life on the whole - very boring at times. There were one or two high spots, however, as when a Watch-Keeping Operator reported a suspicious trace on the recorder. The Duty Officer failed to reconcile the trace with shipping movements, of whose ETA and ETD we had previously been notified. Frantic telephone exchanges between XDO and PWSS established that it was an old Dutch submarine, which was occasionally used for training purposes, to give aspiring submarine 'killers' an opportunity to practise their craft.

One day, I was informed by the 'Powers that Be' that it was considered good experience for us ASFD officers to be given sea training in this old banger. The night fixed for my initiation was a stormy monsoon night. Anyone familiar with that coast will agree that it really can be stormy, with gale force winds prevailing around the clock. Anyway, come 2000, I betook myself to the harbour. I whistled up the duty boat and was ferried out to the submarine, which was anchored some 400 yards from the jetty. Boarding was something of an acrobatic feat, as there was no gangway and one had to jump from the wildly-moving boat on to a rope ladder dangling over the side of the submarine. With my heart in my mouth, I jumped and just managed to grasp the ladder before the boat fell away.

It was pelting down with rain and there was no-one on the bridge. With some difficulty, I found my way into the control room, where the Dutch equivalent of our CPO Cox'n asked me my business and then led me to the wardroom, where I was greeted by the Captain and his Chief Engineer, who were sharing a companionable schnapps. After welcoming me and offering me a drink - which I declined for fear of dropping in the drink on my way back - he informed me that it was quite impossible for him to put to sea that night, but he would be glad to entertain me some other time. I breathed a sigh of relief, because I honestly had no desire to go jaunting about the Bay of Bengal on a night like that - particularly under water!

On one occasion, one of our RIN ratings, newly married and very homesick, went AWOL. I logged him 'Absent' and, after the statutory lapse, as a deserter. Some three months later, much to my astonishment, I received a letter from him expressing a desire to return to duty. We had no choice but to turn him over to the police. He was duly picked up, court-martialled and sentenced to ninety days hard labour and dismissed the Service. I felt sorry - his only crime was an overwhelming desire to spend a little time with his wife.

We were not without excitement. One day, the OOD received a phone call from NOIC's Secretary. FOCRIN was in Madras and had expressed a desire to pay us a visit - we had precisely thirty minutes in which to prepare to receive him. Fortunately, one of our RN Leading Seamen was an ex-destroyer man and knew how to make the usual noises on a Bosun's pipe. This, with the sentry's 'Present Arms' and the line-up of Officers, CPO and off-duty hands, made a quite presentable reception, with which the great man, through his ADC expressed himself well pleased.

Being the only married officer aboard, it was our pleasure - my wife's and mine - to entertain the officers and, on occasion, the RN personnel at our flat, which was conveniently situated near the Station. Many a convivial evening was enjoyed, the last being our farewell party. It was a rollicking do as, apart from our own officers and RN ratings, we enjoyed the company of the BMO and several officers from the Base. We consumed all my quota of spirits and beer, plus what others had brought, ending up with four bottles of Colombo arrack - the contribution of the Chief.

In March 1945, I was drafted back to Castle Barracks and thence to HMIS MACHLIMAR, as Chief RIN Instructor, A/S FD School. With me were two Sub-Lieutenants and a Midshipman. A third subbie acted as assistant to a RN Lieutenant, who was in overall charge of training. We had a motley crowd of trainees, mainly RIN, but also men from the Royal Navy, from the Royal Sinhalese Navy and even a few from what was left of the Royal Navy, Straits Settlements. I was now on the CO MACHLIMAR's staff and had to take my share of School's activities, including helping out the permanent OOD day and night. I was allotted a cabin in the Officer's Mess and was supposed to spend my days at the School. VE Day came and went - the war, our war, was coming to an end and then came VJ Day.

The CO, (Commander J Sanders RN) had ordered a ceremonial parade, to which he had invited sundry Army and Air Force dignitaries. The parade was under the command of the School's Executive Officer, Lieutenant Commander HM Darbyshire, RINVR. Each Division was commanded by its own Divisional Officer - I commanded mine, which consisted of three officers, four CPO's and PO's and some eighty ratings. With no rehearsal or practice, the parade was a shambles. Somehow or other, I managed to get my Division inextricably mixed up with the others. There we were, milling around, Commander Darbyshire blowing his whistle and doing his nut, until order was finally restored by a handful of shouting and aggressive RPO's.

After the parade, I caught the liberty truck into Bombay. It was wonderful to see Colaba Causeway revealed in all its splendour, and squalor, lit up at night. My wife and I and a few bachelor friends went to the Yacht Club for drinks. Flora Fountain and the adjoining area were a blaze of light. Servicemen and civilians were milling around in a frenzy of joy - it was a scene to remember.

On our way back, we were treated to a solo sword dance by a Scottish soldier and, a little later, we ran for our lives to avoid the noisy attentions of a bunch of BOR's. We retired to bed in the early morning, very tired, very drunk, but rejoicing the insufferable Nip had been beaten at last.

The next weeks were spent in closing down the ASFD part of the School and packaging up the equipment for return to Bath. I returned to DALHOUSIE on the 19th July 1945. After hanging about for some days and badgering Lieutenant Cohen RINVR, of the Drafting Office, a job was found for me with the RNFPO, as a courier, humping His Majesty's Top Secret Mail all over the Indian sub-continent. Others of my colleagues were given Base jobs or sent on courses. One, I met in Calcutta, where he was the Mess Manager - all very different from what we had trained for.

I was anxious to return to civvy street and to civilian employment, although a permanent commission was on offer with the Indian Navy. With a growing family and the sure knowledge of impending Independence, I preferred to opt out. On the 10th October 1945, I went on Class 'A' Release leave. We left Victoria Terminus at 7.00pm. A number of my Service friends were there to see us off and I don't mind confessing that there were tears in my eyes. I loved, and still love, the Service.

In early 1943, I was appointed CO of HMIS HASCHEMI, based on Vizagapatam, relieving Lieutenant Courtney, RINR, for some three months whilst he was on sick leave. HASCHEMI at this time was doing a patrol of some ten days in the Bay of Bengal. On return to Bombay, I was summoned to discuss a proposal which was this – would I take a party, consisting of a CPO, Leading Seamen, an Electrical Artificer, two AB's and a cook to Trincomalee and report there to a Captain RN. On asking the purpose of the party and reasons for proceeding to Ceylon, I was informed that it was a 'Volunteer Job' and, if I accepted, I would be fully informed on reporting at Trincomalee. This all sounded rather strange. However, the party was assembled and we proceeded by train via Madras, Dhanascodi, Talamanar and finally reported to SNO, Trincomalee.

This turned out to be no cloak and dagger mission and why the original secrecy I never understood. Our party was to await the arrival of HMS EMILE BAUDOT, a French Cable ship handed over to the RN by the Free French. Her CO was a Commander RNR, First Lieutenant, RNR and a T 124X crew. We were to report to EMILE BAUDOT on arrival, for the purpose of laying a defensive loop cable system across the approaches to Trincomalee harbour.

This system of underwater defence was devised after the sinking of HMS ROYAL OAK at Scapa Flow, in the early days of the war. Very briefly, by way of description of the loop system of underwater detection, lead sheathed cable was laid in a pattern on the sea bed, covering the approaches to a port. These loop cable patterns were connected to a shore recording post. If a metallic body crossed the loops, an induced current gave the shore recording post an alarm, and, if no surface vessel was observed at the time of crossing, it was assumed that a submarine vessel had induced the current and appropriate defensive action was taken by HDML's.

After some six weeks, the loop system was laid and completed. I was summoned by the CO of EMILE BAUDOT, to be informed that the ship had orders to proceed, I believe to Madras, but I was to remain at Trincomalee to await the arrival of a self-propelled lighter from Colombo, carrying some hundred tons plus communication cable. Our cable party function was to be the laying of this cable, which, so far as I can remember, was some three to four inches in diameter; extremely heavy and very inflexible. The lighter arrived in due course, with a native crew. Apart from being self-propelled, no mechanical aids existed on deck -rope stoppers were our only means of checking a cable run.

So, after six weeks' experience, my crew and I found we were the undisputed experts. A preliminary survey of the harbour was made and, with the assistance of a very large squad of Cochin State labourers, as a shore party, the cable was 'draped' around the harbour, with shore ends landed at China Bay and ashore elsewhere. We also laid cable from two gun emplacements on islets just offshore, outside the boom defence. As I never had any adverse reports from Trincomalee, I assume the system worked.

The Cable Party was now established and I believe we were destined at one time to have a RIN Cable Ship. I once heard a whisper that INVESTIGATOR might have been converted. Our next assignment was to Madras, where the loop system was out of action. We located the fault and effected the repair.

On return to Bombay, I was appointed to NOIC's staff, (Captain Curtis RINR) and told to proceed to seaward and board HMS BULAN, another RN Cable Ship, straight from the UK. I was to extend the courtesies of the RIN to the ship and pilot them to a suitable anchorage in Bombay Harbour. BULAN was an ex-P & O Straits passenger vessel, with a long fore-deck. In conversion, she had bow sheaths fitted to her semi-clipper bow, for cable laying. Twin screw, she was handy and manoeuverable. Her CO was Lieutenant Commander John Donaldson-Palmer RNR. Two RNVR Lieutenants; Radio Officer; Four RNR Norwegian Engineers; T 124X crew.

The Cable Party was again seconded to HMS BULAN, which had arrived to lay the Bombay Harbour loop defences. This was in due course achieved. A very happy ship, she had a magnificent wardroom, being the former saloon from her passenger carrying days. During her conversion, her CO was somehow able to have a corner bar with stools and optic measures installed. She even had a piano on board and Saccone and Speed had furnished her well with liquids.

After completing the Bombay loop system, the ship was in Alexandra Dock, loading cable for the Karachi loop system. We lay opposite to the FORT STIKINE. We were three days on passage to Karachi when we heard of the explosion in Bombay Harbour. After arrival at Karachi and carrying out a preliminary survey, the loop system was laid, the RIN Cable Party being involved. I had a particularly nice function to perform. I was housed ashore on Manora Island as guest of the Port Commissioner's very charming wife in a delightful old Portuguese house. The Cable Party's job was finally to supervise the landing of the shore ends on Manora beach.

BULAN now returned to Bombay, where the loop system required repair. I should state here that the loop system in Bombay was laid in the dhow anchorage area. Off shore, waiting for the flood, one can well imagine the delight of a dhow crew, on hauling in their anchor, to find lead covered cable coming over the bow. Certainly, on charting the lay of the cable recovered, dragged far beyond the original lay, a substantial quantity was unaccounted for. The repair was effected and the Cable

Party reluctantly came ashore.

By this time, a further Cable Ship had arrived on station, HMS KILMUN. She was, I understand, originally a First World War escort vessel of the 'K' class, operating, I was informed, between the Mersey and Port Said on convoy escort. I further believe HMIS HASCHEMI was originally also a 'K' class escort named KILDIN. This is all hearsay, but sounds possible.

Cable laying was now at a low ebb and it was obvious that the RIN did not require a Cable Ship. We were, as a party, appointed to assist the King's Harbour Master, Bombay, a Commander RNR, to lay trots of buoys in creeks to the eastward of Elephanta Island. His first question was 'What do you know about buoy laying?' His comment to my answer was 'That makes two of us.' With his excellent guidance and help, we were loaned an LCI from which the ramp was removed. The trots of buoys were for the purpose of mooring small craft in the creeks preparatory to the 'push' against the Japs. Whether these buoys were ever used, I do not know.

However, I was given the assistance of Lieutenant A Hill RNVR from HMS BULAN and, somehow, we did manage to lay the trots of some seven or eight moorings to each. Sinkers of some fifteen hundredweight plus kept either end of the trot in position, (we hoped!).

The Cable Party was now really superfluous and, after tidying up, such as storing cable on Colaba Causeway and returning equipment, the job was finished. For the record, the Cable Party consisted of: S D Gordon, as CO, CPO's Daud Hussain and E A Patel, L/S Kadir. The AB's and cook's names escape me. Lieutenant A Hill RNVR and Lieutenant F Cox RNR rendered much assistance in the buoy laying episode.

14

Administration and Law

REMINISCENCES OF A RETIRED CGO by AH HAMMOND

The heading will probably raise the question as to what on earth is a CGO? The abbreviation is for 'Civilian Gazetted Officer' - a term coined, so far as I can remember, to cover those civilian officers, other than those on loan from the Royal Navy, in the complement of the Royal Indian Navy Headquarters. It did not exist either in RIN authorised complements or in formal Government of India sanctions. It was not used in the Army or Air Force, although officers of equivalent status existed in those Services in both peace and war. The RIN had no peacetime Headquarters in Delhi or Simla, it being solely represented by a RIN Liaison Officer attached to the Defence Department.

A few personal details outlining how and why I became a CGO - I was born in Guildford, Surrey on the 10th April 1906 and in 1921 I was denied entry to the Royal Navy, firstly as an ERA and secondly as a Boy Seaman, by that miserly gent Stafford Cripps' budget cuts. I joined the British Army, (Royal Sussex Regiment) in September 1922 - falsely stating my age as eighteen. I served in Northern Ireland and Malaya before arriving in India in March 1926. Throughout my service I had worked in various regimental administrative posts and, on being medically down-graded because of a football injury, I became a permanent 'ink-slinger'. An infantry career being no longer possible, I sought a transfer to the Indian Army, first to Rawalpindi Brigade Staff and then to Army Headquarters (India) where, on discharge in 1930, I took civilian officer status.

I worked in the Supply and Transport Directorate and the QMG's co-ordination section on war planning until 1940, when I was transferred as a Branch Superintendent with the Department of Supply which was then being formed. I worked in Simla, Calcutta and New Delhi, latterly being appointed as an Assistant Secretary to the Government of India. In September 1943, at the instigation of the Military Finance Department, I volunteered to serve in Naval Headquarters, (India), which was then being vastly expanded. Whilst waiting to take up my appointment as Staff Officer, (Works) I was able to assist several Staff Officers with information from the Army, Air Force and civil organisations through my peacetime contacts. Then came a summons from the Admiral, who said that he had heard that I knew everyone worth knowing in New Delhi and who 'requested' me to take over the post of Establishment Officer. He wanted a rapid re-organisation and quick results - I told him that this could only be achieved by 'bending the rules' - I knew how, but I would need everyone's support and, in particular, his support when I got into difficulties with the Military Finance Department. He guaranteed 101% from all. Later, when I did need it there was no hint of disapproval and by means of DO (demi-official) correspondence, the FOC invariably won my battle.

My job covered administering the needs of over 1,000 officers, ratings and civilian clerical staff in matters of pay, allowances, recruitment and promotion of clerical staff, petrol and food rationing, purchase and maintenance of office furniture and equipment, allocation and maintenance, (through the Public Works Department) of office accommodation, obtaining Government quarters, road, rail and air travel, plus a thousand and one other jobs which no one else wanted. It took time to organise, but with some trojan work by my Section staff, headed by the Superintendent, a Sikh named Puji and a Hindu cashier named Saxena, we rapidly became a smooth running outfit. I particularly remember the support I received from all ranks, senior and junior alike and their readiness to ask for and accept advice from me and my staff.

With the approval of the Chief-of-Staff, Chief-of-Administration and the Naval Secretary, I set up a Promotion Committee for civilian staff, to which the heads of the branches and sections concerned were co-opted. Allocation of accommodation in the South Block Secretariat and the 'G' Block hutments was a constant headache, aggravated by the Admiral's frequent demands for 'musical chairs'. It fell to my lot to work out allocations and, on one occasion I was under so much pressure from the interested parties, that the Naval Secretary locked me in the Admiral's waiting room and demanded two alternative solutions. He got them and, although I was not over popular with those made to move, they were generally accepted in good spirit.

Then my career came nearly full circle and my boyhood ambition to be a sailor was almost realised when the FOC appointed me as his Assistant Naval Secretary in place of Tony Srinivasan, who was going on a Long course. Although by Viceregal edict not allowed to go back into the Services, at last I was as near to the 'sharp end' as was possible. 1944 was a good year - I thoroughly enjoyed the job and, in particular, I much appreciated the respect of all with whom I came in contact - senior and junior alike.

To this day, I do not know what was thought of a secondary school educated, ex 'pongo' infantry lance-corporal getting such an appointment - albeit in wartime.

Before I move on, let me relate an amusing incident. The clerical staff were recruited and trained centrally by an Army organisation and, one day, we received and posted to the Engineering Department an Indian copy typist, who was promptly returned by Commander Jimmy Green on the grounds of his not being able to type. We sent him back for re-testing and he came back to us with a certificate of competence. We finally resolved the puzzle when it was discovered that, whilst he could copy printed matter, he could neither read nor write. He had taught himself on a ramshackle machine in the bazaar to reproduce the forms he saw in print. We kept him and he was one of the best copy typists of the printed word in the office - mistakes and all!

Later on, with promises of promotion to a senior appointment, I was lured into moving over to the Personnel Department. The promises were pie-crust and the job I did was a sinecure, but I enjoyed the rest after starting my war in 1937, when we changed over from a 10.00am to 4.00pm five-day week to a twelve and sometimes fourteen hour day, seven days a week, until I went on eight months long leave, after fourteen years, in April 1947.

Before I close the account of this period of my life, I would like to relate two experiences in Calcutta. Whilst OS (E) at Captain Digby-Beste's headquarters, (DSTO) and with FOCRIN's approval, I went to assist an RN captain who was forming a special office, planning shipping for the invasion of Burma. He could get little help from anyone, including the NOIC, but with local contacts, including my one-time boss, the DGMP, General 'Lakri' Wood, I managed to get him all the equipment and staff required and also, through the Chief Officer WRINS (Mrs Cooper) a Second Officer WRINS as a PA.

On another occasion, when those horrible little yellow men bombed them, I managed to be in Kidderpore Docks. Fortunately, the bombs turned the wrong way and missed four nearby munitions ships. Later, some idiot informed me that, being in the specified war area, I was entitled to the Burma Star. I informed him that I would not dishonour the memory of the fighting men lost and wounded, which included many of my friends and colleagues, by accepting it. Whilst I was on leave, Partition took place and, on advice from General Wood, I opted to serve in Pakistan.

I left the UK in October 1947 and, whilst in Bombay, experienced two incidents, one good and one bad. The good one was that I was offered the appointment of Director of Victualling, Royal Indian Navy, but, as it did not carry a permanent senior promotion, I did not accept it. The bad one - I heard a regular RIN two-and-a-half striper bombastically state what he was going to do to the Pakistan Navy. On arrival in Rawalpindi, I became DAQM and later, the AWMG (Works). I travelled all over West and East Pakistan, being the first unescorted British officer to tour the whole of the military cantonments in the North West Frontier Province and Baluchistan.

I came home in November 1949 on premature retirement, to secure the future for my wife and three children, (who had been with me throughout), including a further pension. I eventually went on pension in May 1951. Incidentally, it may not be generally known that my Indian/Pakistani pension, like every other civilian employee, including the Indian Civil Service, from Provincial Governor downwards, carried a maximum of Rs.500 per month. This amount had been fixed in 1867 - the oldest pension scheme in the world.

There is, however, one outstanding case on record. A civil surgeon, after eighteen months service in Bengal, was invalided out; came home; recovered; joined the British Army; became a Colonel; died in his nineties and received the pension throughout. His name was Coussmaker and he invented the first artificial limb.

FORM OF DAILY SERVICE FOR USE IN ALL DEPARTMENTS OF THE GOVERNMENT OF INDIA

Anon.

PRAYER:

Let us pray:

O Lord, grant that this day we come to no
decisions,
Neither run into any kind of responsibility,
But that all our doings may be so ordered as to
establish
New and quite unwarranted Departments,
For ever and ever,

Amen.

HYMN:

O Thou who seest all thing below,
Grant that thy servants may go slow,
That they may study to comply
With regulations till they die.

Teach us, O Lord, to reverence
Committees more than commonsense,
Impress our minds to make no plan,
But pass the baby when we can.

And when the tempter seeks to give
Us feelings of initiative,
Or when alone, we go too far,
Chastise us with a circular.

Mid war and tumult, fire and storms,
Strengthen us we pray with forms,
Thus will they servants ever be
A flock of perfect sheep for Thee.

Amen.

PROBLEMS OF A JUDGE ADVOCATE

by GW WALKER

Amina, in this Vale of Tears,
Sojourning but eighteen years,
Feels the sap of youth upsurging,
Has no man to ease its urging,
(Rahman, in this time of strife
serves his country not his wife).
Amina takes the dimmest view:
Hints, that they, perhaps, have known
What it is to sleep alone
(Hopes they have, for if they ain't
She's too modest to explain't);
Threatens, for their kind approval,
Suicide or self - removal.
    NHQ, though deeply moved,
(In their time, they too have loved),
Harden their official heart -
Leave Amina in the cart.
        Since from NHQ proceeds
No relief for nightly needs,
Philosphic'ly inclined,
Amina thinks she'll change her mind,
Rahman sundered from her bed,
Someone else will do instead,
But, (although for want of love bored),
Ev'rything must be aboveboard:
Let no kept boy, on the make,
Cut himself a slice of cake;
Bed id bed - let none disparage,
But her terms are strictly marriage,
NHQ must please endorse her
Plaint for Rahman to divorce her.
        J A counsels strict adherence
To discreet non-interference;
Repercussions lie in wait,
Terrible to contemplate.
        Next thing, she'll be asking, (bless her),
Volunteers for a successor!
        But it doesn't rest with me:

15

The Communications Branch

by HC BIRD and other Signals Officers (see Acknowledgements)

By 1930, the last traces of the 'Troopship Regime' of the Royal Indian Marine (as the Service was then called) had disappeared. With the arrival of the new sloop 'HINDUSTAN', together with the existing ships and under the eagle eye of the Flag Officer Commanding, Vice-Admiral Sir Humphrey Walwyn KCSI, KCMG, CB, DSO, a sea-going squadron was now in being. Training in all branches became intensified over the following years and it is the object of this narrative to record the training organisation and subsequent expansion to meet the requirements of war in the Communications Branch of the Royal Indian Navy.

In 1930, the centre of the Signals world rested at the foot of the Breakwater in the Naval Dockyard, Bombay. It consisted of a small single-storied building housing the office of the Squadron Signal Officer; lecture rooms and a small Radio Station. Adjacent to this building was the Port Signal Station - a square two-storied stone tower with a signal mast and flag deck adjoining. The station watch-keepers, school staff and ratings under instruction were accommodated in the Depot-ship DALHOUSIE alongside the breakwater. The total strength of the Branch, ashore and afloat, at this time was of the order of 200. Signal traffic was of a routine nature and chiefly visual - little use being made of radio except to ships on passage.

With the gradual acquisition of modern ships and more co-operation with the East Indies Squadron of the Royal Navy, the Royal Indian Navy became a fully-fledged member of the Dominion Navies. Officers and men drafted to the United Kingdom to man the new ships were able to take courses at the appropriate Royal Naval Establishments and bring back up-to-date ideas on training and equipment.

In 1933, Lieutenant MHStL Nott RIM, qualified in signals at HM Signal School, Portsmouth and, on his return to India, was appointed Squadron Signal Officer. There can be no doubt that the capability of the Branch to expand and sustain the enormous increase in Signal responsibilities that arose at the outbreak of the Second World War in 1939, must lie to his credit. By 1936, the existing Port Signal Station was proving quite inadequate to cope with the increasing volume of traffic. It was replaced by a new Signal Station built on the Breakwater; accommodation for the Signal Staff being provided on the ground floor. At the same time, a Signal Distributing Office was established in the main Administrative Office in the Dockyard. This move, together with the removal of the office of the Squadron Signal Officer to the Administrative Office, released valuable space in the small Signal School for instructional purposes.

In 1935, planning commenced to establish a modern radio complex to meet the needs of an expanding Service. A radio-link had been established with Whitehall W/T Station, using a small high-frequency ship's transmitter, sited in the Signal School. Reception of H/F was difficult, due to interference from Dockyard machinery and there was no way of overcoming that problem. It was accepted that, so long as Naval Headquarters remained in or near the Dockyard, some form of remote reception would be required. As regards the transmitting station, sufficient space for the necessary buildings and associated aerial arrays was not available within the limits of the Dockyard or the city of Bombay.

The Army authorities controlled a large area of land at Colaba, which, from a technical point of view, was an excellent reception site, being free from both physical and electrical interference. After considerable argument, the Defence Department agreed to allot to the Navy a sufficient area for a Receiving Station; a Radio Direction Finding Station; Aerial arrays and Staff Quarters. The next problem was to find a suitable site for the transmitters. This was found near the village of Mahul, some fourteen miles inland from Bombay City. As soon as accommodation became available, Warrant Telegraphist Mr Bert Spence moved to Mahul to supervise the erection of the buildings and installation of equipment as it arrived from the United Kingdom. Both the Receiving and Transmitting Stations were operated by landlines from a Remote Control Office, established adjacent to the existing Signal Distribution Office at Naval Headquarters in the Dockyard.

It had been established custom that radio equipment for the Service should be obtained from Admiralty sources. Due, possibly, to the financial restrictions imposed on the Services, little advance had been made in the design of radio equipment - this applied particularly to Shore Station W/T equipment. It was felt that here was a golden opportunity to break with tradition and turn to the commercial world for at least some of our requirements. An order was placed with Marconi at Chelmsford for two eight kilowatt and one eleven kilowatt transmitters. These were installed at Mahul - they were H/F crystal controlled and gave years of trouble-free service.

The electrical installation of equipment at both the Receiving and Transmitter Stations was carried out by Dockyard Staff, under the supervision of Commander NT Patterson OBE, Manager of the Electrical Department in the Dockyard. Landlines from the Remote Control Office to Receiving and Transmitter Stations were provided by the Bombay Telephone Company and, by the middle of 1939, the complete scheme was in full operation - just in time.

Up to the early 1930's, recruitment for all branches of the Service was mainly from the Ratnagiri District, south of Bombay. All signals publications were in English, so those recruits with a knowledge of English were earmarked for the Signal Branch. After their new-entry training in 'DALHOUSIE', they were drafted to the Signal School. As the Service expanded and higher educational standards were required, the general policy for the recruitment of boy entries shifted to the Punjab and other northern States, where generally, a higher standard of education existed, with a more advanced knowledge of English. In the case of recruitment for the Signal Branch, the standard was set at Matriculation.

This policy was continued until shortly before the outbreak of war, but thereafter, increasing numbers of new entries were recruited from southern and central India and from the Anglo-Indian community.

In 1935, with the return to India of Lieutenant HC Bird, after his Long Signal course in the UK, and on his being appointed Officer-in-Charge of the Signal School, Staff training duties were separated and the Staff Officer, Signals was able to devote all his time to staff matters. Up to 1937, the output of communications-trained boys was rather less than one hundred annually. After the international crisis in 1938, a review of personnel requirements clearly showed that, when war did break out, an enormous expansion in all branches, of both officers and ratings, would take place. There had been a gradual increase in the Signal establishment over the past few years and, with more ratings coming forward for higher-rate courses, the existing Signal School was becoming hard-pressed for accommodation and expansion within the Dockyard was out of the question.

In 1940, the training of boys for the Signal Branch was transferred to the newly-commissioned Boys' Training Establishment, HMIS BAHADUR, at Karachi.

Prior to the opening of Bombay Central Railway Station, the terminal of the Bombay, Baroda and Central Indian Railway had been in the centre of Colaba. This had now been abandoned, leaving a large area of deserted platforms and rusting railway lines. This site was viewed with a 'lean and hungry' look by the Navy, and the Defence Department was asked to try and obtain the land for a new Signal School. This they did with remarkable alacrity and a scheme was prepared to provide accommodation and training facilities for both officers' and ratings' training. Provision was also made for a bungalow for the Commanding Officer.

As soon as approval in principle was given, the site was cleared, building commenced and, in April 1941, the new Signal School came into operation. The School was originally under the administrative and disciplinary control of the Commanding Officer of the RIN Depot, but later, it was made an independent command and was commissioned as HMIS TALWAR, with Lieutenant Commander George Bailey RIN in command. Later still, the old sloop, HMIS CORNWALLIS was allotted to it for practical sea-going training.

The huge increase in the number of Special Service ratings entering the Service necessitated their training being cut down to five-and-a-half months, including the New Entry course. This was unavoidable, but it resulted in the drafting of inadequately-trained communications ratings to ships and shore stations. However, by 1944 the situation had considerably eased and it was possible to extend the training period to approximately eight-and-a-half months, including two months in a sea-going training ship.

Besides the instructional staff of forty-four ratings and a ship's company of 260, the Signal School had accommodation for a total of 930 ratings undergoing training. Seventy officers and 930 ratings were the maximum accepted at any one time. The establishment was purely a RIN commitment and most of the training was done by RINVR officers, but Admiralty had built some classrooms and loaned a few instructors. Among the courses undertaken in HMIS TALWAR were: Reserve Officers' Short and Long Signals courses; Ordinary Signalman's and Ordinary Telegraphist's preliminary courses; Ordinary Radar Operator's and Radio Mechanics' preliminary courses, (until the opening of the Radar School, HMIS CHAMAK); Visual Signalmans' 111, 11 and 1 courses; Wireless Telegraphists' 111, 11 and 1 courses, Convoy Leading Signalmans' courses; Convoy Yeomans' course; Leading Coders' course; Petty-Officer Coders' courses etc. Signal training remained in HMIS TALWAR until the new Combined Training Centre was opened at Cochin after the war.

The outbreak of war saw a large increase of the staff at Naval Headquarters and the old administrative building in the Dockyard began to bulge at the seams. The large increase in radio traffic and ever widening distribution of signal copies required further increases in both Signal and Telegraphist staff. A multi-storied building near the main gate of Bombay Fort was taken over for the RIN and the Signal Branch occupied one floor with the Remote Control Office, Signal Distribution Centre, Cypher Office and offices for the staff.

When the Flag Officer Commanding and his staff moved to New Delhi, more accommodation became available for any further requirements and it was assumed that no further moves would be necessary. However, the even tenor of our lives was rudely shattered by the fall of Singapore, the advance of Japanese naval units into the Bay of Bengal and the air-raid on Colombo. Bombay Fort, built by the Portuguese in the seventeenth century and brought into the possession of the Crown as part of the dowry of Catherine of Braganza, contained three large dungeons at the base of one of the main walls. These rooms were considered reasonably bomb - proof and large enough to accommodate the three Signal Offices. As there was no natural ventilation, air-conditioning had to be installed, which caused problems with the high humidity in Bombay. However, as physical security was considered more important than physical comfort, work was put in hand to make conditions as good as possible. The floors were tiled, walls plastered and painted and, in due course, the Remote Control Office, Signal Distribution Office and Cypher Office moved into the new quarters and remained there for the rest of the war.

*   *   *

Up to the beginning of 1939, the custody and use of cyphers had been the responsibility of the Supply Branch and, in the RIN, any cyphering required had been dealt with by the Admiral's Secretary. It was then decided to hand over this responsibility to the Signal Branch - which, in effect, meant the Staff Officer (Signals). As can be imagined, the need to train a nucleus of staff became an urgent necessity. As there was no volunteer organisation to call upon, the only solution semed to be to call for help from amongst the Officers' wives. The response was immediate and an initial class of some thirteen ladies was formed and lectures began.

It was around this core that, when hostilities began, sufficient numbers had been trained to enable a twenty-four hour watch to be instituted. As soon as they became available, RINVR Officers were trained - mostly on the job - and soon found themselves in charge of watches of some twenty ladies. As the cypher traffic increased, the supply of Officers' wives ran out and selected civilian ladies were taken on. It should be recorded that the cypher ladies received no financial reward for their services for nearly two years after war started and transport at night was only available through the generosity of a Parsi gentleman. With the formation of the Womens' Royal Indian Naval Service, those cypher ladies who so wished joined that Service - those who did not, remained as civilians.

*   *   *

In 1938, the Admiralty had suggested that a Radio Direction Finding Station in the Indian Ocean area would be of considerable value and this had been included in the Bombay Fort scheme.

The station was sited to the seaward side of all other buildings at Colaba and its geographical position and orientation of the receiving masts were established with the greatest possible accuracy. On completion of the Station, training was carried out and when war broke out, a twenty-four hour watch was maintained on selected enemy frequencies. Bearings of U-boats and surface raiders were transmitted to the Admiralty within a matter of seconds. The station at Colaba obtained bearings of the 'Graf Spee', which, with bearings from other D/F stations, resulted in her being tracked down before the River Plate battle.

While, in the early days, there was no direct evidence that Japan would join in, it was decided to monitor as much Japanese W/T traffic as possible, so that the disposition of their naval forces could be noted. To this end, selected ratings were trained in Japanese morse and soon a steady stream of intercepted traffic was being forwarded to Naval Headquarters in Ceylon, to be collated with similar reports from other stations.

For many years, Indian Naval forces had patrolled the Mergui Archipelago, the Nicobars and other island groups in the South Indian Ocean and were well aware of the Japanese interest in this area. On more than one occasion, Japanese fishing vessels, (so called), were found to have sophisticated Marine Survey equipment on board. There are a number of anchorages among the Islands and probably the largest and most secure is at Nancowry in the Nicobar Islands. These Islands lie some 250 miles north-west of the entrance to the Malacca Straits and, as any naval forces advancing westwards would most likely enter the South Indian Ocean by this route, the possibility of setting up an observation post in the area was studied and it was concluded that a coast-watching station at Nancowry might well prove of considerable value.

As the operation was primarily one of communication, it was handed over to the Signal Branch to plan and set up the Station. Because no suitable transmitter was available, Mr CN Bamji, the Radio Instructor Officer at the Signal School, designed and built a small H/F transmitter to work from a petrol generator. Masts were pre-fabricated in the Dockyard and an ever-growing list of stores gathered together. The PWD in the Andaman Islands had been requested to arrange for a hut to be made and sent to Nancowry.

With the usual last minute rush and bustle which seems to bedevil any project, Lieutenant Commander HC Bird RIN, with Sub-Lieutenant E Lodge, RINVR, two telegraphists and a mountain of stores, embarked in HMIS PARVATI, under the command of Lieutenant SG Karmarkar, RINR, and sailed for Nancowry.

On arrival, the hut was found to be ready for occupation, so all hands turned to, sorting stores and equipment. Within a week, the masts had been erected, equipment installed and all was ready to commence transmission. At midnight on the 2nd November 1940, Lieutenant Commander Bird and Sub-Lieutenant Lodge went ashore to try to get through to Calcutta for the first time with the newly-installed transmitter. On starting up, the petrol engine driving the alternator for the transmitter caught fire and Lieutenant Commander Bird almost lost his life when he slipped and trapped his leg in the equipment. He was very promptly rescued by Sub-Lieutenant Lodge and the fire was extinguished.

Subsequently, Sub-Lieutenant Lodge received a Letter of Commendation from the Flag Officer Commanding, Royal Indian Navy, which stated that his 'prompt action . . . was responsible for preventing what might have been a very serious fire, resulting in the loss of the hut and equipment' - no mention of his having saved Lieutenant Commander Bird's life.

With the Japanese landings in Malaya and the command of the sea having passed to them, there was no bar to their progress into the Indian Ocean, however many sighting reports may have been made. So in these circumstances, the Station was abandoned.

*   *   *

The expansion of the war to south-east Asia led to the appointment of Naval Officers-in-Charge of Naval Bases at all the major ports in India and the increased activity of minesweeping and in-shore patrol flotillas. Visual signalling arrangements were reviewed at all ports, resulting in new Signal Stations being built at Calcutta, Vizagapatam, Chittagong, Cochin and Coconada. Port W/T Stations, with associated Cypher Office facilities, were established to support these activities and to communicate with convoy escort vessels using the ports. A W/T Station was later established in New Delhi, to link Naval Headquarters with the ports and with Admiralty, via Bombay Fort W/T Station.

In September 1942, when the RIN took over responsibility for V/S and W/T communications at the Bahrein base, a qualified Signal Officer, Lieutenant E Lodge, RINVR, was appointed as Staff Officer (Signals), to the Senior Naval Officer, Persian Gulf and RIN ratings manned all signals services at Bahrein and Khor Kwai. The RIN had earlier taken over these services at the Naval base in Aden, in order to relieve Royal Navy personnel. Another Signals Officer Lieutenant NG Whitmore RINVR, was appointed to Aden. A radar station was established on Quoin Island in the Straits of Ormuz, for which the RIN was fully responsible - Lieutenant Rimmer RINVR was in charge.

* * *

In February 1944, a Naval Signals Directorate was set up within Naval Headquarters, New Delhi to cope with the increased work - load. Commander HC Bird OBE, RIN, was appointed as Director of Naval Signals (India). The appointment of Staff Officer (Signals) lapsed and the task of giving assistance to Port Signals Officers and to communications staffs at sea was undertaken by the Fleet Signals Officer.

Among the officers who formed the staff of the new Directorate were : Lieutenant Commander T Sheppard RIN, Lieutenant E Lodge, RINVR, Lieutenant DJ Hastings, RINVR , Lieutenant AJ Harris MBE, RIN, Lieutenant AGS Bryson RINVR, with Lieutenant Commander (S) KT Quick RINVR and four Indian RINVR officers in the cypher office. RINVR Officers provided the Naval Member and Secretary on the SCBI, a combined Board, working with SACSEA, responsible for the allocation and co-ordination of all frequencies in their own and adjoining theatres. Other members came from the RAF, US Forces and the Indian Post Office. Radar was originally the responsibility of the Signals Directorate, but, shortly afterwards, a separate Radar Branch was formed and a Staff Officer (Radar) - Lieutenant Commander DJ Hastings RINVR, was appointed to Naval Headquarters.

* * *

In July 1943, a Specialist Signals Officer, Lieutenant E Lodge RINVR, was flown to the UK to study modern methods of communications - security, as practised in Whitehall and in other Naval Establishments. On his return to India, he joined the Directorate of Naval Signals in New Delhi and he introduced appropriate measures for signals security throughout the Royal Indian Navy.

With the considerable technical improvement and, in many cases, with the complete rebuilding and reorganisation of the Indian Naval wireless stations from 1942 onwards, the Indian ports and New Delhi formed, within two years, an efficient part of the naval world - wide wireless organisation. Bombay Fort continued to play its part as an important link with Whitehall, South Africa, and the south-west Pacific. Calcutta, in particular, with its up-to-date remote reception and transmission and acres of rhombic aerial arrays, developed into a very fine radio station, necessary for the operational role which it played

Signals Directorate — Naval Headquarters (India) — 1944
(Sitting — left to right) Sub Lt C Nanda,RINVR; Lt(S) Khanna,RINVR; Lt AGS Bryson, RINVR;
Lt DJ Hastings,RINVR; Lt Cdr T Sheppard,RIN; Comdr HC Bird,OBE,RIN; Lt Cdr(Sp) D Quick,RINVR
Lt AJ Harris,MBE,RIN; Lt KK Sanjana,RINVR; Sub Lt(Sp) FF Coutino,RINVR; Chief Yeoman IA Thakur,RIN

during the war. From three lines manned in 1943, fifteen lines were in operation the next year.

To illustrate Bombay Fort's role; some important signals received and transmitted come to mind:-

i   Wavell's signal from Singapore to Churchill giving the warning that surrender was now inevitable (1942).

ii   Auchinleck's signal to Churchill from the Middle East, giving his requirements of tanks and other equipment for the eventual offensive from El Alamein (1942).

After the fall of Singapore, Bombay leased an IRCC, high-powered HF transmitter in Poona, (keyed from Bombay) to supplement the main transmitters at Mahul. For geographical and topographical reasons, Bombay was much more effective as a HF Station that Colombo and was a vital link with the East Indies Squadron after Singapore fell.

Naval Headquarters was heavily involved, with the other Services and the Indian Posts and Telegraph Department, in the planning and subsequent utilisation of the internal LT network for the Indian sub-continent (1942 onwards). This cost twenty crores of rupees. The extension of the Defence Teleprinter Network in India to the RIN was a significant step in reducing W/T traffic and increasing the efficiency of communication between Naval Headquarters, New Delhi and the major ports.

The Base Wireless workshops at Calcutta and Bombay were fitted with up-to-date lathes and coil-winding machines, greatly facilitating the repair and overhaul of wireless equipment in ships. Special test - equipment provided circuit analysers, oscillators and valve test boards. Base workshops at Chittagong, Vizagapatam, Madras, Cochin and Karachi were also provided with this equipment. Special test equipment to service the latest types of transmitters and receivers was provided for Bombay and Calcutta.

A great improvement was made in 1944, compared with the previous campaigning season. Chittagong wireless station was completed in 1943 and eight lines were manned in 1944. More than a hundred signal ratings were employed. On 'D' Day in Burma, the Royal Indian Navy manned communications organisations at Calcutta and Chittagong were stretched to the limit, but they played a vital role in the successful operations culminating in the recapture of Rangoon. When South-East Asia Command was formed in New Delhi in 1945, Naval Headquarters W/T station had to cope with enormously increased traffic, particularly between the Commander-in-Chief, East Indies and Admiral Mountbatten's Headquarters.

When Singapore was re-taken in January 1946, Bombay Fort W/T Station noticed that Admiralty were having great difficulty in establishing regular W/T communication. Warrant Telegraphist Bert Spence, who was the Officer-in-Charge, Mahul, suggested that Bombay Fort could help and assistance was, therefore offered to Admiralty. For a time, Bombay Fort was receiving and re-transmitting all traffic to and from Admiralty and Singapore.

The following is a copy of a signal received from Admiralty:-

FO BOMBAY (R) FOCRIN, C-in-C EIS from ADMTY.

The recent prompt action by Bombay W/T in providing a W/T link to Singapore to clear congestion on service 6 was most effective and much appreciated.

* * *

Shortly after the outbreak of war, some of the smaller craft used for harbour patrol duties in Bombay were not fitted with radio and, in any event, all ships maintained W/T silence. A dedicated Parsi pigeon fancier, Mr BK Shroff, persuaded Vice-Admiral Sir Herbert Fitzherbert that carrier pigeons might prove a satisfactory means of passing messages to shore when ships were out of visual touch. Mr Shroff was commissioned as a Sub-Lieutenant (Sp) RINVR and was appointed as Officer-in-Charge, Pigeons.

A small white pigeon loft was erected at the corner of the lawn outside the Officers' Mess in the Dockyard in Bombay and special miniature signal forms were designed by the Signals Branch. The birds, with a message tube attached to their legs, were put into baskets and delivered daily to the Port Signal Officer, who handed them over to ships' officers when they called for their Recognition Signals before setting out on patrol. The birds were to be released should it become necessary to communicate with base when out of V/S range and, in any event, before the end of the patrol. Whether or not any important messages were transmitted by this means is not known - what is known, however, is that one bird was released from HMIS PATHAN, but before it could clear the ship, it was overcome by engine room fumes and it fell down the funnel.

16

The Engineering Branch and the Bombay Naval Dockyard

RIN ENGINEERING MEMORIES OF PC CARD and others

The Engineer Officer cadre of the Royal Indian Marine/Navy at 1929/30 showed a pattern of ad hoc recruitment in small numbers since World War I. The reason was the run-down of the Service and the Inchcape Report findings. How much effect came from the Indian Army as the main plank of India's defence policy can only be conjecture, but a 'dead hand' of Military Finance was soon found to affect Naval functions by Naval newcomers. The scene in 1929 showed Engineer Officers of pre-World War I, World War I and post-World War I entry and then a batch of eight Sub-Lieutenants at the end of 1929. At that time, there was one Indian Engineer Officer, then Lieutenant DN Mukerji. Thereafter, came a trickle of Indian and British recruits, to maintain numbers, up to World War II.

The outbreak of World War II brought an influx and rapid expansion of numbers, from civilian sources, who served in RINR and RINVR cadre. It is to be noted that this ad hoc recruitment up to World War II, of officers who had engineering training and experience, was different from the normal Royal Navy's pattern of a regular intake, in numbers needed, through a comprehensive pattern of education and training, prior to sea service.

There were two areas of service for Engineer Officers in the RIN, generally known as 'Service' and 'Survey'. The RIN was responsible for providing staff for the Mercantile Marine Department of the Government of India, functioning in Indian ports. Basically, the Engineers either served afloat or in the Mercantile Marine Department or in a number of various other appointments within the 'Raj'.

It is worth looking for a moment at what went on in the pre-World War I to World War II years. Pre-World War I activities were in trooping etc and World War I brought the War into the picture. Post-World War I activities were a mixture of servicing lighthouses etc, care and maintenance parties in the ships of the DUFFERIN era; of shore appointments in Government Dockyards - Calcutta, Bombay, Rangoon; in Port Blair as Engineer and Harbour Master, (and, from accounts of that particular appointment it was a most interesting one, largely for the reason of considerable independence and opportunity for responsibility. For one or two junior officers, an annual event for several weeks was a stint in stock-taking checks in the Naval Stores Department. There was also an appointment of a similar nature at the Naval Henjam Coal Depot, in the Persian Gulf.

Looking at this picture of varied appointments and responsibilities from fifty or more years ago, brings out the value of the pre-recruitment engineering training and experience which became available to the Head of the Engineering Sections, the Engineer Captain, when making appointments. This, by contrast with the more formal RN training, may have been a valuable feature in filling these different appointments, which has responsibilities and duties - a fact perhaps not appreciated at the time.

All officers were required to have a qualification in Urdu, which needed study, for which the necessary tuition was paid by the individual. I take issue with those who query the necessity for the up-grading of the knowledge needed. I had passed the preliminary Urdu examination when the new order, requiring the Lower Standard Urdu examination to be taken within a certain time, came along. This entailed further study during World War II. In my case, after taking the forenoon part of the examination, I was informed that, in error, I had been tested for the Higher Standard and the Lower Standard test was given in the afternoon.

Looking back, it was a good life - it was something worth doing with a challenge. One grumbled at the time over petty events but there was a good mixed bag of hard work, sport and the excitement of new places. Then, with World War II, came the test of the experience gained.

Until recruitment from the Punjab began in the early 1930's, Engine Room Ratings were recruited virtually entirely from the Ratnagiri district. Although they were largely without a formal education, their tradition of centuries of fishing and sea-faring made them ideal and hard working. Their discipline was excellent, as a small anecdote relates. The writer's first appointment on arriving in India was as junior Engineer in PATHAN, (only two Engineers were carried). During the first experience of boiler cleaning shortly after, knowing no Urdu, a Leading Stoker started to 'take the Micky' out of the new boy by not understanding my effort to communicate that I did not like the way he was working in the boiler. A few moments later, the Chief Stoker, one Said Ali, came on the scene and the situation rapidly changed. Strict discipline was re-enforced immediately by action and word of mouth from Said Ali and it had a permanent effect for the year served in PATHAN.

Ratings were not trained as Engine Room Artificers, but their watch-keeping abilities were good. However, the commencement of the Punjabi Muslim input of Stoker boys, brought a change. The arrival of HMIS HINDUSTAN from the UK in 1931 emphasised the need for new and modern ships to have properly trained crews and shore based training became mandatory. This commenced with a Stokers Training School being started in a small Dockyard building in 1932. Captain (E) H Harvey, (then Lieutenant Commander), was in charge and the writer was his junior assistant. Training, based on the Stokers' Manual, was introduced in DALHOUSIE.

Methods were primitive. To teach coal firing for HMIS CORNWALLIS, an empty forty gallon oil drum, with no ends, was slung and could be adjusted for height and also angled. This represented a furnace door - soil substituted for coal. Stokers' Manual training was also carried out in ships by Engineer Officers. The STS highlighted the need for more sophisticated and comprehensive training and from it came the Mechanical Training Establishment.

Commander (then Lieutenant) J Covedale-Smith underwent UK training in Royal Navy Mechanical Training Establishments and, in the latter part of the 1930's, the RINMTE came into being. Its first home was a building in the Dockyard near the Signal Station. Progress was rapid, in particular for the planning and initiation of courses in basic knowledge and development of skills for rates to Artificer levels. The emphasis for speed in output increased just prior to World War II and, with the oubtreak of war.

Expansion of the normal Dockyard functions and the MTE's need for more space led to a move to the Castle area and expansion of activities to provide a nucleus engine room complements for new ships. Demand intensified and older seagoing men from the Merchant Navy were recruited and sent for basic training to the MTE also. This in turn produced pressure with older men and young men with a background of secondary education, all new to Naval discipline. Problems arose, but were overcome and the manning problem was reduced. Arising out of the problems was the situation where a number of young men, (Artificers under training), were sent to jail. Virtually all were of the Roman Catholic faith and the Roman Catholic Archbishop of Bombay sent a senior member of his staff to the Officer-in-Charge of the MTE to express the Archbishop's complete agreement with the action taken.

Pressure and problems dictated a removal of the MTE from Bombay to Lonavla, where HMIS SHIVAJI was born. Several miles of ghat track separated SHIVAJI from Lonavla itself and whatever bright lights existed there for the liberty watch. SHIVAJI is noteworthy from the aspect of move of plant from Bombay pumps, boilers etc, to form a working, steaming nucleus of machinery for training purposes. The writer had the pleasure of seeing from time to time the machinery being installed, 3,000 feet above sea level on the western ghats and particulary of the aforesaid boiler having a ride, by road, on a tank trailer up the ghats.

One hitherto unrecorded event should be put in the history of SHIVAJI. FOCRIN (Admiral Godfrey) decided to inspect progress of the Establishment, then in the throes of pregnancy, just before birth. The area was rocky, rough, bumpy and by no means cleared of scrub and jungle bush. FOCRIN was driven around the area in the Establishment jeep - a new means of propulsion for the Admiral. He asked the driver to kindly steer towards a tough, strong and by no means small sapling. The order was obeyed, with a resulting severe collision and succeeding series of bumps and jolts. The Admiral, it is understood, expressed his satisfaction for the vehicle's road worthiness!

Thus, the present day HMIS SHIVAJI's descendant at Lonavla is the descendant of foresight and efforts made half a century ago and is one proud record held by the Engineering Branch of that period.

In the late 20's and early 30's the only ships which the RIM/RIN had were as follows:-

Sloops:

CLIVE - laid down in the UK about 1913 and finally built between 1919 and 1921. Displacement 1,748 tons; speed twelve knots. Two Babcock water tube boilers, oil fired and twin screw geared steam turbines.

LAWRENCE - built in the UK 1919; displacement 1,210 tons; speed - twelve knots. Propulsion as in CLIVE.

These two ships were of much the same 'yacht-like' design - built as Despatch Vessels for carrying VIPs around, looking after Lights etc. Captain (E) Trenoweth was LAWRENCE's Engineer Officer for her delivery voyage from the UK. He had served in HMS ERIN (battleship) during World War I.

CORNWALLIS - built in the UK in 1917 - ex-HMS LYCHNIS, of the old Flower Class. Displacement 1,383 tons; speed twelve knots. Two coal fired marine boilers, with single screw, four cylinder triple expansion engine.

CORNWALLIS could edge up to sixteen knots in favourable conditions - ie good coal and trained boiler room crews; clean condenser, (and no jelly-fish to block intakes!); cool sea temperatures and balanced engine.

Patrol Vessels:

PATHAN - built in the UK during World War I - ex-RNPC 49. Gross tonnage - 605; speed nineteen knots.

Two Yarrow water tube boilers, oil fired and twin screw geared steam turbines.

BALUCHI - Similar to PATHAN.

These two ships were the only true 'warships' in the Squadron until HINDUSTAN arrived from the UK in 1931.

Target Towing Trawler:

MADRAS - No construction details available.
One coal fired marine boiler and single screw, three cylinder triple expansion engine.

Survey ships:

> PALINURUS - No construction details available. Gross
> tonnage - 444. One coal fired marine boiler and single screw,
> three cylinder triple expansion engine.

> The 'old' INVESTIGATOR - built by Vickers in 1907.
> Displacement 1,172 tons; speed thirteen knots.

> Two coal fired marine boilers and single screw, three cylinder
> triple expansion engine.

> This ship was replaced by the 'new' INVESTIGATOR, (ex-Cable
> Ship PATRICK STEWART) in 1933.

Depot Ship:

> The hulk DALHOUSIE was moored alongside the Dockyard
> breakwater and was used as a training and accommodation
> ship. She had no machinery - lighting etc being supplied from
> shore supply.

It is also worth noting that the Dockyard had a tug, (whose twin
sister had earlier been sold to the Sultan of Zanzibar), and there was also
the Dockyard Dredger CACHALOT.

The first modern ship, HINDUSTAN, arrived in Bombay in 1931,
having been brought out by a Royal Navy delivery crew. She was a
Bridgewater Class sloop - displacement 1,190 tons - speed sixteen knots
and she mounted two - 4 inch and four - 3 pounder guns. Propulsion was
by three drum Admiralty boilers and twin screw geared steam turbines.

General memories about some of these ships may be of interest. I
served, on first arrival in Bombay, for twelve months in PATHAN and
then joined the newly arrived HINDUSTAN as junior, (No 3) EO.
Lieutenant Commander (E) Harold Harvey was the Engineer Officer in
charge and Tom Elliott (like myself a Sub-Lieutenant) was No 2 EO.

The shake-down cruise was to Karachi, Henjam and Muscat. The
fresh water supply to the Captain's quarters was, to say the least, dodgy
and occasioned Captain Turbett some annoyance. The supply frequently
ran dry and the 'Chief' was sent for. By the time the latter reported to
the Captain, a 'miracle' had always happened. The serious side to this
comment is, of course, the age old designer's problem of priorities, weight
and space and evaporators to produce fresh water were of too small
capacity and in the most difficult place for cleaning the coils. If modern
technical reports are to be believed, 'space age' technology has virtually
removed that particular bugbear.

As far as can be remembered, there were no major breakdowns
preventing our ships going to sea - one exception was when CLIVE ran all
her main turbine bearings. The EO and his staff did a splendid job in
refitting the ship to full operational status from their own resources. This

happened in Trincomalee where, at that time, no help could be given from shore. Another example is when, in 1933, CORNWALLIS re-tubed her condenser with Ship's staff. This was also carried out in Trincomalee, where new tubes were available.

Another repair worth mentioning is the work done on CLIVE's main engine forced lubrication system pipes. The ship, on full-power trials out of Colombo early in 1937, lost lubrication pressure. The main engines were shut down and sustained no damage. Admiral Bedford was flying his Flag on a cruise to 'show the Flag' to the Andamans, Akyab and the Arakan coast. Captain Percy Learmont was CO. A great deal of brazing had to be carried out to effect repairs on work and age-hardened brittle copper pipes, which was satisfactory. Later in Bombay, flexible pipes were fitted to eliminate the trouble.

There is one final chapter to CLIVE's thrust-bearing work described above - it took place on the same cruise as the forced lubrication pipes fractured, mentioned above. The Admiral was holding exercises and CLIVE's Engine Room sealed orders called for an examination of the main engine thrust shaft bearing. The Engineer Officer registered his objections, referring to the work done not many months earlier and asked the Captain to sign the E/R Log entry, noting this objection in RED. The Captain refused and another test exercise was substituted.

In regard to the RED entry, another need arose when INDUS was on passage to the Thames for the 1937 Coronation. An overnight stop was made off Southend Pier. The First Lieutenant instructed the EO to maintain steam for immediate notice, all night. This order, entered in RED in the E/R Log Book, was taken by the Engineer Officer to the Captain, then Captain AR Rattray, for his signature, as it was considered to be one likely to cause damage to the M/E turbines. The Captain refused to sign and a longer period of notice was substituted. In the event, INDUS did not have to make any emergency move and passage up the Thames proceeded peacefully the next morning.

It is interesting that INDUS, over a year later, after having returned to India and been on her visit to Australia, came in for refit in Bombay and amongst the defect list work items was one for repairs to turbine blading.

Lieutenant Commander G Taylor contributes a memory of HINDUSTAN about 1940. It concerns the 'Allens of Bedford' blast injection diesels installed. These diesels needed precise preventative maintenance and experienced handling to give trouble free service, even when new in 1931. He pays a well earned tribute to the skill of the ship's Chief Mechanic, one Bauhudin, a Ratnagiri rating, who, alone and unaided kept the two diesels going for weeks on end, under war conditions.

The pre-World War II situation of plant and equipment in the Engineering Department of HMI Dockyard, Bombay, of the whole Yard, in fact, was of old, dated and worn machinery. The hydraulic machinery for dock gates, capstans and cranes in 1939 was virtually half a century old - slow and cumbersome - and needed much care and attention for trouble-free working. From memory, on only one occasion did a failure take place, when, towards the end of the war, the wet basin gate gave trouble.

HMI Naval Dockyard – Bombay   Aerial photograph taken just before the outbreak of war

This record reflects the care given to the plant over that half century.

Similarly, the Department's machine shop reflected the same story. It was obviously naive to expect machine tools made to designs at the turn of the century to handle materials with characteristics of hardness, toughness and strength not then known and to be able to remove metal at rates several hundred per cent more than Grandfather had dealt with.

Warned by Munich, a modernisation plan was prepared and submitted to Naval Headquarters for the Government of India. This plan covered virtually the whole of the machinery and plant and foresaw the need for increased space. Its cost ran into many lakhs of rupees. It was not approved and a Colonel of Military Accounts made the comment that age alone was no valid reason to scrap and renew. It is to be noted that, less than twenty-four hours following the first Japanese bomber over Calcutta, the modernisation scheme was approved in toto.

By this time, the United Kingdom required all the plant capacity it had and our needs were difficult to meet. It resulted in a modernisation scheme having to be carried out on an ad hoc basis, with Lease-Lend help from the USA, spread over several years. The first new machine tool the Department had had for years was a small six inch centre lathe, received from the Custodian of Enemy Property, from a cargo seized just after war started. Some of the gains from modernisation many be mentioned, which were most beneficial. A long bed lathe was received which made it possible for main propeller shafting up to just over sixty feet in length to be handled, instead of twenty feet, as in the past.

Foundry capacity was upgraded by improving Iron Cupola melting capacity and introducing modern methods to produce higher grade and better quality iron and two modern high speed melting furnaces for non-ferrous castings were installed. A small basic testing laboratory was set up to give essential data on the qualities of metal produced. A young Parsi man employed in the Department was given training and ran this unit.

A Millwright's section was set up, to deal with the installation of plant and to maintain it. The Department fortunately obtained the services of an ex-GIP Railway foreman millwright to build up from scratch and run the new section. It is worthy of note that little or no disruption of normal work took place through new plant installation, in spite of a full load of work on ships and the 'Factory' working twenty-four hours daily for six days and twelve days on Sundays.

World War II brought a need for motor vehicle maintenance and repair facilities. Until then, the Yard, (NSO) had three motor vehicles. Expansion of the RIN and the arrival of RN establishments brought many more vehicles into the Yard's responsibilities. The maximum at one time reached around a thousand. MED set up a workshop near Bombay Race Course for preventative maintenance and repair. A foreman, who had walked out of Burma, with General Motors training, was engaged. It is pleasing to reveal that he very satisfactorily took charge of the unit, running it in a trouble-free manner.

Machine Shop work with the outbreak of World War II was not adequately handled, since new and tough materials led to problems of output and quality of finish. This led to the formation of a Tool Room by MED, given to the charge of a young man, an ex-GIP Railway Apprentice Tool Maker - an outstanding individual. The Department was lucky with him. With a minimum of equipment, heat treatment, grinding etc, and a stock of cutting steels (ex-Custodian of Enemy Property, largely) he built up the basic tools for the Machine Shop. When this was done, all old tools were withdrawn one week-end and replaced with new. Stocks of new tools were adequate for maintenance and this painful but necessary exercise proved itself and gave the results that had been expected.

The Blacksmith's Shop had a new air supply to its forges and this air was also made available throughout the 'Factory'. MED had no Drawing Office prior to World War II. Plans were stored in a small room off the MED's office. A Drawing Office was established on the first floor of the 'Factory' where, in the Boer War and World War I periods, lightweight small lathes had operated. The Drawing Office was built up by and in the charge of an Engineer Officer who, in civil life, had been employed by Babcock & Wilcox. He recruited and trained staff and formed an up-to-date filing registry for plans and drawings, many being photocopied on micro-size film for space purposes and storage.

An emergency training plan for manning new lathes and other machine tools was put into practice. Limited training scope - one man for one machine - it worked, though the subject of much criticism. It was intensive and simple in character and effective, as it was supported by an efficient overseeing system from Chargemen and the Admiralty Foreman who had arrived by this time.

Whilst considering the Machine Shop, it is to be recorded that, at the height of the UK's production problems in World War II, Churchill desired to know what Indian production was. He had an inspection carried out - Government and civilian sources of production - by an experienced and well thought-of Engineer - Sir William Stanier - and Locomotive and Railway Chief Mechanical Engineer from the Midland Railway. In due course, he examined MED's 'Factory', accompanied by a number of senior engineers from civilian ship repair yards, the Indian Railways etc. He made the pleasing comment that it was the only workshop so far seen by him which was fully utilising its installed plant. The remark produced a response from his companions, who accused MED of paying higher rates for good men than they were paying.

One item of work was making and trial of limpet mine casing. It had a 'Top Secret' categorisation and the decision was made to have this item carried out as a normal one with no secrecy. This was done and the Millwright Section did it. We were told later that it had been used in the Singapore area. Military Intelligence monitored the work for any hint of information being circulated, but there was none, either in or out of the Dockyard.

To this can be added the story of HMS KIMBERLEY's main engine gear wheel work. The Commanding Officer of the ship personally examined progress on it and he was not satisfied with the way it was being carried out. The very old 'Joseph Whitworth'-made lathe was first of all checked for its accuracy and steps were taken to ensure it would run at very low speeds and not 'seize up'. It was operated by day only as, after dark, the soil under the machine bed moved and caused unwanted trouble. Temperature differentials, making movements between the bed and the soil, ie, foundations and soil, were thus avoided. The Captain's distress and his suggestions to improve affairs were passed to the Admiralty civilian Machine Shop Foreman with frequency. Eventually, steps were taken to curtail these twice daily visits and the ship later carried Prime Minister Churchill in the Mediterranean.

The Munich crisis brought a flurry of planning. One aspect was the arming of Merchant Navy vessels. It was known that the Sewree scrap yard had had gun rings from ex-World War I armed vessels dumped there. An inspection found them, but there were no orders to purchase them. When World War II was imminent, a second inspection revealed that they had all been sold to Japan!

As Singapore fell to the Japanese, a number of Chinese Admiralty engine fitters came to Bombay and proved themselves invaluable in the Dockyards. MED's staff increased to about six Naval Engineer Officers, about six civilian Foremen, locally recruited and six or eight Admiralty Dockyard civilian staff were seconded from UK Naval Yards. Their training and experience with detailed knowledge of repairs was very valuable.

It should also be recorded that Yard expansion brought a tremendous amount of electrical work, to supply light, power etc for buildings and plant. This was carried out by the Yard's Electrical Department, smoothly and efficiently and their co-operation and co-ordination was greatly appreciated. There was always an excellent relationship, which dated back to earlier pre-war instruction given by the Electrical Engineer - Commander (Sp) NT Patterson ('Pat', as he was respectfully known), to the 1930 batch of Engineer Officers who were sent to him for instruction.

A state of affairs, perhaps unique, existed in the middle of 1945. The whole of the Dockyard went on strike. This continued and negotiations between the two parties were without results, apart from demonstrations outside the Dockyard. Then Government allowed a lock-out to be declared. This was in July/August 1945. There were a number of RIN ships in Bombay and some in the Yard for repairs. A plan was devised for assistance from the Engineer Officers where possible, to keep the idle Dockyard plant in a state of preservation. This action was being commenced at the time of Partition in August 1947, when the writer handed over to his successor, Commander (E) A Briggs RIN.

THE ENGINEERING BRANCH OF THE RIN, 1929-47, by GW WATSON

As an introduction, the training of the batch of recruits of which I was a member included three apprentices - one each from the Royal Dockyards, Chatham, Portsmouth and Devonport - one ex-apprentice from the railways, two ex-apprentices from private shipping firms, one junior engineer from a merchant shipping line and one ex-Keyham. No one had academic qualifications except that I was a member of the Whitworth Society.

After an interview and medical examination on the same day in the India Office in August 1929, we were kitted up, at our expense, and proceeded to Portsmouth for Divisional and anti-gas courses. On completion, we embarked in the troopship NEVASSA and arrived in Bombay in December 1929. The stench of Bombay nearly made me resign and return to the UK. All new entries were drafted to sea-going ships as soon as possible.

My first ship was CORNWALLIS as Junior EO. The Senior Engineer was the **first** Indian Officer in the Service (Mukerji) and the Chief was a senior two-and-a-half (Thomson). There were no ERA's in those days and EOs were expected to carry out certain maintenance work. The Senior Engineer and Junior EO were watchkeepers and divisional officers. Engine Room complement in sloops was four mechanics, Chief Stoker, Leading Stokers and stokers similar to RN ships of similar class, with a watch and station bill arranged in three watches.

There were the usual complaints from the Engine Room Department regarding stokers being given upper deck jobs by the First Lieutenant, especially at 'clear lower deck' for hoisting boats etc. In harbour, Junior EOs had to land at 0600 for 'square bashing'. This was not at all popular, especially in Karachi, in the desert, where swarms of flies attacked one's bare legs above the knee, (we were in shirt and shorts), and Captain Learmont was in charge bellowing 'the position of attention is the position of maximum rigidity - STAND STILL!'. Another chore given to Junior EOs, was to take the records of fire control instruments by standing **outside** and peering through the spy hole in the blast shield of 4" guns at full calibre shoots. Why our ear drums were not permanently damaged will never be known.

The amount of steaming done was less than in the RN, owing to the Service being run by the Controller of Naval Accounts. The amount of fuel burnt per annum was strictly limited by a niggardly budget, so EOs spent some of their time working out maximum mileage at most economical speeds, commensurate with the requirements of the FOC for exercises and 'showing the flag' cruises. The RN (East Indies Station) used to 'pipe-down' every afternoon when in harbour. Not so the RIM - the CNA wanted his pound of flesh.

As far as can be remembered, there were no major break-downs preventing our ships going to sea - with one exception - when CLIVE ran all her main turbine bearings. The EO and his staff did a splendid job in refitting the ship to full operational status from their own resources. This happened in Trincomalee, where at that time, no help could be given from shore. Ships were clean and well maintained by ships' staff. This was quite an achievement as the CNA also cut to the bone the amount of money available for naval stores.

RN ships of similar size to the RIM ships carried one EO only, but four ERAs were also in the complement. Owing to a shortage of EOs at the time, I was appointed to the INVESTIGATOR, as the only EO in the ship in 1930, as a very junior Sub-Lieutenant. The ship did a full season surveying in the Mergui Archipelago. In addition to the ship sounding the ocean from dawn to dusk each day, three motor boats had to be kept operational on coast-lining duties over the same period. We carried one spare motor boat engine and, owing to the possibility of a defect developing, which had been experienced the previous year, engines had to be changed in rotation every 300 hours. To complicate matters, it was found that bolt holes in engine couplings were of a different size from those in the shaft flange. The EO then turned new coupling bolts on an old lathe on the quarter deck, which was driven by a large belt from the sounding winch. Mechanics were unable to use a lathe. After the boats returned from coast-lining, the EO, one mechanic and one stoker worked far into the night changing engines.

I was really 'thrown in at the deep end' during my service in INVESTIGATOR. There was no help available from anywhere, but it was a marvellous experience being in charge and on one's own. An examination had to be taken for promotion to Lieutenant. This was held approximately two years after entering the Service and, if successful, the Officer was promoted after three years.

Leave was granted in the UK after three to four years' service in India. There was no local leave, as the exigencies of the Service never permitted it. The leave amounted to twelve months, but EOs were expected to study for the Extra First Class Certificate of Competency, at their own expense, and to sit the examination during their leave. The object of sitting the examination was to qualify as an Engineer and Ship Surveyor after training with the British Board of Trade. If successful, the Officer could be considered for service in List 2 if required.

During the early 1930s, two new ships were added to the RIN - HINDUSTAN and INDUS. These were sloops and similar to RN ships of the same class. Each ship carried three EOs, as we still had no ERAs. Service as Lieutenant lasted for three years and, during this time another examination for promotion to Lieutenant Commander had to be taken and passed. Also, an examination in Urdu had to be taken and passed.

Munshis (teachers) had to be paid for at the officer's expense. Some officers who had an aptitude for languages went on and passed the Interpreter's examination and studied other Indian languages, such as Hindi, Marathi and Gujerati.

As, during my first home leave, I became a student again at the Poplar School of Engineering and Navigation; during my second leave I sat the Extra Chief's examination and again became an Extra Chief (failed narrowly). However, NHQ thought this was good enough and I was drafted to Glasgow, on the staff of the Chief Engineer and Ship Surveyor, Board of Trade, for training as an Engineer and Ship Surveyor. After twelve months' service in Glasgow and at Head Office, Westminster, I qualified as a BOT Engineer and Ship Surveyor.

On return to India in 1938, preparations were being made for World War II and I was appointed Manager, Constructive Department. This was the most hard-working and interesting part of my career in the RIN. Many Indian coastal craft were requisitioned for absorption in the RIN and had to be armed and converted for either M/S or A/S duties in HMI Dockyard, Bombay. I can only think of three - BHADRAVATI, PARVATI and ST ANTHONY - there were many more.

The majority of the increased load of work involved the Constructive Department, viz, strengthening decks for gun mountings and M/S winches; compensating hulls where holes were cut for A/S domes; fitting guns, winches, depth-charge throwers and racks; fitting magazines, wardrooms and mess-decks; converting heads from Indian to European style etc. Finally, an inclination experiment to check buoyancy calculations and fitting ballast to give the ships acceptable stability and then sea trials.

Facilities in the Dockyard were inadequate, so many portable air-compressors, generators, welding sets had to be purchased, also oxy-acetylene burning sets and pneumatic tools. I cannot remember hearing a cheep out of the CNA at that time. Fred Hopkins, (my Assistant from the Admiralty), the Parsi Senior Foreman, foremen and chargehands, shipwrights and myself worked like stink and all hours. There was a fine spirit in the Department.

Just before the outbreak of war, I was appointed to CLIVE as EO, and served in the PG and Red Sea. In 1941, I was drafted to the UK as Engineering Overseer on the staff of the Admiral Superintendent, Contract Built Ships, Newcastle-upon-Tyne, for twelve ships building in the UK for the RIN. These were: sloops - two at Thornycrofts, Southampton; two at Yarrows on the Clyde; minesweepers: two at Blyth; two at Renfrew; four at Greenock. Additional duties were as interviewing officer for choosing extra Reserve and Volunteer Reserve EOs required, also assisting in commissioning the ships and attending basin and sea trials.

I was appointed EO of GODAVARI - one of the Thornycroft sloops and stood by her building. EOs of these ships, in addition to being in charge of the Engine Room and Electrical Departments, were also damage Control Officer of the ship; in charge of Central Stores; responsible for the operation and maintenance of the gyro compass and fire-control table and expected to assist with cypher duties.

In 1945, when Coastal Forces were being built up for the invasion of Burma, I was appointed Base Engineer Officer, Vizagapatam and, thereafter, Deputy Director of Post-War Planning, New Delhi.

This latter group consisted of Director - Captain Jefford; Deputy Director - myself; Assistant Director - Lieutenant-Commander GP Frazier. We dwelt in the 'corridors of power', where the composition of the post-war RIN was being dreamed up. FOC and Staff Officers, including Captain Jefford did the dreaming; Jeep Frazier's job was writing papers of justification for the Director to submit to the powers that be; my job resembled that of a glorified draughtsman - drawing up endless tables of ships, shore establishments, complements, stores, armaments etc. Commander-in-Chief India, FOC and Staff Officers changed their minds every time the clock struck - so there was plenty for our group to do.

The mutiny intervened and I was appointed a member of a Board of Enquiry, visiting various shore establishments. On completion, I went home on my third leave - no courses or examinations this time. On return, I was appointed SEO Bombay, until voluntary retirement at the end of 1947.

During the period covered by the previous chapters, there were occasionally problems with labour in the Bombay Dockyard. The following two letters are interesting in that context.

1. Dated 3rd June 1938

Sir,

I wish to bring to your notice that three so-called officers under your services in the Stores Department are men who don't like to face their opponents on the open road, but are great heroes in the Dockyard, taking the upper hand of men who try to earn an honest living under them.

It is high time you not only looked into the matter but took action.

Enquire into the salaries of the men according to abilities and you will find that the best men are given a dog's life, not because they haven't guts, but because it's their daily bread they have to consider.

I may now mention their names; they are three physical wrecks, Mr EVO Johnson, Mr F Hearn and Mr JB Hawes, the three men who like fighting behind the goal instead of on the field. Bribes, gambling and drinking are the three good points of these civilian staff of the Royal Indian Navy.

If you haven't got the courage to deal with this case, the Congress Committee will show you and the British Government (how) to govern the situation. Since you can't rule this place, it is better you all cleared out instead of spoiling our motherland, India. Do you ever accept complaints from your subordinates - if you have not, the results are above.

I can say lots more but time and space does not permit me.

I close now hoping things will improve, because I am a respectable citizen and will not lower my social standing for bribe-takers, gamblers, drunkards, not in moderation but in extreme.

Blame who you wish, but this is the truth.

2. Dated 20th January 1939

Royal Indian Naval Dockworkers Mass Meeting

A call to assemble at a meeting given at short notice was never responded to so spontaneously as witnessed at the Elphinstone Circle Gardens, when over 1,200 workers of all Departments of the RIN Dockyard assembled to hear the say of their respected leaders.

Mr MJ Lopes, the President of the Welfare Benefit Fund and Union of the Dockyard, the hero of the day, was the person whose outstanding achievements of the day were to be recorded.

Opening the proceedings, Mr Daji Kamla, Vice-President, introducing Mr Lopes to the gigantic assembly and requested all to hear patiently what he would say and requested him to address the meeting.

Mr Lopes, addressing, first thanked all the workers who partook of the demonstration held at the office of the Captain Superintendent of the Dockyard this morning, according to the Resolution of the General meeting held yesterday and extolled the extraordinary discipline of the workers in maintaining very good behaviour throughout the ordeal, which was the first and, he said, the best of its kind in the history of the Dockyard workers.

Continuing, he said that today was a Red-Letter day for the workers of the Dockyard.

Then Mr Lopes read the petition addressed to the Captain Superintendent and ably translated the same in Marathi to the assembly. He then said how he was interrogated by Commander Card and Mr Hamilton, to both of whom he replied that the demonstration is held to place the grievances of the workers of the ME Department before the Head of the RIN Dockyard and only to him the matters concern.

Later Commander Jefford, (Commander of the Yard), a responsible officer was the next officer who enquired of him as to who was the leader of the demonstration. He replied that I was the President of the Welfare Benefit Fund and Union of the Dockyard and was there to place a petition of the ME Department workers before Captain Nicholl, as the Manager, ED, did not take notice of the petitions of the aggrieved workers.

Commander Jefford, Mr Lopes said, behaved in a strictly gentlemanly manner and handled the situation in a very pleasant way. Had he not done so, very unpleasant results would have taken place, seriously damaging the reputation of the Dock Workers and Officers.

Whilst handing the petition to Commander Jefford, Mr Lopes said that he was entrusting the papers into his hands because he was confident of the good and kind nature of the officer and relied on a gentleman's word that the petition was in safe and proper hands and that due consideration and favourable reply would be given to him, through the Head of the Dockyard, on Moritus.

Resolution

This meeting resolves to place on record the gentlemanly behaviour of Commander Jefford in handling a situation of great consequences and that his action is appreciated by all workers of the Dockyard and a copy of this resolution be forwarded to him for information.

Mr Ibboo, Boilermaker, terminating the meeting requested all workers to continue working in such manner as to give no cause for complaint whatsoever.

(Signed) NJ Lopes
President Dockworkers' Welfare
Benefit Fund and Union,
RIN Dockyard, Bombay

A manuscript note on the bottom of this letter by Captain Nicoll reads: 'Commander Jefford, it seems, was the hero of the day!'

THE BOMBAY DOCKYARD AFTER PARTITION by A BRIGGS

At Partition, the directive for the Bombay Dockyard was to scrap the traditional RN organisation and to re-establish on the lines of the US Navy yards and to bring production up to commercial efficiency. Also, every effort was made to use all facilities to the maximum, in view of the Fleet expansion. I was appointed Acting Captain (E), as Industrial Manager, to achieve this, assisted thoughout by ex-RIN Indian officers and IN officers of the 'L' Branch. Construction was covered by myself, with a senior Admiralty civilian. Foundries were supervised by an Admiralty civilian and a young Parsi graduate in Naval Architecture arrived in 1949.

The industrial activities were divided into five sections: Engineering; Electrics; Construction; Maintenance and Production Control. There was one RN officer for Engineering; one IN officer for 'L'; me for Construction; one IN officer for Maintenance. A Production Control Centre was started, supervised by an Admiralty civilian and later taken over by an Anglo-Indian foreman from Engineering. The RN Commander (E) did two years and was then relieved by a Commander (E) IN (ex-RIN). Job cards were introduced and all work reduced to operations and planned to a critical path – (years ahead of the UK).

The top floor of the Engineering Machine Shop was converted into a general offices for managers and staffs and included the Production Control Section and Drawing offices. The Brass Foundry was moved from Engineering alongside the Iron foundry. The space thus gained was converted into a line fitting shop. Boat building was all concentrated in one area. The old Captain Superintendent's offices were converted as classrooms for the new apprentices entry, while the old Constructor machine shops were converted for apprentice practical training.

The lower halters of Duncan Dock were removed, which made possible the docking of INS DELHI. Two lease-lend dockside Portal cranes lying in packing cases, were installed – one between the dry docks and the other at the west wall of the wet basin. A complete cradle with hoisting gear, (also lease-lend and in packing cases), was installed, capable of taking all the yard craft and saving valuable dry dock requirements. These installations were by 'Maintenance', (Bob Sinha) – a superb job.

There were three Unions in the Dockyard – Congress, Communist and Socialist. A Works Committee was formed, with the Managers and Union representatives and the Industrial Manager as Chairman. There were no restrictions on items to be discussed and meetings were held weekly. All labour, (6,000 odd), were classified into trades and other designations and scales of pay for these different grades were worked out and approved by the Government of India - (the scales were index-linked). Apprentice entry to the different trades was introduced - Lieutenant Commander (E) Dick Jefferies (RN) was in charge.

The Accounting system was surveyed by Messrs. Power Samus Ltd. and a mechanical system introduced to process clock cards, job cards etc, and a realistic on-cost was established. This allowed indigenous manufacture for NSO and also for outsiders, such as Port Trust etc. Estimates and actual costs of refits were realistic.

Sir Alexander Gibb and Partners were appointed to survey the Yard, with a view to extending the breakwater to Ballard Pier, so forming a vast wet basin. They also investigated the problem of enlarging the submarine dry dock. A plan was made for the establishment of a Steel Foundry.

These vast changes in the Dockyard were made possible by the superb work of the ex-RIN Engineer Officers taken over at Partition, Sinha, Bushan, Kochar, Warner, Sharma, Baswani, being just a few.

17
Education and Training

"A COAT OF MANY COLOURS" by HR MILLS

Before the war, I was in the Education Service of the Cochin State Government, holding the appointment of Principal and Professor of Physics in the Maharaja's College, which consisted of 1,000 students and was affiliated to the University of Madras. I was the only European in the State Service.

The day before the outbreak of war, the 2nd September 1939, while I was in Bombay playing rugger for the Mofussal in the annual All-India Rugger International, I received a telegram, sent on to me by my wife who was in Cochin, instructing me to report to the Naval Officer in Charge, Cochin, Captain LS Wadeson RIN, in connection with my volunteering for service in the RINVR. I fortuitously met Captain Wadeson on the train going back to Cochin and was appointed Paymaster Lieutenant RINVR the next day. The Maharaja and the Dewan of Cochin readily agreed to my secondment for the duration of the war.

My official and social contacts among the Port authorities and Government officials were found useful in providing information on local affairs for the NOIC, who initially arrived without staff to start from scratch organising the defences of the Port and to establish a Naval Office - on a rather barren island, which had not existed ten years before, as it was built up of mud, sand and oyster shells from the dredging operations which had made Cochin Harbour into one capable of berthing large merchant ships and passenger liners.

By 1936, well-built Port offices, some residences for Port officials and a good hotel had been constructed, but the rest of Willingdon Island, as it was named, remained a large expanse of mud and sand, which soon attracted tropical vegetation of all kinds. It was soon destined to play a prominent part in the development of the States of both Cochin and Travancore (later to become Kerala).

The Naval base at Cochin at the outbreak of war was deemed to be of considerable strategic importance, as the finest port and harbour in south-west India. It grew rapidly during the first few months of the war. Several RN and RIN officers joined the staff and five small local naval defence vessels, rapidly converted from merchant vessels, for defence and minesweeping duties, were based at Cochin.

It is worthy of note, as an example of the way in which all kinds of help were used in the emergency and the shortage of facilities, that my troop of senior Sea Scouts of the Maharaja's College were employed, in uniform, as signallers and messengers, quite voluntarily, for shore-to-ship communications. Their only reward was an occasional trip to sea. Several later joined the Royal Indian Navy.

A dozen or so were taken to Bombay in one of the RIN corvettes to participate in the 'Navy Day' held there. The Flag Officer Commanding RIN was well aware of the importance of training boys and youths from an early age to take up careers in the Navy, as there was an acute shortage of suitable recruits.

At this time, there was considerable unrest among students all over India. Their national hero, Mahatma Gandhi, was put in prison by the Government, because of his anti-war propaganda and acts of civil disobedience. As Principal of a large college, I had to use tact and understanding to avert violent demonstrations. I recall that on the occasion of Gandhi's birthday, the student council leader and several of the senior students came to see me and asked permission to celebrate the Mahatma's birthday. I had to think quickly - I had joined the Navy only a week or so previously - but I felt that a simple meeting of students, such as would be approved by Gandhi himself, would be in order, provided that there were no inflammatory speeches or unseemly demonstrations. This the students agreed to and thanked me. The students withdrew, but, within ten minutes, they came back to see me again with one more request. 'What is that?' I asked. 'Sir, we would request you please to preside over the occasion'. Again, I thought rapidly and decided that, if it were right for the students to have a little celebration, then it must be all right for me to preside over it. I acceded to their request and the meeting of the whole College went off in a calm and dignified manner, as Gandhi himself would have wished. One student read a portion from the Bhagavad Gita; one a portion from the Koran and, I recall, I read an appropriate passage from the Bible.

The Resident of the Madras States, Sir Claremont Skrine, (the Viceroy's representative), paid the State one of his regular visits a week later and, at an interview I had with him, I said to him 'Sir Claremont, I have an admission to make. Last week I presided over my students' celebration of Gandhi's birthday, at their special request'. I was apprehensive, to say the least, of what his reaction might be to the incident. He beamed at me and said 'Mills, you did perfectly correctly and I am very pleased that you dealt with the situation so satisfactorily'.

By the end of November 1940, NOIC Cochin was instructed to commence the degaussing (protecting against magnetic river) of the local flotilla and to make a start on HMIS INVESTIGATOR, which was then in Cochin. The technical instructions, marked SECRET and in the form of pages of tables, were, to the ordinary ship's engineer, something of a mystery. As Secretary to NOIC I was able to glance at the tables and saw that the figures were simply expressions of Ohm's Law. So, shooting my neck out, I had the temerity to write a note to NOIC suggesting the number of DG coils and their specifications, required in various zones for the job.

To my surprise, my note was forwarded to Bombay, with the suggestion that I might be advantageously employed in Bombay on

183

degaussing duties. Within a week, I was transferred to Bombay (I left my wife and three small children in the Principal's house in Ernakulam, on the mainland). I became the first RINVR officer to carry out degaussing work under the Sea Transport Officer, Mercantile Marine Department. I had an excellent colleague in Lieutenant (E) TB Bose RIN, an engineering graduate of Calcutta University.

Our routine job was to calculate the precise ampere-turns for each ship, based on the ship's dimensions and its position, if known, when it was built. We had then to ascertain the power available from the ship's generators and plan the switchboard on the Bridge, so that the ship would be safe in various magnetic zones. Contracts had to be placed with Bombay contractors, eg Mazagaon Dock, and the work had to be supervised and finally tested to meet Admiralty requirements.

An interesting part of the job was to meet the ships' Captains and Chief Engineers and explain to them the working of the degaussing installation, including the compass corrector coil, in accordance with the official pamphlets issued for merchant ships. After a few weeks, I became conscious of a few raised eyebrows and even censorious glances, cast at my white 'Pusser's' stripes, particularly when discussing the ship's generators and the need for compass correction resulting from degaussing coils. Eventually, and apparently without any official sanction, I was quietly told by my senior officer to go and buy a couple of purple, (Engineering Branch) epaulettes. I did just that and immediately felt accepted in the Engine Room, in the holds and on the Bridge. In addition, we had the good fortune to initiate several RINVR officers with electrical experience into the work.

The RIN made an important contribution to the protection of merchant ships, as many ships came to Bombay without degaussing equipment, since shipyards in neighbouring friendly countries were unable to meet the heavy demand. Bombay frequently had to complete, as a matter of extreme urgency, degaussing jobs which had been started in Australia or Singapore.

Even after DG coils had been fitted and tested with meticulous attention to the regulations, including the requirements for compass correction, it was important for the success of the work to be tested to ensure that the ship's magnetic field had been reduced to well within the limit of sensitivity of the magnetic mine. This was done by running the ship over a testing range, which consisted of a series of sensitive magnetometer coils set in Bombay harbour, connected to instruments on shore, capable of recording photographically an accurate profile of the ship's magnetic field, from stem to stern. The recordings were analysed and the ship's DG equipment was then adjusted to eliminate any excessive magnetic fields from the ship at the depth of a few fathoms. Degaussing the many merchant ships, including troopships from Australia, calling at Bombay, became an important activity in the Dockyards and excellent co-operation was received from several contracting firms, notably Mazagaon Dock.

Degaussing in Bombay during the early days of the war had its human side. I give an example of the kind and cordial welcome I received from the Captain of a large Dutch ship on completion of my job and making sure that he was fully familiar with the installation. It was well past lunchtime on a Saturday afternoon and he was due to sail that evening. He received me in his cabin and overwhelmed me with his gratitude for what the Navy was doing to win the war, and what the British people were doing to help the Dutch people in their plight of having their country overrun by the Nazi army.

His cabin was decorated with charming photographs of his family, from whom he had had no news for over a year. He seemed at the point of breaking down and was glad to have a sympathetic listener outside his own crew. As I was, for all practical purposes, off duty and about to disembark, he insisted on my having a drink and he poured me out a liberal glass of Bols gin, in order to toast our families and the end of the war.

He was most anxious that I should accept some small token of his appreciation of my friendly chat with him and then opened one of his lockers stacked with cartons of cigarettes, insisted on my taking a carton and ordered his steward, in Dutch, to take it to my car at the foot of the gangway. It seemed churlish to refuse, although I am a non-smoker. I was, however, totally unaware that the steward, acting on instructions, actually dumped about six cartons on the back seat of the car.

Now, odd as it may seem, I am allergic to gin and, under ordinary circumstances, never touch it, so, as I began to feel queasy and started to come out in a cold sweat, I expressed my thanks, took a fond farewell and managed to muster sufficient control to descend the gangway to the car, whose driver gave me a suspicious look - I must have looked awful. I certainly felt awful and managed to collapse on the back seat and heave a sigh of relief.

My relief, however, was short lived. As the car sped round the dock towards the main gate, I realised that I was surrounded by half-a-dozen large cartons of cigarettes, with no authorisation for such a cargo and I also realised in a flash that the Dock security police, stationed at the gate, were particularly punctilious in the execution of their duty. As a newly joined RINVR officer I had an immediate premonition of being stopped; taken in charge for being under the influence of drink, as, indeed I was after that disastrous single gin and then being court-martialled for smuggling.

I just managed, by reflex action and just in time, to sweep the incriminating cartons onto the floor of the car, muster up a smile and return the salute of the duty policeman, who fortunately recognised me as a regular degausser. As mentioned, I am a non-smoker, but I had no difficulty in disposing of the excellent cigarettes among my RIN shipmates - who much appreciated the kind thought and generosity of a lonely and anxious Dutch Merchant Navy Skipper calling at Bombay.

The Flag Officer Commanding the Royal Indian Navy was fully aware of the pressing need for an adequate supply of recruits and particularly for the facilities for the training of boys to the required standards in education, technical skills, discipline and loyal commitment to the Service. By December 1941, a Boys' Training Establishment was nearing completion at Chinna Creek, Karachi. My eleven previous years in the Indian Education Service were now put to use by my appointment as Headmaster of the new school, HMIS DILAWAR, under Commander NBS Hewett RINVR. My first task was to go on a recruiting expedition to the Punjab to get the boys. While the Punjab was a regular recruiting ground for the Indian Army, parents and boys were a little apprehensive about joining the Navy, especially at a tender age and having no experience of the sea or ships.

The recruiting party included a medical officer, a schoolmaster and several smart CPOs. We were thus able to conduct a medical test, an educational test and a test of physical fitness of a very simple sort, which included running, jumping and throwing. Railway warrants were issued to the successful recruits and I was most gratified to see the boys arriving on the appointed day at HMIS DILAWAR. We had a great time getting the school started and the boys kitted up and out on parade.

We had no educational books or equipment, so, with a couple of 'schoolies', I ransacked the school suppliers in the bazaars of Karachi and managed to acquire some simple science apparatus, maps and elementary books. I was pleased to be able to get a supply of elementary science books, prescribed for Indian Junior Schools, by Mills & Menon, published by Macmillans.

The naval training, discipline and physical training were in good hands and, with co-operation from HMIS BAHADUR a few miles away, the School began to make its mark. I was able to keep in touch with the training establishments in Bombay and I ran several training courses for schoolmasters and instructors on teaching techniques, as many teachers and instructors had had no such training. I believe I was the only Engineer Branch Volunteer Reserve officer serving as Headmaster of a Boys' Training Establishment.

In Bombay, thanks to the friendly enthusiasm of Lieutenant AB Goord RIN, who was then the Officer-in-Charge of the embryonic Anti-Submarine School, I became interested in an instructional problem which he was experiencing. At that time, the School had no Attack Teacher and no means of simulating echo and doppler effect, (Brian Goord was using a ukelele!). With the co-operation of the dockyard stores and Lieutenant Goord, I managed to design and make an experimental 'Change of Pitch' simulator, thus temporarily solving a problem in the difficult task of explaining doppler effect to men under training. The design details of this apparatus were submitted to Admiralty, who showed considerable interest and circulated them to British A/S schools.

HMIS DILAWAR soon began to make a valuable contribution to the Service and provided experience, not only for the boys, but also for schoolmasters, many of whom had been recruited with no adequate teacher training or experience - part of my time was devoted to running courses in the techniques of teaching. After about eight months, I was transferred back to Bombay, (still wearing purple stripes), with instructions to set up classes for the training of Electrical Artificers and Seaman Torpedo men. These classes were to form the nucleus for a new Torpedo School, which was nearing the completion on Rozi Island, in the State of Jamnagar bordering the Gulf of Kutch.

This establishment was to be under the command of Commander B Ward RN, who had recently arrived from the United Kingdom.

Lack of equipment, furniture, stores etc, caused many problems in the setting up of the School but in Bombay, we had an enthusiastic team, working in makeshift accommodation for classrooms and workbenches. Our main task was to assemble the classes, organise time tables and carry out simple basic training in ships' electrics and, at the same time, to collect all essential equipment, apparatus and stores and to transport the lot to Rozi Island, as soon as possible, in HMIS NARBADA.

Within a few months, HMIS VALSURA became a fully-fledged training establishment, with several hundred ratings, including six Torpdedo Gunners Mates from the Royal Navy, as well as several RIN schoolmasters. I was appointed as the Chief Instructional Officer, as well as Sports Officer and I was able to get my wife and three small children to join me in VALSURA from Karachi. We were happy to have temporary hutted accommodation. My recollections of VALSURA are very pleasant; we managed to take a pride in the establishment and to enjoy the natural beauty that the game reserve of Rozi Island provided, thanks to the benevolence of the Jam Sahib of Nawanagar.

We had acres and acres of hard sand for every kind of sport. Our ship's concerts were all a great success and there was no lack of talented participation. In odd spare moments, I used to strum ribald songs on an old ukelele, (using only four chords). This came to the ears of the Commanding Officer, who was very anxious to form a small corps of buglers, to help regulate the establishment and so he instructed me to train four buglers from scratch in the main calls - Reveille, Colours, Divisions and Liberty Men.

This assignment was apparently a part of my duties as Sports Officer and Chief Instructional Officer, but it was an assignment that severely taxed my loyalty to the RIN. My only bugling experience was as a member of a bugle band in the Boy Scouts in 1920. Fortunately, HMIS VALSURA was ideally situated for bugle practice, as it was on a large, uninhabited, semi-desert island, so that I could take my potential buglers well beyond the usual pain zone, where we could safely blow to our heart's content, without creating serious disaffection in an otherwise happy ship. This odd appointment did not entitle me to any further change in the colour of my stripes.

At one time, we experienced a severe epidemic of malaria which, at its peak, put out of action about fifty per-cent of the total establishment and placed a very heavy burden on Medical Officer and sick berth attendants.

During my time at the Torpedo School, I submitted various schemes and suggestions to FOCRIN, which were forwarded to Admiralty, with mixed success, among them:-

1.   A method of checking the zone settings for the degaussing system in a ship, by means of a simple device consisting of a magnetometer supported a few feet above a DG cable.

*(Sitting, left to right) W/Sm Ahmed RIN; CWO AW Baigent RINVR; W Elect A Down RN;
Lt HR Mills RINVR; Lt JR Smith,MBE,RN; Lt WLN Jones RINVR; Lt NV Anandker RINVR;
Sub Lt S Sen RINR.*

First Class of EA's – HMIS VALSURA – November 1942

2. A method for adjusting the B coils of a compass compensating coil system when the ship was in harbour, heading ninety degrees or two hundred and seventy degrees.

It was respectfully pointed out that the procedure prescribed in DG Pamphlet No 4 (Admiralty Compass Observatory) was incorrect. However, despite strong support from an eminent Indian scientist, the fault was not admitted.

Later, the procedure proposed by the RIN was completely vindicated by the publication in the USA of 'Navy Department Degaussing Manual - Degaussing, Compass Compensating Coils; Installation and Adjustment'.

3. A series of graphs, as part of an introductory lecture on Torpedo Control, showing the precise mathematically calculated courses relative to ships. This was done with the encouragement and guidance of Lieutenant J Bayliss RIN.

In a letter to FOCRIN the Captain of HMS VERNON, the Royal Navy Torpedo School, wrote:-

'The introductory lecture in Torpedo Control . . . has been studied with much interest in HMS VERNON. The well executed graphs show clearly the points explained in the lecture.

Such a lecture is of great value when teaching officers already possessing considerable qualifications in Torpedo Control and are required thoroughly to investigate torpedo control problems. Advantage has already been taken of the graphs contained in this lecture in HMS VERNON.'

4. The General Staff Branch, Research Department of the Indian Army asked if the Navy could assist in the problem of detecting camouflaged pill-boxes, used by the Japanese during the Burma campaign and ascertain, if possible, if they were occupied.

The suggestion was made that the use of infra-red photography might solve the problem of detection. A solution to the more difficult problem of detecting any occupants, might possibly be achieved by the use of heat-sensitive apparatus.

Soon after my family had arrived from Karachi and settled down, my predestined career as a rolling stone continued to unfold, as Commodore G French RN had arrived in Naval Headquarters as Director of Training and he had on his list of priorities the formation of an Electrical Mechanics Training School at Marve, as a source of electrical mechanics for the RIN Landing Craft Wing.

And so, my time at VALSURA ended in December 1943, when I was appointed Officer-in-Charge of the Electrical Mechanics Training School, attached to the RIN Landing Craft Wing at Marve, near Bombay. (In this job, I resisted the suggestion that I should assume **green** stripes, but, by this time, I was promoted to Lieutenant Commander (E)).

Just before Christmas, I left my family on Rozi Island, under instructions to start the Electrical Mechanics Training School from scratch, in two derelict houses, pleasantly situated on the seashore at Marve, about ten miles north of Bombay.

It was a challenging and worthwhile exercise to collect the tools, a couple of diesel engines with generators and control panels and then to instal the machinery to simulate a Landing Craft. This work entailed numerous trips into the Bombay Dockyard to collect all the necessary gear for our workshops and classrooms. In this work, I was ably and enthusiastically supported by Electrical Sub-Lieutenant MK Lele RINVR and Sub-Lieutenant (E) JB Barkley. In a matter of three or four weeks, we had gear installed, workshops fitted out and classes started.

We had one small setback on the 14th April 1944 — the date is indelibly engraved on our memories, as it was on this afternoon that the SS FORT STIKINE, carrying 1,318 tons of live raw explosives, blew up, flattening 300 acres of Bombay Docks; turning twelve other ships into scrap iron; showering destruction over an area a mile wide and creating a tidal wave that lifted the stern of a 4,000 ton ship fifty feet into the air and left it on the roof of a shed. The full death count is unknown to this day.

That very morning I had taken a small working party into the docks to take delivery of a new 'Crown' diesel engine, of the type used in landing craft, for instructional purposes in our School. Despite being assured a few days previously that the engine would be ready for collection on that morning, we found that the storeman had not received the requisite piece of paper signed by his superior for the release of the engine. We were told that this would be put right if we called the next day.

Sadly, the whole of the store, and the engine, was demolished that afternoon by the great Bombay explosion. Although we did not get our engine, our trivial disappointment paled into insignificance against the ghastly tragedy of that afternoon. We were at least fortunate in not being obliged to take delivery of the engine on that fateful afternoon, and possibly, of being blown to pieces.

The Electrical Mechanics Training School, situated about ten miles out of Bombay, had a horrific view of the distant explosion. We were all sitting outside the School at about 1600 and the School had arranged a passing-out tea party and had invited friends from the Landing Craft Wing for that Friday afternoon. We were amazed to see a huge 'mushroom' cloud form and hover over Bombay and then, about fifty seconds later, we heard a shattering BOOM, followed about a minute later by another. We had no idea what had happened, but it was quite obvious that a tremendous explosion had taken place. Although we were all anxious to get into Bombay to offer any help needed, we were instructed to remain where we were and await orders.

I was particularly saddened by the catastrophe, as one of my good friends, Lieutenant (E) Burke RINVR, whom I had helped to initiate into degaussing work a year or so before, was in the Docks at the time of the explosion and was actually going to a nearby ship when the FORT STIKINE blew up. No trace of him was ever found and it fell to the lot of my wife to help console Mrs Burke and, a few weeks later, to see her and her small boy off on a ship going to the UK. The tragedy was made the more acute as they had lost a boy aged two years, only a few weeks before, through appendicitis. A graphic and detailed account of the catastrophe was published in 1960 in the book 'The Great Bombay Explosion' by John Ennis, published by the Berkley Publishing Corporation of New York.

A couple of weeks after the explosion, a Service was held in the Bombay Cathedral to commemorate those who had lost their lives. The Service was attended by representatives of all the Services involved, including the RN, RIN, Army, Port Authorities, the Mercantile Marine, Fire Brigades and Dockyard workers. The Cathedral was filled and the Bishop conducted the service with due solemnity.

At the end, the Bishop came forward for the Blessing, but there was a small hitch while he was waiting to be handed his crozier. This he eventually received hurriedly and a little awkwardly, so that it was in danger of falling. A Royal Navy rating who was following the ecclesiastical ritual with keen interest, was heard to whisper to his shipmate: 'The Bish nearly forgot his boathook drill!'

While at the Landing Craft Electrical Mechanics School in July 1944, I received a letter from the Director of Training, Commodore GA French CBE, RN informing me that I was to be transferred to Naval Headquarters, New Delhi as Assistant Director of Training under Instructor Commander V Lamb RN, who was being flown out from the UK in August, with the prime object of forming an Instructor Branch. It was suggested that I might have to change my purple stripes for green Special Branch stripes for a while, but this I was able to resist, since my ultimate 'home' was to be the Instructor Branch (blue stripes).

First, a little history of the Schoolmaster Branch of the RIN which preceded the formation of the Instructor Branch. Early in 1938, as war clouds were gathering in Europe and threatening the whole world, it was realised, with increasing urgency, that adequate expansion of the Royal Indian Navy, in an age of modern technology, would require greater attention to the educational standards essential for the training recruits and for the up-grading of seamen, petty officers and warrant officers.

At that time, the total authorised educational establishment of the RIN was a Schoolmaster Branch, which consisted of one Chief Petty Officer Schoolmaster and two Petty Officer Schoolmasters and their pay was very low. An important step was taken in February 1938 by the appointment of Headmaster Lieutenant DJC Smith RN, whose brief was to develop and raise the standard of education.

'Schoolie' Smith (by which name he was affectionately known throughout the Service) was a remarkable man. An excellent 'mixer', he toured India on recruiting tours and quickly made a name for himself as a smiling ambassador for the Service. He achieved an enviable rapport with the people of India of all classes and creeds and the Service owes him a special debt of gratitude for his valuable efforts in overcoming prejudices and instilling a sense of confidence in would-be recruits. He completely revised the Higher Educational Test and the Educational Test (India) and he prepared general educational syllabuses for practically all RIN establishments and ships.

Improvements in pay and status assisted recruiting and, by the end of 1943, the Schoolmaster Branch cadre had increased to forty Warrant Schoolmasters and 180 CPO Schoolmasters. With the strengthening of the Branch, education within the Service made rapid strides and by the end of 1944, the RIN Educational Tests compared favourably with those of the Royal Navy and the standards achieved throughout the Service had risen significantly. 'Schoolie' Smith was appointed Deputy Director of Education at Naval Headquarters in February 1944, with the rank of Headmaster Commander. He left India to return to the Royal Navy in October 1944.

Talking about the Schoolmaster Branch reminds me of a course I conducted for CPO Schoolmasters in Karachi, during which I emphasised the importance of **understanding,** as being all important in learning and **remembering.** As an example, I wrote on the blackboard a simple sentence that had meaning, followed by five short nonsense words. After about ten seconds, the sentence and nonsense words were erased from the blackboard. Towards the end of the session, I invited each member of the class to recall the sentence and five nonsense words and flippantly added that I would give Rs. 10 to anyone who could give the correct answer.

I had carried out this demonstration several times before in various places and made the point that nonsense words were almost impossible to remember. I was feeling confident this time I had made my point, when a CPO Schoolmaster rattled off the nonsense words perfectly and without hesitation. I could only offer my congratulations and hand over the prize of Rs.10 with the comment that some people had special types of memory denied to others.

The next day, CPO Romer, in class, presented me with a rather nice dictionary (priced Rs.10) and confessed that he had been involved in a small course some weeks previously and was wise to my little demonstration, as I had used the same sentence and nonsense words then, which he had made a special effort to memorise. The dictionary was a retribution to salve his conscience! We all had a good laugh - my point had, in fact, been made and my instructor status was intact. There were no losers - although I may have been guilty of breach of some section of KR and AI. I still have that well thumbed copy of Chambers Twentieth Century Dictionary, inscribed on the flyleaf 'To Lt Cmdr HA Mills, RINVR, with best regards from AP Romer, BA, CPO Schoolmaster, Karachi, 5-11-44.'

Instructor Commander Victor Lamb RN, duly arrived in August 1944 and he and I got down to work, preparing and revising courses and syllabuses, to meet the demands of the rapidly expanding service. A major problem confronting the RIN was recruiting men and boys with adequate educational backgrounds, particularly in English, arithmetic and general intelligence. Recruiting officers were specially aware of this problem, as were Schoolmasters and New Entry Training Establishments, such as HMIS AKBAR at Thana.

In this latter establishment, Commander BW Lucke RINR had remarkable talent and interest in devising and standardising educational tests, though he was not a professional educationist. He, with my encouragement, drew up a series of tests in English, reading and

192

arithmetic and some tests in Urdu. These were easy to administer, quick to carry out and objective in producing test results that could be statistically standardised. The tests were based on tests approved by the highest authorities in the United Kingdom. It is interesting to note that, on demobilisation, Commander Lucke returned to the UK and became a successful professional schoolmaster.

The Chief Recruiting Officer in Bangalore recommended that the tests which we devised should replace those being used to test RIN recruits under the Indian Army system. In a letter to the Recruiting Directorate of the Adjutant General's Branch, he wrote:

> In place of the reading and spelling tests sent out by you, tests which were given by Lieutenant Commander Mills, RINVR have been introduced . . .
> . . . These tests are practical and can be given without difficulty to a large number of recruits at a time. . .

After the inevitable delays caused by Government of India 'red tape', the Instructor Branch came into being in November 1944. A report in RINLOG, the monthly magazine of the RIN of December 1944 states:

> The first batch of recruits to the newly-formed Instructor Branch of the Royal Indian Navy have recently undertaken advanced technical and mathematical instruction of RIN officers undergoing specialist training.
> The Instructor Branch is also responsible for the general supervision of all educational work in the Navy and will ensure that educational facilities for officers and ratings are available wherever they are required.
> Ratings in the Service have always had access to educational instruction in their leisure hours and the RIN has more than 200 schoolmasters, (Headmaster Lieutenants, Commissioned Warrant Schoolmasters and Chief Petty Officer Schoolmasters), who hold training classes and voluntary classes in all shore establishments and in some ships at sea. These classes are extremely popular and well-attended.
> Officers of the new Branch rank as Instructor Lieutenants and Instructor Lieutenant-Commanders of the RINVR. Their uniform has distinctive cloth of light blue between the gold stripes.
> They are recruited from candidates between thirty and forty years of age, who have been trained in a recognised univeristy and have taken an Honours degree or equivalent in Mathematics, Physics or Engineering, (Mechanical or Electrical).
> The first batch of Instructor Officers consists of Indian graduates with considerable teaching experience and all except three in the Instructor Branch and the Schoolmaster Branch of the Royal Indian Navy are Indians.

After a few months in Delhi, I was transferred by Commodore French to Bombay as Staff Officer, Education. This enabled me to carry out work I had been hoping to do, namely, to run courses for officers and senior ratings on Instructional Techniques. During my six years as an RINVR officer, I had received no formal training and it was only in the last few months of my service that I was deputed to attend a course run by the Army Staff College at Dehra Dun on Instructional Techniques. I attended this course, which lasted only one week, with Headmaster Lieutenant Kew RN who came out from the UK to strengthen our Schoolmaster Branch. He was a most likeable colleague and we enjoyed the course, which was extremely well run and a model of how such a course should be run for the Services.

Incidentally, the Officer-in-Charge of the course was a Major Dennis Foreman, who had lost a leg in France and who later became the Director of the British Film Institute, received a Knighthood and played an important part in directing the film 'Jewel in the Crown'.

Although I had had a year's training as a teacher, (Cambridge Diploma), I nevertheless learned more in a week at Dehra Dun on this course than I did in a year of the usual teacher training. I mention this as, when I returned to civilian life and took up jobs as a Technical Educational Adviser to the Government, I realised how little effective training was being given in industry.

In the early 1950's, there were practically no qualified training instructors in industry, although there was a tremendous need for skilled men. Training was carried out by anybody who was on the verge of retirement, or on the principle of 'sitting by Nellie'. I thereupon began to turn my experience in instruction techniques to some effect by writing a book on the techniques of technical training, which came out just at the time when the Government was starting the Training Boards and taking proper training seriously. To my surprise, the book was a great success -it has sold all over the world and has gone through eight reprints and editions - all started off by my attendance at Dehra Dun and later supplemented by a short course I attended in Portsmouth, run by the RN.

I just managed to get deputed to attend this RN course through the fact that, by the end of 1944, I had been in India just seven years without any UK leave and so qualified for sixty days leave, which I accepted with some misgivings, as this leave did not, of course, apply to my wife and family. My wife nobly insisted on my taking this opportunity to see our families at home and seeing something of the RN Instructor Branch at work.

It so happened that, at this time, Captain Martin Nott, who had taken over from Commodore French as Director of Training, was about to proceed to the United Kingdom to visit various Training Establishments and for a little well earned leave. He characteristically suggested that I might usefully accompany him on his crowded programme, which included establishments in various parts of the UK, including Scotland. This proved to be a most enjoyable and rewarding trip and gave me a new insight into training and the Instructor Branch. During our tour together, I came to

194

see what a really great man Captain Nott was and what an irreparable loss to the Service his sad death in an air crash shortly afterwards really was.

In a characteristically friendly and enthusiastic letter after our tour, Captain Nott suggested that I might consider remaining in the Royal Indian Navy, instead of accepting an educational post at the Ghazi College in Kabul, Afghanistan, which I had been offered - but that is another story. I eventually left India on 14 May 1946.

"MY TIME WITH THE RIN" by GA FRENCH

I had been commanding HMS HAWKINS for over a year, employed on Ocean Escort to large troop convoys between the Clyde and Aden and the Indian Ocean, at a time when the Eastern Fleet was coming together in Kilindidi, after the loss of Singapore. Despite the Home Fleet's early lesson of enemy submarines penetrating our harbours - eg the sinking of the ROYAL OAK in Scapa, the Eastern Fleet had regarded themselves as immune to this threat, until a Japanese submarine penetrated Diego Suarez and fired a torpedo at an 'R' Class battleship. Sir James Somerville at once took precautions against this threat and a drill was organised to 'Exercise submarine attack in the harbour'. The warning was to be a single flag signal, followed by a continuous sounding of the siren. So when I visited Bombay with a large troop convoy, I made the appropriate Executive signal. Nothing happened so, when I went to call on Jack Rattray, then Commodore, Bombay, he asked me with mild surprise what all the fuss was about.

In June 1943, the ship docked in Simonstown for a short refit, when I got a signal from Admiralty. 'To proceed to New Delhi, on priority passage, as Director of Training and Inspector of Training Establishments, in the appointment of Commodore, 2nd Class'. I handed over my lovely ship and travelled by train to Durban, whence I embarked in a Sunderland flying boat and flew to Cairo, via the plains of Kenya, up the Nile and Khartoum. In Cairo, my priority was down-graded, as I was not going to an operational area; so, after four nights in Shepherd's Hotel, another Sunderland took me to Karachi and thence landed me on the lake in Gwalior on the 24th July 1943. Thence to Delhi, where I was met by Lieutenant Spiers RINVR, who told me that I was on loan to the Royal Indian Navy. I thought that I was going to a British Combined Ops job, as I had been on Winston's Joint Planning Staff before joining HAWKINS.

Admiral Godfrey was on tour and I was shown into an empty office, with no carpet, an unconnected telephone and a mouse. The next day, I was met by Mrs Torpy, more or less in the clothes in which she and her husband had escaped from Burma - and feeling just as bewildered as I was. I was given a room, 'Hutted Scale Mark III', I think it was called, with a bed, a mosquito net, a chair, a table and a shower. This I found in some contrast to my lovely cabin in HAWKINS, who, pre-war, had been the Flag Ship on the China Station.

Admiral Godfrey returned the next day, explained his reasons for my appointment and broadly the problems ahead. I was introduced to the Staff at NHQ - John Lawrence was Chief of Staff; Philip Mare was Chief of Administration and 'Suji' Thomsom was Chief of Personnel. I was shown my hutted office adjacent to the main building and the initial staff were Lieutenant Commanders Chakravarti, Chatterji and Lele and, on the educational side, Schoolmaster Commander 'Schoolie' Smith RN (Retd). Mrs Torpy and I were the newcomers and Mr Bannerjee the excellent stenographer.

The problems broadly facing FOCRIN at the time are best described in the chapter of Patrick Beesly's book 'Very Special Admiral', in which he deals with John Godfrey's period as Flag Officer Commanding, Royal Indian Navy. It must be remembered that, at that time, FOCRIN was subject to the Army command of the Commander-in-Chief, India and was not an autonomous authority himself.

The war perspective was gloomy and urgent, with the European Front being top priority; the various US/British plans for the attack on Europe; a grave threat by sea from the Japanese Fleet; General Slim and his wonderful 14th Army in their fight in the Burma campaign; problems with China and the appointment of Mountbatten to SEAC.

The first thing John Godfrey (whom I had served twice before - a kind man with a brilliant brain; not easy to serve - a quick temper which was soon forgotten) realised was that the big problem facing the RIN **internally** (as opposed to its relations with the Eastern Fleet, Army and general war effort) was that it had over-expanded at a pace at which it could not be **trained,** due to lack of facilities. It was about 2,000 strong when war started and, by July 1943, it was nearer 20,000 and still on the increase with recruiting. It was to deal with this that John Godfrey signalled to the First Sea Lord for the appointment of RN Captain with up-to-date war and training experience - hence my appointment.

I was able to see the various points of view - of the clashing of the various external problems, being a term-mate of Mountbatten; recently one of Sir James Somerville's captains; an inside knowledge of the British direction of the war and action experience in Norway etc.

My internal dilemma, which of course, was most important, was that though I knew what was needed in the RIN, I knew nothing of India; its outlook; way of life or language - which was the life-work of the India-specialised RIN European Officer. Not unnaturally, though very kind to me, some regarded this external injection with some suspicion, especially as it involved opposing some of the current expansion policies.

But my staff were kind - the Indian officers taught me a lot and, by good fortune, Jimmy Streatfield-James (an ex-Dartmouth cadet), and I, had family friends in the UK in common. He and I did much touring together, so he taught me a lot about India and, I think, brought an impetus and sense of urgency and a wider view to the RIN. Philip Mare, that very likeable old dear as CO (A) was understanding about this and we never really clashed on anything, including the slowing down of taking in Indians with no knowledge of the sea, putting them into uniform and sending them to sea.

As soon as I had measured this problem and examined the composition of my small staff, I decided the best thing to do was to establish the priority of needs; get my staff to draft the outlines for Government and FOCRIN and set out to visit the main training areas, taking with me an appropriate staff officer and Mr Bannerjee and of course, by faithful bearer Abdul, who really taught me so much - not the least that 'you can't hurry the East'. Having been brought up on Kipling, (still, in my mid-eighties, a tower of strength to me) I was fascinated by the country, but baffled and at times, frustrated by 'petty nonsenses'. I found DFA (N) - as we do in the UK now - a bit of a trial at times, but decided that 'pleading' was more profitable than arguing, which is what the breed, (and in the UK) love.

A good start had been made on modern establishments, but still inadequate for the expansion. Above all, there was no Officers' Training School (on the lines of 'King Alfred' in the UK). So premises were obtained in a large house in Bombay and Commander Passmore-Edwards was selected to command, initiate and start. Ratings' training was still inadequate and was done in the Barracks, but a large New Entry training establishment, just outside Bombay, HMIS AKBAR, had been planned and construction was starting.

We also visited the Signal School and the A/S School in Bombay, the Torpedo and Electrical School, HMIS VALSURA, with a RN Commander as CO, under the benevolent wing of the Jam Sahib of Nawanagar, and the Gunnery School, HMIS HIMALAYA at Karachi. Also at Karachi were the Boys' Training Establishment, HMIS BAHADUR, (Commander Neal Hewett RINR, whose father had been a Captain in the Royal Indian Marine), and HMIS DILAWAR, for young ratings.

When I got back to Delhi, I had begun to get a measure of the job and realised that touring in my capacity as Inspector of Training Establishments would occupy much of my time and that I must have an experienced 'India-wise' Deputy to co-ordinate staff activities and deal with NHQ whilst I was on tour. I managed to get Commander Neal Hewett out of BAHADUR and he was ideal. A seaman himself with a long India tradition and a fine chap. So I now had Training staff and Educational staff, working together, whilst I got on 'in the field' to educate myself, assess the needs and to shake up the chaps and encourage them.

A very delightful personal souvenir of the time is the invitation to Viceroy's House, on the 13th October, to the farewell party to Lord Linlithgow, the outgoing Viceroy and another, marked 'Secret', to the 'assumption of office of Viceroy and Governor General of India of Field Marshal the Viscount Wavell'.

By now - four years after the outbreak of war, I realised that enormous changes had taken place in UK training and equipment, upon which the RIN depended. I had not seen my family for nearly two years and was fairly 'whacked'. John Godfrey, who had been DNI (shamefully treated by Winston) realised this and arranged for me to visit the UK. Accompanied by Lieutenant Commander Chakravarti I left Delhi and flew to Britain. Between the 17th December 1943 and 22nd February 1944, we toured the UK. My wife was working in the Admiralty at the time and was seconded as my secretary, which combined business with pleasure (or, at least family contact) and in the period we visited every main British Training Establishment. We had no 'leave', nor did we waste time.

The routine was: travel to relevant training establishment; 'Chakkers' and I would 'suck out' all we could; return to our Pub, where my wife would mend 'Chakkers' socks (and mine) and type all I dictated to her on my day's findings and, after a night's rest, move on - a most interesting and valuable visit.

This included a very interesting time with Admiral AB Cunningham, First Sea Lord and a very revealing interlude at the India Office. The latter was obviously my 'base' in the UK, though I only saw it once. The Civil Servant who was the official link between the India Office and Admiralty was Mr Bull. One day, in his office, discussing problems in India, I said 'You know the train journey between Bombay and Delhi . . .'. He looked at me with some surprise and said - 'Oh! - but I have never been in India'!

I have the following extract of a report in a paper:

A nice compliment was recently paid to the Royal Indian Navy by the Commander-in-Chief, Portsmouth, Admiral Sir Charles Little GBE, KCB. During the recent visit of the Director of Training to the UK, Sir Charles Little gave a luncheon party to Commodore Maundrell CIE,RIN, Commodore and Mrs GA French, Lieutenant Commander Chakravarti RIN and Lieutenant Jurdon RINVR. It was a memorable event for those of us who were present, taking place, as it did, in Portsmouth Dockyard, where HMS VICTORY, the very heart of the traditions of the Royal Navy lay adjacent to the most modern craft which warfare in 1944 demands. One felt that the spirit of this great sailor, who led the British Fleet to victory at Trafalgar in the timbers of the VICTORY and laid the foundations for a hundred years of peace in Europe, was looking down approvingly at the Spirit of the Navy in 1944, including representatives of the Royal Indian Navy now gathered.

Back in Delhi on the 22nd February, thanks to the zeal and efficiency of my wife, I was able to present FOCRIN with a complete typed copy of my report on all the establishments we had visited in the UK and on the 23rd February, I set out for Tour No 6 to Bangalore, Madras, Bombay and Kolshet, returning on the 3rd March.

Another abiding memory is the train journey from Vizagapatam on the 8th July, arriving in Calcutta on the 9th. Jimmy James and I had a first class compartment to ourselves until, at some stopping point which I cannot remember, a USA Top Sergeant got in. Jimmy had, of course, been in the country for many years and spoke some of the languages and was thoroughly versed in the customs of different religions. Within a quarter of an hour of arrival, the USA man started to give us the benefit of his views. They ranged over all aspects of Indian life, particularly the conduct of the war. It was a very long time before he drew breath, having nearly exhausted his armoury of enlightenment, at which point, I asked him how long he had been in the country. I am not sure if his reply was three weeks or three days - but it certainly was no longer. When I told him that my companion had been over twenty years in the country, he became slightly less informative - to our great relief.

My fourteenth tour, I think, must have been on the occasion of the official opening of the Gunnery School, HMIS HIMALAYA by HE the Governor. A very splendid occasion, of which I have two pages of photographs. Many Indian officers, including Vice-Admiral Vasu Kamath, then a (G), were present. This ended my war-time loan to the Royal Indian Navy, but little did I know that this was to be the beginning of a much longer one, later on, after Independence.

I left Delhi by air on the 20th October 1944, to await a flight to the UK. I left Karachi on the 22nd October in a mail-carrying Wellington bomber and spent the passage lying on the mail bags - not the type of air travel to which people are accustomed today. I remember, being limited to 60 lbs of luggage and to save weight, I started in white shorts, but had to end up in blue uniform and so I put the latter on over the white and changed in Malta, thus enabling me to arrive in the UK on the 24th October with some fresh fruit for my family.

We landed at Lyneham airport, near Swindon, but it took me nearly as long to travel home to Dorset as it had to fly from Karachi, as I had to travel by train to London in order to change over to the line for Dorchester. After a very short leave, I joined the Admiralty as Deputy Director of Plans (to Admiral AB Cunningham) until 1946. Then, the first Imperial Defence Course post-war, (where I first met my close friend Brigadier 'Joe' Lentaigne) followed by, in 1947, Chief of Staff to FM Montgomery's Top Level Staff exercise 'Spearhead' and, June 1947 to 1948, commanding NORFOLK as Flag Captain to C in CEI.

At the end of 1951, I was invited to return to the Indian Navy as Chief of Staff to my old friend and one-time contemporary, Admiral Pizey and my wife and three children arrived in Delhi the day King George VI died in February 1952. Then there were the most interesting and valuable years, well described in many books - the best being 'Freedom at Midnight' - recommended by Mountbatten himself. I still have regular contacts with many Indian friends and an Indian godson - now over thirty years old.

18

The Gunnery Branch

IN THE RIN, 1934-47, by AT BOND and others

When the Royal Indian Marine became the Royal Indian Navy in 1934, the Service had only seven armed ships - LAWRENCE, CLIVE, CORNWALLIS, INVESTIGATOR, PATHAN and MADRAS. Two more - HINDUSTAN and INDUS - were added in 1935 and all nine were in commission at the outbreak of war in 1939.

There was a small and somewhat rudimentary Gunnery School located in Bombay Depot within the Dockyard as was the Armament Depot (run by the Indian Army) and the Squadron Depot and RIN Dockyard facilities remained the same until the outbreak of War on 3rd September 1939. The Gunnery School had drill 4" of MK IV 3" HA/LA (later) twelve pounder and three pounder Guns and Mountings and close range AA weapons plus small arms and the normal instructional equipment for the Squadron's pre-war armament with the exception of a 4.7" Mounting. Gunnery Officers: Lieutenant Commander PH Learmont RIM was the first officer to qualify at HMS EXCELLENT in 1929 followed by Lieutenant Durston RIM in 1932, Lieutenant JE Cornish RIN in 1937 and Lieutenant A W Beeton RIN in 1938.

Following the outbreak of war the conversion and arming of local Merchant Coastal Vessels requisitioned mainly from Bombay Shipping Companies was carried out in the Bombay Dockyard with astonishing speed. These ships were mainly armed with twelve-pounder guns and depth charges were fitted to the faster ships whilst minesweeping gear was fitted to the slower ships.

Local Naval Defence flotillas at Karachi, Bombay, Cochin, Madras and Vizagapatam were formed mainly from these converted Merchant Ships until later in the war the RIN's own building programme of modern sloops (modified Bittern and modified Black Swan class) Bathursts, Bangors, Bassets etc provided escort, patrol and minesweeping ships built as fighting ships. By 1940 the RIN had forty ships in commission and this number was to treble before the end of the war in 1945. The pressure by the end of 1940 on the Dockyard was such that urgent steps had to be taken to move specialist schools elsewhere. Also with the greatly expanded service the original Gunnery School became completely inadequate very rapidly. Negotiations had been underway to build a completely new and modern Gunnery School at Karachi on Manora some two miles north of HMIS BAHADUR, the new Boys' Training Establishment. This was finally approved in late 1940 or early 1941 and site clearance and preparation commenced in 1941 by JC Gammon Ltd under the directions of the Indian Army (Sind District HQ Karachi). Meanwhile thanks to Honorary Lieutenant (later Honorary Lieutenant Commander) Sir Dinshaw Petit, Bart., RINVR, the Gunnery School was moved to Il Palazzo, a large mansion on Malabar Hill leased for the purposes and a practical firing range was established on the foreshore of Lieutenant Sir Dinshaw Petit's own Malabar Hill House.

This firing range meant that practical anti-aircraft firing practice became possible immediately. However during 1941/42 low angle full calibre practice firings became very restricted due to the lack of a Gunnery School Firing Ship which could not be made available for operational reasons.

In July 1942, a Naval working party in charge of a qualified G Officer was appointed to oversee the construction of HMIS HIMALAYA (the name chosen for the new Gunnery School of Karachi). This included responsibility for the installation of the new Guns, F/C equipment etc, on the Firing Range at Manora, instructional equipment in the Battery, AA Dome Teacher etc.

Between 1939 and 1942, nine officers had qualified as Gunnery Specialists in HMS EXCELLENT and in the subsequent war years a further six officers qualified as Gunnery Specialists in the UK and two as Gunner, Ordnance and Weapon Engineering Officers.

Now, HMIS HIMALAYA, commissioned on 26th November 1943 with accommodation for sixty-six officers, eight warrant officers and six hundred ratings, was to become one of the most modern naval Gunnery Schools of its type. The construction costs plus equipment amounted to some £2,700,000, half of which was borne by HM Government and half by the Government of India. HIMALAYA was equipped to train officers and ratings in all aspects of gunnery up to 4" Guns as installed on the most modern sloops. The School was built to enable further expansion to provide training facilities in the armament of modern Destroyers and Cruisers when required to do so. L/A and A/A Firings could be carried out to seaward with every type of weapons used in the service and in 1944 HMIS LAWRENCE was attached to HMIS HIMALAYA as Gunnery School Firing Ship.

From this time until the end of the war, many Reserve Officers underwent specialist courses in HMIS HIMALAYA and many RIN Gunners also qualified in the School. (Further details can be obtained from "World War II Fact File - British Escort Ships", by HT Lenton and from the relevant issues of "Janes' Fighting Ships")

The HIMALAYA Firing Point was extended for the second time in April 1945 with additional weapons for the intensive training of Coastal Forces Gunnery Rates for the operations on the Burma coast. Also additional fire control gear consisting of Rangefinder Director MK III W AFFC MK III and DKC MK II was installed. This brought the firing range up to date with the latest modified Black Swan Sloops. The end of 1945 saw the pressure on training and on the ships themselves ease substantially after VJ Day and the end of hostilities against Japan.

Unfortunately the RIN Mutiny in February 1946 resulted in HMIS HIMALAYA being placed on a Reserve (care and maintenance basis) from April onwards and Gunnery Training was never fully resumed before Partition in August 1947 and HMIS HIMALAYA was recommissioned as HMPS HIMALAYA as the combined Training Schools for the Royal Pakistan Navy, later the Pakistan Navy.

19
The Landing Craft Wing

REMINISCENCES OF T SHEPPARD

On December 22nd 1983 there appeared an obituary notice of one Major-General RH Hutton. Those who participated in the 1944/45 Arakan campaign might recall a small Brigadier, under an enormous bush hat, directing troops of 74 Brigade and later 51 Brigade, in amphibious operations in the Mayu peninsular, at Akyab, at Myebon and at Kangaw, the last-named being the scene of what was described in the official history as 'one of the bloodiest battles of the whole Burma campaign'. Reggie Hutton was awarded his first DSO when, in the Mayu Range, he captured a series of strongly defended Japanese positions, having personally reconnoitered them alone with his orderly. He won the Bar to his DSO in Kangaw. The RIN Landing Craft Wing was heavily involved in Kangaw, as well as many other landings in Burma.

In 1942, a decision was made to form the Wing. As there was already a great shortage of personnel for the manning commitments of what might be termed the orthodox navy, arrangements were made to transfer military personnel to the RIN for training in amphibious warfare. Many Army officers volunteered to change, being attracted to the novelty and excitement of Combined Operations. These joined the RIN, RNVR and RINVR officers also in the 'Wing'. The sepoys were not familiar with the world of the seafarer and so it was decided to transfer whole units. Two Battalions, the 9/1 Punjabis and the 15/13 Frontier Force Rifles, with large drafts from the Jats, Rajputs, Dogras and Bombay Grenadiers were eventually absorbed into the Wing and trained as seamen. Stokers and Engineroom ratings were mainly from General Service. These were largely HO ratings, many former motor-mechanics, and predominantly from southern India. Signal ratings to be trained for Beach Signal Stations were also from General Service.

The training of instructors - from General Service - began in November 1942 at Marve, to the north of Bombay. These officers then moved to Mandapam, to the new RIN Landing Craft School, commissioned as HMIS HAMLA.

In January 1943, the transferees from the Army began to arrive at Mandapam, which was eventually to house 250 officers and 3,000 men. Training in naval structures, seamanship, boat-handling, rope-work etc, went ahead, overcoming the many initial difficulties and growing pains inherent in such an operation. Most ratings had never seen the sea and were, in their off-duty hours, to be seen in groups gazing in wonder at this

204

new phenomenon. The mixture of races, religions and background led inevitably to friction and problems, but eventually the ratings and their officers welded together in flotilla units, with high morale and good esprit de corps.

After their initial training, the first flotillas were moved, in June 1943, to the Combined Training Centre in Bombay, for exercises with the Army. The first contingent consisted of 3 LC (A) flotillas, 1 LC (P) flotilla nd 2 LC (M) flotillas. Two Beach Commandos and a Beach Signal Section had also been formed and these too were sent to Bombay in August and September 1943. It had been planned that Force 'G', which arrived in the East Indies from Madagascar, should be used for a major amphibious assault in Burma in 1943/44. The Landing Craft Wing, which had trained with two divisions of the CTC, were earmarked as part of the Force 'G'. Force 'G' was, however, recalled to the Mediterranean and the RIN flotillas were left in India. In the spring of 1944, No 2 CTC was opened in Coconada and commissioned as HMIS JEHANGIR.

Meanwhile, in the 1943/44 'season' in the Arakan, two LC (M) flotillas and one LC (P) flotilla were employed in the more limited operation, working largely with three Royal Marine Commando and fifteen Corps. During the 1944 monsoon, the LC (M) flotillas were withdrawn to Chittagong, whilst the LC (P)'s remained with fifteen Corps Headquarters in the Naaf River. At the same time, other flotillas were training at HMIS HAMLAWAR at Marve and HMIS JEHANGIR at Coconada.

In late December 1944, more flotillas moved to Chittagong and it became apparent that the time had come for major operations in the Arakan. The first objective was Akyab and this was recaptured on January 3rd without opposition. However, it was a valuable exercise for all the combined operations personnel, as well as the Army (74 Indian Division) and 45 Marine Commando. Some casualties were caused in a sneak raid by Zeros on the creek where the landing craft were moored. LCM's of 46 flotilla were detached to support the 82nd West African Division in the Kaladan valley.

The next major operation was the landing at Myebon, which took place on January 12th 1945. This was strongly opposed, by shore artillery, mortars and mined beaches. It was a classic combined operation involving close air support and bombardment from HMIS NARBADA, (Captain MH Nott RIN) and HMIS JUMNA, (Commander KRU Todd RIN) (who had carried troops subsequently used in the assault). The landing was carried out by 42 Royal Marine Commando. Owing to heavy opposition, the subsequent waves of assault troops were put ashore on a second beach, as were the necessary stores. On D+1, 74 Brigade were landed and passed through the Commando brigade on the bridgeheads.

For the next few days, our LCA's were working with commandos in reconnaissance and mopping-up operations on the west bank of the Myebon river and putting in small parties of troops from 74 Brigade at various points in the chaungs.

Kangaw was the next major target for the amphibious forces. The object was to cut off the Japanese forces moving towards the coast,

The RIN Landing Craft Wing go in — Burma 1945

retreating from the West Africans. The Kangaw beachhead was defended by a whole Japanese brigade and had, according to the records, the biggest concentration of Japanese artillery yet encountered in Burma. Fierce hand-to-hand fighting ensued and casualties were heavy on both sides. The landings were carried out again by the Royal Marine Commandos, with 51 Brigade as follow-up troops. Fighting continued in this area until the 12th February, with the Japanese fleeing southwards towards Dalat and NARBADA and JUMNA and, later, CAUVERY, (Commander FWW Harvey), were working in the chaungs, supporting the landings and harassing the retreating enemy.

Ru-Ywa was attacked by our amphibious forces on February 16th, another operation designed to cut off the retreating enemy. Possibly unique in amphibious warfare, the RIN craft were supplied from the air, by Dakotas dropping supplies at the beachhead by parachute. Again, the RIN sloops were active in bombarding Japanese positions.

While these operations involved Royal Marine commandos and 25 Indian Division, concurrently 26 Division were being landed also with Royal Marine Commandos in Ramree, (January 21st) and Cheduba, (January 26th). Heavy units of the Eastern Fleet, including HMS QUEEN ELIZABETH, supported the landings at Kyaukpyu. HMIS KISTNA, (Commander SG Karmarkar), was part of the bombardment force. Again, there was heavy fighting and our landing craft and beach parties were engaged. The last major landing on the Arakan coast was at Letpan, also involving the 26 Division. This was carried out on March 13th, and led to the capture of Taungup early in April. HMIS CAUVERY and JUMNA supported this landing, again transporting troops for the assaults, as well as bombarding enemy positions.

All these Arakan landings had the objective, not only of the recapture of territory from the Japanese, but also to provide airfields for the support of the 14th Army fighting up-country. RIN landing craft were then withdrawn to India, to train for Operation 'Zipper', the landings planned to occupy Malaya. HMIS JEHANGIR was very busy right up to the dropping of the atom bomb. Some LC personnel were sent to Egypt, to train and take over LC (I)'s, as, hitherto, the RIN had operated only minor landing craft.

The above story of the Landing Craft Wing is an endeavour to record its activities up to the end of the war. It is necessarily brief and somewhat sketchy; based on private notes and extracts from various official documents which are in the author's possession. It is not possible to record fully the extraordinary achievements of this force, the overcoming of enormous difficulties of supply of craft and spares, the continued improvisation to maintain the craft in a state of readiness, the utter lack of facilities for the crews operating on the coast, the hazards of the chaungs with large tidal ranges, the welding together of the crews from diverse backgrounds and cultures - it is, however, very satisfying to recall the unstinted praise, not only from senior Naval Officexers, (RN and RIN), but also from the distinguished Generals of South East Asia Command - Oliver Leese, Philip Christison and the Divisional Commanders, Wood and Lomax; to say nothing of the Supremo himself,

Lord Mountbatten.

In July 1984, another obituary appeared in the 'Times' - that of Lieutenant General Colin Hardy, formerly Colonel-Commandant of the Royal Marines. Among his achievements was mentioned his leadership of the Commando Brigade at the 'epic landings at Myebon'. Those who were there, both at the beachhead and in NARBADA, will remember Hardy as an unflappable and decisive commander - and a good friend and loyal supporter of the RIN Landing Craft Wing.

There must be a wealth of stories to be told about HMISs HAMLA, HAMLA II and JEHANGIR - the Landing Craft Bases at Marve, Coconada and Varsova.

I noticed a reference recently to the setting up of a Radio Base at Coconada. That was JEHANGIR and, when the cyclone hit the East Coast of India in '44 (?), the entire base was inundated with five to six feet of water and the radio tower was the only dry spot, being the only two storey building in the Base.

The W/T ratings on duty stayed dry - the rest of us were up to our necks in water, while the local frogs and snakes were all looking for a dry head to sit on! It was quite a mess.

Landing Craft and local fishing boats were all adrift and crashing through cabin windows and doors. Diesel oil was floating up from the underground tanks and mingling with the flood.

When the water receded, much of our equipment and personal effects were washed out to sea, leaving many of us 'fully equipped' in exactly what we stood up in - a pair of pyjama pants and a sou'wester! (sort of curtailed the effectiveness of 'Divisions').

JEHANGIR was formerly a Burma Shell base, complete with railway spur and concrete slipways adjacent to the Coconada Canal, which was originally constructed by the Dutch. In addition to the slipways, we had a monstrous contraption - an open-ended hoist, on tracks, which could be pushed and pulled about by a D-8 bulldozer. When pushed down the beach into the sea, a landing craft could be floated into it, hoisted out of the water and towed up the beach for repairs. This machine was affectionately known as 'Jehemie'.

One of the Lieutenant (E)'s wrote to his wife and casually mentioned 'Jehemie' several times. She didn't get the picture and responded by enquiring if 'Jehemie' might be Jehangir's wife!

20

Marine Survey

AN OUTLINE OF THE MARINE CAREER OF WILLOUGHBY GEORGE BEAUCHAMP, 1864-1922, by PC BEAUCHAMP

WGB was born at Great Hampden Buckinghamshire on August 1st 1864 to Willoughby James Beauchamp, then Land Agent to George Cameron Hampden, a relative of the Earl of Buckingham and Elizabeth Maria, nee King, daughter of the Rector of Bradenham, Bucks.

WGB, who was distantly related to the Buckingham family through a great aunt and whose father had been Rector of Monks Risborough, was described in his day as the strongest man in Buckinghamshire, being said, at the age of fourteen, to have lifted with one arm a 100 lb sack from the ground into a wagon. He was also a most kindly person, for in his petition requesting that WGB be presented for schooling at Christ's Hospital, which he lodged three years before his death at forty-six, he was obliged to state that, although his salary as Land Agent amounted in all to £300 pa, he was supporting not only his own six children but also two young children from India (probably the Grims). WGB was duly presented to Christ's Hospital in September 1872 by the Honourable Henry Dudley Ryder who later became the 4th Earl of Harrowby and features in the Book 'Lady Unknown - the Life of Angela Burdett Coutts', he being a Governor of Coutts Bank.

So WGB, the second of the six children in age, became a Bluecoat, but, during his second year at the age of ten, his father died (leaving all his estate to his wife, which consisted of some small savings at less than £400). WGB was then discharged from school by his mother at the age of fifteen, with his final certificate showing Honourable Mention in French and good diligence and skills in Drawing, Music, Maths and Chemistry. He was sent to Germany to learn some of the language before returning to his home in Great Missenden.

In 1880, WGB, was apprenticed for four years to Messrs JH Allan of 2 Leadenhall Street, London, (Shipowners), for whom he served on the iron barque SEA QUEEN (873 tons) trading at the time between London, Gopalpore, Caligapatam, Madras and Chittagong.

This vessel had a crew of twenty-six, (mainly British and Scandinavian, although two were discharged for theft and arson on his first voyage). There were also seven apprentices in all at the start, but two were time-expired on calling at Chittagong and another left by mutual consent. During these voyages, his records show that he worked himself up the ladder from 4th to 1st Officer. It may have been that, between voyages, he was able to earn some extra cash by employment as a constable with the Calcutta and Bengal Police.

Following completion of his apprenticeship in November 1884, with the Master, G Thurston, giving him an excellent report, he waited in England until taking his Second Mate's Certificate in London and then, on April 1st the following year, he sailed for India, the voyage taking nearly eight weeks. On arrival on May 25th, he was posted to the TENASSERIM, which was a 1,760 ton 250 HP transport, stationed at Bombay.

After serving six months in the TENASSERIM, WGB was posted on two weeks special duty with the Marine Transport Office in Madras, where he would have been able to see his brother, Henry, another ex-Bluecoat boy who had come out on the salt and had been writing for the Madras Mail. (Henry was later to become Editor of the Madras Mail and make a complete translation of 'Hindu Manners, Customs and Ceremonies', which became a standard work). On return from special duties, he spent nine months attached to the hulk SERIMAMIS, awaiting the return of TENASSERIM from the Hydraulic Lift at Hog Island, which was described by his son Harold in the book on the Wadia family's contribution on shipbuilding in India. During this time, he passed the BOT examination on the deviation of the compass and underwent a period of training and assessment. At the end of August 1885 he was promoted directly from Third to First Grade Officer, subsequent to which he served a seven months spell in the ENTERPRISE.

In November 1887, WGB was appointed to the Marine Survey Department as an Assistant Surveyor, 4th Class. He joined the wooden paddle steamer INVESTIGATOR, under Commander Albert Carpenter, DSO RN, which sailed for the Nicobars and Port Blair in the Andaman Islands. The Superintendent of the colony of Port Blair was then Colonel T Cadell, VC, BSc.

INVESTIGATOR completed a mapping survey of the Andamans and the West Coral Banks on the scale of 1" to 1 mile. A dredge to haul sponges was used in this work, a method copied from the Norwegian North Sea vessel VORINGEN. In the annual report, WGB was described as 'showing aptitude in mastering some of the details of marine surveying'.

While still in the Andamans, WGB joined the INVESTIGATOR's steam cutter, 'Boat Party No 1', in December 1888 working with the QUANGTUNG (an iron paddle steamer of 560 tons and 150 HP, which was then acting as the Andaman Penal Settlement guard ship). Port Blair harbour and the deep water between South Andaman and the Archipelago were charted, with North Button and Wilson Islands also being surveyed. Under Lieutenant MH Smyth RN, in charge of the Boat party, 'Mr Beauchamp made a 3" to the mile chart of Diligent Strait and a 1" to the mile chart of the Strait to Port Blair'.

During the recess, WGB took six months leave in England, during which he married Emily Greaves, daughter of the Reverend Joshua Greaves, Vicar of Great Missenden.

In 1889, now under Commander RF Hoskyn RN, WGB was promoted to First Grade Officer and was the most junior of his peers - named Searle, Livermore and Dobson - in INVESTIGATOR. Leaving Bombay, she corrected the chart positions of the Laccadive Islands and coaled at

Colombo. After surveying for shoal ground at Great Basses Light, south of Ceylon, she called at Port Blair, en route for Rangoon, to land the Boat Party. Thence, Great Cow Island was surveyed, as was also Gopalpur on the Ganjam coast and Bimlipatam as the party made its way back to the recess office. On May 16th 1890, the recess office was duly opened at Poona – (to be closed again in October, as was the annual routine).

While in Poona, WGB would have learned of the birth of his first child, Willoughby Greaves, on April 5th, who was later to found and become Captain of the Canadian RNVR and a CBE.

A year later WGB, now No 2 of the Marine Survey Boat Party assembled with the other members in HMIMS LAWRENCE on October 7th for passage to the north of the Persian Gulf. The Director of the RIM had specifically ordered a survey of the Bahmishir and Shatt-el-Arab rivers, on a scale of 1½" to the mile. The bench mark was made on the British Telegraph House at Fao.

The party was commanded by Lieutenant GS Gunn. HMIMS COMET, a steel paddle steamer stationed on the Tigris at Baghdad was sent to assist. She was only of 16.7 tons, but had a 50 HP engine and two Nordenfelt guns. The entire Bahmishir river was apparently sketchmapped in one day, whence the party rejoined LAWRENCE at Basra in Iraq. (HMIMS LAWRENCE, at that time a steel paddle steamer, was normally stationed in the Gulf as a Despatch Vessel, but here we find her journeying out once again to return the party to Bombay).

Appointed Acting Commander in September 1891, WGB was promoted Assistant Surveyor 3rd Class, (Officiating) and No 3 to Commander Hoskyn and Lieutenant CV Smith RN in INVESTIGATOR. About this time, newly promoted Commander Gunn reported on Commander Hoskyn's death in hospital, but not before, on October 25th 1891, the good Commander and his wife had been witness to the birth of WGB's second son, Harold Charles, who was to reach the rank of Commander in his father's old Service, later to become the RIN. Emily was then living in the 'Neutral Lines' in Poona – presumably during the recess.

INVESTIGATOR then commenced the season's survey along the west and eastern coasts of India, encompassing Deogarh Harbour, Minikoi, Madras, False Point Devi, the Laccadives, Colombo, Coconada, the Cardimums, and the Godavari rivermouth.

On return from leave WGB was appointed Assistant Surveyor, 2nd class, responsible directly to Commander FF Oldham RN. This season INVESTIGATOR covered much the same course as the previous year, including Kiltun, Pere Mul Par, Colombo, Pinnair, Chitlac, Aukutta, Madras, Minikoi and the Kistna rivermouth.

The following year's annual report shows that INVESTIGATOR completed the season by working off Kistnapatam, Nellore and the Bombay approaches. It states that the pumice bed on Kardamat 'might well have been deposited by the Krakatoa eruption.' From May 5th 1893, WGB went on twelve months furlough to England, to study at the Royal Naval College, Greenwich, and in May the following year he was recalled to replace one of the two RN Lieutenants, who had both been recalled to

England. He was promoted to Assistant Surveyor, 1st Class.

INVESTIGATOR commenced the season surveying the Indus and the mouth of Hajaro, where Commander Oldham's report logs no less than twenty-three cases of beri-beri on the lower deck. Other areas mentioned in the report as being surveyed were further points along the west coast of Hindustan, including Calicut, the Palk Straits, the Delft Isles, Colombo and Karivatu.

Sub-Lieutenant Hand rejoined INVESTIGATOR at this time from sick leave. Hand because renowned in later years for his skill as a marine artist.

In 1895 WGB was appointed Senior Survey Officer on RIMS NANCOWRY - a wooden screw steamer of 70 tons, with an emplacement to carry a nine-pounder gun 110 HP. He was accompanied by Sub-Lieutenant Hand. The season began with a survey of Palk Strait from Kankasanturai. NANCOWRY was despatched to Trincomalee with orders to survey Paumber Pass, coal at Calicut and rendezvous with INVESTIGATOR at Marmagoa - thence to Bombay, where the recess and charting office was to open on May 8th. NANCOWRY also surveyed the Indus coastal delta 'the remarkable gorge of the Swatch', Bassein Creek and the rivers Thana, Penn and Ambu. 'Enormous changes' were found compared with the old chart of the Kakaiwari mouth. There was again beri-beri on the lower deck.

NANCOWRY finished the previous season by surveying the Panvel Creek, as far as navigable for river steamers. On 15th May 1896 the crews went into recess. But, following leave, WGB, again in command of NANCOWRY, was despatched from Bombay, in tow of RIMS CANNING, (a steel screw steam trooper), with orders to proceed via Paumben Pass to Port Blair, coaling en route at Trincomalee. From Calicut, she traversed the Bay of Bengal under her own steam, not requiring to use the deck cargo of seven tons of coal, as favourable winds sped her across in six days.

After correcting sightings and measurements relevant to the retriangulation of the Andaman Islands and soundings up to the Krishna and Barahua Light Vessels off Rangoon, an unsuccessful search was made for a shoal reported by SS VITA. (Such fruitless searches following reports by merchant vessels are referred to annually). Towards the end of the season, parts of the Gulf of Martaban were surveyed and water snakes were frequently seen - on one occasion, 'four being shot from the ship in the space of five minutes'. Once more, Christmas and New year appear to have been spent at sea.

On return to Bombay by April 29th 1897, WGB was detached to complete a large scale plan of Madras Harbour and Roadstead, on a scale of 24" to the mile. This was finished by July 4th. During this time he would have stayed with his brother Henry, who was already writing articles for the Madras Mail.

At sea, the following season, WGB became No 1 in the INVESTIGATOR under Captain TH Hemming RN. She left Bombay on October 11th, calling at Colombo and Port Blair for coal. Subsequently, surveying was carried out in the Andamans, Table Island, Cleugh Passage and Coco Channel.

INVESTIGATOR reached Moulmein, Burma on Christmas Eve and made a plan of the port on 6" scale. She then made magnetic observations in the Bay of Bengal and into the Gulf of Martaban. 'The magnetic observations were required to correct Admiralty charts and were of the first importance to seamen', said the annual report, somewhat defensively. After return to Bombay, WGB was in temporary charge of Marine Survey for some months while Commander Hemming was on leave, following which he took six months leave in England himself.

On return on April 1st 1899 WGB was permitted to revert to the general service of the RIM Defence Squadron and was in temporary command of LAWRENCE on a journey from Bombay to the Gulf, from which he returned on October 15th 1900. It was during this temporary command that he would have learned of the birth of his third son, Lawrence King, who was to serve a distinguished career, reaching the rank of Commander RN.

WGB was then Staff Officer, Bombay Dockyard. In 1902, his brother Henry, Sheriff of Madras and Editor of the Madras Mail was made a CIE. The Annual Report of the RIM for 1903-4 reports his promotion to Commander and states that he carried out the duties of Assistant Director until a Commander Elderton assumed charge. On April 27th 1903, his youngest child, Evelyn Frances Joyce, was born in England. She was to marry an eminent and much loved general practitioner in Gerrards Cross.

From 1903 to 1905, WGB was in command of CLIVE which, in her role as a troopship, (iron, screw steamer, 2,722 tons, 2300 HP), brought the Somaliland Field Force to Bombay and moved the King's African Rifles from Berbera to Mombasa and Chinde. In September and October she brought the 123rd Outram's Rifles and other units from Aden to Bombay and in November and December shipped troops to Mauritius and Singapore. For this service, WGB received the Somaliland clasp to his Africa General Service Medal, 1902-4.

In 1905, WGB was briefly in command of both CANNING and DALHOUSIE, but between May 1905 and February 1906 he was officiating Port Officer at Chittagong. During this period, Bombay Dockyard saw the passage of no less than 65,000 troops between such distant ports as Berbera, Hong Kong and England. The Dockyard also saw visits from the Prince of Wales and Lord Kitchener. GH Hewett was Director of the RIM in these years, being promoted to Admiral (Royal Navy) in 1907.

July found Commander WGB as Assistant Director of the RIM (vice-Captain Elderton) but, at this point, he transferred back to the Marine Survey as Surveyor-in-Charge. The Survey was then in recess at Coonoor, with teams drawing charts of the previous season's work on the approaches to Muscat, Aden, Kuwait, Rongat Bay and Colebrook Passage. Admiral Sir Archibald Day in his book 'The Admiralty Hydrographic Service, 1795 to 1919', says that the Marine Survey's responsibility for the Persian Gulf was at this time in doubt, when the maintenance of Indian tide gauges at Kuwait, Bahrein and Bushire were reviewed in 1906. INVESTIGATOR was having defects made good in Bombay at this time

RIMS INVESTIGATOR 'ONE'

215

and, because of her age, the Government of India made the decision to replace her.

WGB now received speedy promotion, due to Captain Hemming's retirement because of deteriorating eyesight. Captain TH Hemming RN, when in HMS DART surveying the coast of Queensland, lost the sight of his right eye due to the bursting of a soda water bottle. Two years after being invalided, he was passed fit for active service and appointed in charge of the Marine Survey of India in 1897. In 1903 he was put on the retired list, but the regulations permitted his continued employment until he retired in 1906, when he handed over to WGB. He was the last RN surveyor to hold an appointment which had been in force since 1882.

As Surveyor-in-Charge, WGB had supporting him Lieutenants Gray, Mills, Headlam, Robinson, Campbell and Dawson when INVESTIGATOR sailed for the new season on September 10th 1907. Her task was to complete the survey of Kuwait harbour and any additional work specified by the Political Resident.

Bushire was reached on September 19th for coaling and then special work was completed for the Indian Government at Khor Abdullah and Khor Zobeir, (the approaches to Basra Harbour, Iraq), before Kuwait was reached two days later. After further coaling and making deep sea soundings en route, INVESTIGATOR arrived back in Bombay on November 24th. During her stay in Bombay the Honourable Member of HE the Viceroy's Council, Major General CH Scott CB, RA, with the officiating Director of the RIM, boarded and inspected the ship and the surveying work in hand. In December, INVESTIGATOR proceeded to the Arakan coast of Burma (Andrew Bay, near Sandoway) via Colombo and Port Blair. At Port Blair, the decision was made that NANCOWRY should also be replaced.

At Sandoway, the Deputy Commissioner visited INVESTIGATOR and arrangements were made to survey the coast. Hill peaks were cleared to enable triangulation. Akyab was reached on December 23rd, when the ship was coaled and watered. The Port Officer averred that the Outer Bar had been shoaled, but this proved not to be the case. On December 29th, INVESTIGATOR left Akyab to survey a newly formed volcanic island to the north west of Cheduba Island, at the special request of the Director of the RIM. New Year's Eve and Day were spent in charting this island, after which a survey of the coast and a plan of Andrew Bay was commenced - the Irrawaddy Shoal, close to Kyaukpyu Harbour was surveyed and a hazardous rock found.

A telegram was received from the Director on February 9th, ordering the ship to Rangoon to help two 'home' experts scientifically to investigate the pearl fisheries in the Mergui Archipelago, (notably the islands of Elphinstone, Crichton and High Peak). Fortunately, the plan of Andrew Bay had been completed apart from soundings off Foul Island and the ship arrived at Rangoon on February 12th.

At Rangoon, the two experts, (RN Rudmore-Brown and JJ Simpson) were embarked and Lieutenants Robinson and Headlam sent back to Bombay to make room for them. Captain RE Lloyd, the Surgeon Naturalist and Medical Officer, included in his annual report references to much of his work in assistance to the pearl fisheries at Mergui. He also published a book for Calcutta Museum on the contributions to deep sea fauna made by the Arabian Sea.

WGB commenced his administrations report of 1907 by stating that the two experts were disembarked at Mergui. After coaling at Rangoon, INVESTIGATOR dropped the heavy office kit for Coonoor at Calicut, in preparation for the end-of-season chart making; thence proceedings via Colombo to Bombay in early May. She probably visited Port Blair en route, (for the old NANCOWRY was made over to the Port Blair authorities on April 11th 1907 and the crew were paid off and sent to Bombay).

WGB himself was deputed to the Hydrographic Office of the Admiralty from June 6th to September 13th, and this is referred to in Admiral Day's book, 'The Admiralty Hydrographic Service, 1795-1919'. While in England, WGB may well have visited the two new RIM ships nearing completion, for PALINURUS, (single screw steamer), replaced NANCOWRY at Bombay on July 1st and was commissioned on September 26th and, similarly, the new INVESTIGATOR, (steel, single screw steamer), arrived on October 14th. In the words of his report, 'both ships were thoroughly equipped for modern requirements of surveying vessels and should considerably increase the work carried out'.

For the new season, Commander WGB had with him in INVESTIGATOR Commander Mills and Lieutenants Bingham, Robinson, Thyne and Campbell. PALINURUS was under Commander Hickman, supported by Lieutenants Taylor and Dawson. Before the office at Coonoor was closed, a survey of Madras Harbour and roadstead, which had been prevented due to bad weather in May, was completed. The old INVESTIGATOR undertook her last service trip by beginning the season surveying the coast of India between Karachi and the Hajavro beacon, following the wrecking of S S NITHSDALE.

On November 13th, transfer was completed to the new INVESTIGATOR, upon her commissioning and inspection by Captain Hewitt on November 11th 1907. The older vessel was sold shortly after. She sailed for the Arakan coast via Colombo, pausing to look for breakers reported west of Alguada Lighthouse. Then a coastal survey between Kyaukpyu, Baronga Point and Cheduba Strait was commenced. In late November, Foul Island and Gwa were re-surveyed and a shoal of 2½ fathoms of mud was found where the volcanic island had stood nineteen feet above high water on the same day the previous year.

The mud shoals in the area were found to be still very active and another newly formed shoal was found two miles west of the Terrible Rocks. Some nearby land volcanoes were observed on both Cheduba and Foul Islands, the latter having peaked at 500 feet. Many dangerous coral shoals were detected off Foul Island, which seemed to have attracted large stocks of rock cod and red mullet.

WGB signed his report at Andrew Bay, Sandoway on the 1st April 1908, having just recommended a survey from Nerbudda shoal to Gwa. Signing the same report, the Surgeon Naturalist reported ninety-one cases of ague, 'which was greatly reduced by doubling the dose of quinine'.

Commander WGB now proceeded on Deputation Duty to Bombay, when he handed over his position of Surveyor-in-Chief to Commander CS Hickman. Surgeon Naturalist F H Stewart published 'The INVESTIGATOR's study of Molluscs' under WGB's title and this is now in the British Museum. The previous year, Surgeon Naturalist Lloyd had published drawing of rays and garfish, in a similar report.

For six weeks in March, WGB was deputed for duty in the Persian Gulf and for eleven days on his return was Commander First Grade in RIMS NORTHBROOK. He resumed as Surveyor-in-Charge on May 10th 1909, but, on May 15th, he handed over to Commander Hickman again and went on six months leave out of India. He resumed command once again on October 8th, when, besides Commander Hickman; Lieutenants Headlam, Bingham, Vibart, Dauglish and Sub-Lieutenant Melhuish were also serving under his command in INVESTIGATOR.

On November 12th, she left Bombay to survey Bassein, Diamond Island and the mouth of the Irrawaddy River. The latter was extensively plotted, as much of it had hitherto been scantily charted. Because of the great size of the mouth of the Irrawaddy, most of the work was carried out by astronomical observation, since the land was out of sight. WGB signed his 1920 annual report 'at sea' on April 2nd 1910, before returning to Bombay. On July 8th, he lost his wife Emily.

On September 9th 1910, Commander WG Beauchamp retired, thus vacating command of the Surveyorship which he had held for just over four years. With Captain Walter Lumsden, Director of the Service, Commander Hickman remained in charge of the Marine Survey until the outbreak of the First World War in 1914. At this point, INVESTIGATOR and PALINURUS were seconded as minesweeper and examination vessel respectively.

On May 5th 1911, WGB married Emily Elizabeth Herbert and spent his last years in his house at Great Missenden, which he called CLIVE, after his 1903 command. He died on October 28th 1922, leaving effects valued at £260 to his wife. By 1922, his son, Harold Charles Beauchamp had already served for ten years in his father's old service, having reached the rank of Lieutenant.

21

The Mercantile Marine Department

MINISTRY OF COMMERCE, GOVERNMENT OF INDIA, by FL HEMMING

I joined the Royal Indian Marine in May 1921 as a Sub-Lieutenant and served in various capacities at sea and ashore. After I married, I applied for a shore post, resulting in my being seconded to the Mercantile Marine Department which has, in respect of merchant shipping, responsibility for the administration and surveying duties as listed later.

After training with the Board of Trade Nautical Surveyors in London for three months, and with Ship Surveyors in Glasgow and Clyde shipyards for six months, followed by a qualifying period at the Board of Trade offices in Whitehall and Dock Street, London, the centre for the examination of Masters and Mates in the Mercantile Marine, I was, after a comprehensive examination, appointed as Nautical Surveyor, Chittagong in February 1939, which post was subordinate to the Principal Officer, Mercantile Marine Department, Calcutta District, (then Captain CR Bluett, RIN).

The Nautical Surveyor, Chittagong was a member of the Port Commission, representing, with the Collector of Customs etc, the Government of India interests. He was also Deputy Conservator of the Port; Shipping Master; Naval Reporting Officer; Naval Control Officer - and several other 'bits and pieces' of a naval and/or maritime nature.

When war broke out in September 1939, the Nautical Surveyor's office was rather flooded with cypher and coded telegrams which were largely dealt with by my wife - although in bed suffering from dysentry. Latterly, other means of imparting restricted etc, information were devised, thereby reducing encyphered traffic very considerably. I also found myself as Chaplain's Churchwarden of St. Mary's Church, Chittagong.

It would need much study to compile a history of how the 'Port' duties carried out in the past by the Royal Indian Marine were 'consolidated' into the Mercantile Marine Department in the mid-1930's, but it is clear how, with the total 'navy-isation' of the Royal Indian Marine/Navy it was impractical for the old organisation to continue. I have always felt that I was a bit of an anomaly; never having been, nor having any wish to be, in the Merchant Service. It can, however, be recalled that Bombay had a Port Officer, with both Executive and Engineer Officers of the RIM assisting. The organisation was, I believe, under the local, (ie, Bombay) Government. Port Officers I can recall are:- Captain Sir Henry Morland (knighted when King Edward VII, as Prince of

Wales, visited India); Captain Charlie Stewart Hickman RIM in 1919-20 or so, formerly Surveyor-in-Charge, Marine Survey of India; Captain Wish RIN-1930s; Sir Henry Morland and his grandson, Lieutenant Commander Henry Morland were in the Service. The last was Flag Lieutenant at one time to Admiral Walwyn and then ADC to the Governor of Bombay, Lord Brabourne.

Calcutta, like Bombay, had a similar organisation, with the addition of the Port Officer, (later Principal Officer, Mercantile Marine Department), being in charge of the Bengal Pilot Service, (Hooghly Pilots) together with the Pilot Steamers (usually called 'Brigs') FRASER and LADY FRASER. There was an Assistant Port Officer, (Pilotage) - a senior Bengal Pilot. Port Officers remembered are:- Captain Harrold RIM - 1920/22; Captain Oliver Goldsmith RIM - late 1920s; Captain LWR Turbett RIN - 1930s; Captain CR Bluett RIN - later 1930s; Captain J Cameron RIN.

The Port Officer POMMD was one of the seventeen Commissioners for the Port of Calcutta and the Howrah bridge. Others to represent the Government of India interests were the General Commanding the military forces locally and the Collector of Customs.

In Madras the Presidency Port Officer appears to have had much to do with the minor ports and a number of lighthouses in the Madras Presidency. There was a 'Personal Assistant' - Captain Ruffle - to the PPO - not a Naval officer. There was one Engineer Officer (RIM). Port Officers remembered are:- Captain Sir Ernest Huddleston CIE, CBE, RIM; Captain Charles Ross Campbell DSO, MVO, RIN; Captain Bryan Gordon RIN; Captain John Cameron CIE, RIN and Commander George Malcolmson Osborne-Smith RIN.

The Port Officer at Karachi possibly doubled up with the duties of Deputy Conservator of the Port. It is thought that, inter alia, he exercised some control to the Indian Government Telegraph Cable Steamer PATRICK STEWART, which was not (neither were her officers or ratings) part of the RIM.

Latterly, the last PATRICK STEWART was taken over, reconstructed as Hydrographic Surveying Ship and commissioned as HMIS INVESTIGATOR - the third of the name. Port Officers remembered are:- Captain G N Forteath RIM and Captain C S Scott DSO, RIM.

The Principal Port Officer at Rangoon (with both Executive and Engineer Officers (RIMN) assisting) had control over the Port offices at Bassein, Moulmein, Akyab and Mandalay (all RIMN). Port Officers remembered are:- Captain Anthony Hamilton DSO RIM (1920); Captain A StC Bowden RIM. Port Officers remembered are:- (Rangoon) - Commander Bertram Hughes-Hallett RIM; (Bassein) - Commander Molliet RIM (he died in 1979 aged 101); (Moulmein) - Commander Danson RIM (1921) and Commander CH Corser RIN (1926); (Akyab) - Captain (then Commander) AG Maundrell RIN and Commander Guy Engledue RIM, both mid 1920s; (Mandalay) - Commander Rose-Price RIM. There was also an Engineer Officer at Mandalay (Engineer Commander Theodore Harvey RIN) another at Narayangung in Bengal and also at Port Blair in the Andaman Islands.

When I was appointed to the MMD, the general idea was that officers so appointed should be placed on what was called List Two and that they should be virtually separate from the Service until it came to retirement; that they should be promoted to Commander on the attainment of twenty years service, except for the Nautical Adviser to the G of I and the Chief Surveyor with the G of I who might be promoted to Captain or Captain (E). They would, also, normally wear plain clothes. However, in September 1939, a signal was made by FOCRIN that these officers were to wear uniform.

After the declaration of Indian Independence on the 14th August 1947, Naval Officers seconded to the Commerce Ministry were, with all other RIN Officers remaining in India, transferred to the Royal Navy, (Special List, ex-Royal Indian Navy) and borne on the books of HMS HIGHFLYER - the Naval Base at Trincomalee. Up to that date it was sort of understood that they were borne on the books of HMIS DALHOUSIE, the Naval Depot, Bombay.

This is a precis of the whole story. I was never a Captain RIN, but was subsequently promoted to Captain RN - vide Gazette of India No 1407, dated 21 August 1948.

22
The Radar Branch

by DJ HASTINGS

Radar came very late in the war to the Royal Indian Navy. Some of the Black Swan and Bittern class sloops, which were built and commissioned in the United Kingdom, were fitted with Type 271 radar sets and a few Communications Branch ratings were given basic training in their operation. No Radio Mechanics were trained, however, and the considerable maintenance which was constantly needed on these sets fell on the overworked Warrant Telegraphists in each ship. (The sets could only be operated for about fifty minutes in each hour because of overheating; the sets were not 'tropicalised' and there were constant troubles due to high atmospheric temperatures and humidity; their range, by more modern standards, was poor). No other ships of the RIN Fleet were fitted with radar at that time and, apart from one Royal Navy Radar Maintenance Base in Bombay, no fitting or maintenance facilities for ships' radar existed in India.

Despite opposition from the Finance Department of the Government of India and an acute shortage of equipment available from the United Kingdom, an effort was made in 1943 to get some sort of training started in HMIS TALWAR, the RIN Signal School in Bombay, it having been decided at that time that radar should be the responsibility of the Communications Branch.

This training was initially carried out by a Warrant Telegraphist who, himself had no radar training, but, later, one qualified Radar Officer, RNVR, was loaned by the Admiralty and he took over the responsibility. A small building was erected in TALWAR to house two near - obsolete and incomplete radar sets and a 'dummy director'. It quickly became clear, however, that these facilities were completely useless for the training of radar operators, since the site was completely surrounded by high buildings. (No 'simulators' were available in those days).

Late in 1943, arrangements were made with the Admiralty for three RINVR officers, two of whom were electrical engineers and one a radio engineer in civilian life, to be sent for specialist training in the newly-opened Royal Navy Radar Training School at HMS ASSEGAI in Durban, South Africa.

Difficulties with arranging onward passages to South Africa resulted in these officers being 'stranded' in Mombasa for some weeks, but they were temporarily attached to the Royal Navy Radar Base in HMS GANJONI and, since the whole of the Eastern Fleet was based at Mombasa at that time, they were able to gain valuable experience of the types of radar equipment fitted to all types of RN ships, from battleships and aircraft carriers to submarines. Their specialist course at HMS ASSEGAI occupied a period of four months - two out of the three officers qualified and all returned to India about the end of April 1944, when the two qualified officers were appointed to HMIS TALWAR.

Efforts were made to get some sort of specialist training for radar operators and radio mechanics under way. A near-obsolete type of radar set was fitted in HMIS CORNWALLIS, which operated as a sea-going tender to TALWAR and this enabled some initial training at sea to be given to a limited number of operators.

Shortly after this, the writer was appointed as Staff Officer, (Radar) at Naval Headquarters, New Delhi and was attached, initially, to the staff of the Director of Naval Signals (India).

After a series of staff conferences, it became clear that, with the increasing involvement of the Royal Indian Navy in the war against Japan, radar would be of vital importance to the Service and that three priorities existed:-

1. To arrange for the training of further specialist officers as quickly as possible.

2. To set up adequate training facilities for operators and mechanics in a properly sited and equipped Radar School.

3. To set up radar fitting and maintenance facilities, with trained personnel in the major ports on the East coast of India.

While all the departments concerned in the British Admiralty were consistently helpful, a great deal of time was wasted and a lot of frustration generated by long-winded arguments and a general lack of co-operation received from the India Office in London and the cumbersome red tape of the Finance Department of the Government of India. However, eventually things started to move.

By agreement with the Admiralty, three RINVR officers were sent to the UK for specialist radar training in the Royal Navy Radar School at HMS COLLINGWOOD and, as a follow-up, it was arranged that regular officers of the RIN, who were in the UK on other courses, would be given radar training as and when opportunity offered.

A survey was carried out in several ports in India to determine the best site for the setting up of a Radar School. After a number of possibilities had been examined in detail and rejected, it was finally decided that the best available site would be on Manora Island, Karachi immediately adjacent to the RIN Gunnery School HMIS HIMALAYA.

This site offered the following advantages:-

a. It gave a clear and unobstructed radar 'view' seawards.

b.   Its location offered close co-operation with the Gunnery
      School and with the facilities which it could provide.

c.   Its location offered the possibility of co-operation with
      Service aircraft operated by the RAF and RIAF from
      airfields close to Karachi.

d.   Its location offered the possibility of co-operation with
      all types of ships using the port of Karachi.

Immediately that the basic decisions had been taken, arrangements
were made with the Admiralty for the writer to fly to the United
Kingdom to carry out a detailed survey of training establishments in the
UK, among them, HMS COLLINGWOOD, HMS EXCELLENT, HMS
MERCURY, ASE, Haslemere, HMS VALKYRIE, HMS DRYAD, RNAS,
Yeovilton and to major radar fitting and maintenance bases such as
'Sherbrook House'. Despite the fact that the war in Europe was then
reaching its most critical stages, immense help was given by the
Admiralty and by all the establishments visited.

On return to India in April 1945, an analysis of the lessons learned
on this visit showed, quite clearly, that it was not possible in India to
diversify various aspects of the training problem as was done in the Royal
Navy with separate specialist establishments and that all these diverse,
but inter-related activities would have, somehow, to be concentrated into
one small establishment.

I, therefore, designed and drew the outline plans for the Radar
School main building and its equipment to accommodate Radar Operator
training, Radio Mechanics training, Radar plotting and navigation
training, Radar gunnery control training, Action Information training,
Fighter Direction training etc. With the proposals approved by Naval
Headquarters, the almost inevitable arguments raged with the Finance
Department of the Government of India as to whether permanent
construction was necessary, how much equipment was to be installed and
as to the type of accommodation to be provided for officers and ratings.

When all these arguments were more or less settled, the only
'hiccup' came when, after construction had started, the Indian Army
Engineers, who were responsible for the building works, decided that the
building of a sea wall to protect the main building and the barrack blocks
was not necessary - with the result that the foundations were washed
away during the first monsoon storms. A sea wall was, eventually, built,
but all this added to the delays and frustrations.

Equipment, ordered from the UK, arrived quickly in all the then
current circumstances and was installed as and when parts of the building
were completed. Further problems were created by the delay in Finance
Department in approving the installation of air-conditioning equipment in
the main building, which was absolutely essential to the protection of
scarce, valuable and complicated electronic equipment in the humid and
salt-laden atmosphere of Manora. The delay in providing and installing

Ship's crest of HMIS CHAMAK

HMIS MADRAS

Converted as Radar Training Ship – Tender to HMIS CHAMAK

this vital equipment, meant that much valuable training equipment was frequently out of operation and a vast amount of time was wasted in maintaining such equipment which could otherwise have been devoted to training.

Despite all these frustrations, work went ahead steadily, with superb co-operation from the Commanding Officer and staff of HMIS HIMALAYA, at which establishment the Radar School's officers and ratings were quartered and where a number of radar sets and other equipment were temporarily installed so that some training could continue. A Bathurst Class minesweeper, HMIS MADRAS, was fitted with radar and other equipment and was converted to act as a sea-going tender to the Radar School. HMIS KARACHI, A Basset Class trawler based on Karachi was frequently used for radar training and HDMLs 1261 and 1262 were also allotted for these duties on occasions.

Admiralty had been asked to design a ship's crest for the Radar School. The name - 'CHAMAK' - was suggested by Captain SJ Thomsom CIE, RIN. In Urdu, the word 'chamak' means 'glitter' or 'splendour', but it was mis-translated by 'Suji' to mean 'lightening' and this explains the design of the roundel in the crest. This design was adopted when the School was commissioned as HMIS CHAMAK in June 1945.

The first Commanding Officer of HMIS CHAMAK was Lieutenant Commander JD Manning RINVR and the first training officers were Lieutenants Fleckney, Graves and Parrish, all RINVR, while two Petty Officers (Radar) were loaned to the RIN by the Royal Navy to act as instructors. Unfortunately, training in HMIS CHAMAK started too late to have any real effect on the provision of operators and mechanics during the war with Japan. The failure rate was high and only a handful qualified before war ended.

In September 1945, the training situation was greatly improved by the generous offer of the Headquarters, Base Air Force, South East Asia, to place the facilities of the No 2 School or Air Force Technical Training, Ameerpet, at the disposal of the RIN and for instructors and instructional equipment to be provided. Results from this school were excellent and a high standard was maintained.

At first, proposals to set up radar maintenance bases on the east coast of India met with opposition from the Admiralty, who argued that the Royal Navy base in Bombay was adequate to meet the needs of the Royal Indian Navy and of visiting ships. However, with the shift of emphasis of the war from Europe to the Far East and with the increasing involvement of the RIN in this area, agreement was finally reached.

Base radar workshops were supplied with class 'A' spares and stores for all the sets fitted in HMI ships and boats. A comprehensive range of technical test equipment was also supplied, which covered the likely requirements of any class of ship visiting these ports.

The problem of the shortage of trained technical personnel was solved, temporarily, by obtaining, on loan, the services of four RNZNVR qualified officers and a number of Royal Navy radio mechanics. The main problems encountered were those connected with the electrical breakdown of components, due to tropical conditions and the shortage of spares, particularly transformers, required to rectify faults. Fitting out and maintenance of equipment in HM and HMI ships was carried out successfully at all the bases - merchant ships were also fitted out and serviced. Owing to the changed situated in Burma, it was decided to close down the radar base workshop in Chittagong in May 1945.

Concurrent with the discussions leading up to the decision to build a Radar School at Karachi, consideration was given, at Staff level, to the future composition and status of the Radar Branch of the RIN. Despite some initial opposition from the Signals Directorate, it was finally decided to bring it into line with current practice in the Royal Navy. The writer drafted the RIN Fleet Order which brought the Branch into being towards the end of 1944 and which divided it into two distinct sections:-

a.   Radar Plot Ratings, who were responsible for manning all warning sets fitted, manning action information centres and carrying out all plotting duties in ships.

b.   Radar Control Ratings, who were responsible for all gunnery and target indication sets and for fire control.

The Branch adopted the badges and insignia used in the Royal Navy.

Owing to the instructions into the Service of an increasing amount of new and complex equipment, the Radio Mechanics branch too, was completely re-organised and divided into two sections:-

a.   Radio Mechanics (W), having as their responsibility the maintenance of ship-borne wireless telegraphy and radar equipment.

b.   Radio Mechanics (S), having as their responsibility the maintenance of wireless telegraphy and radar equipment of all types, who normally worked ashore.

These arrangements greatly simplified training and were designed to produce much great efficiency.

Towards the end of 1945, I was appointed as Staff Officer (Radar) to the Rear Headquarters in New Delhi of the Supreme Allied Commander, South East Asia, in addition to my duties with the Flag Officer Commanding, Royal Indian Navy.

Early in 1946, an invitation was received by the Government of India from the British Government, to send a delegation to the First International Conference on Radio Aids to Navigation, to be held in London in May 1946.

This invitation was forwarded by the Commerce Department to the Supreme Allied Commander, with the request that he should make suggestions as to the composition of the delegation. Admiral Mountbatten recommended that I should be appointed as Leader of the delegation and that be accompanied by a senior official of the Ports and Lights Section of the Commerce Department. This was seen as a signal honour for the infant Radar Branch of the Royal Indian Navy. This recommendation was accepted by the Commerce Department and endorsed by the Flag Officer Commanding, Royal Indian Navy.

The Conference assembled in Central Hall, Westminster, on the 7th May 1946, under the Chairmanship of Sir Robert Watson-Watt, (the inventor of Radar), and was formally opened by the Rt Honourable Alfred Barnes, the then Minister of Transport. Twenty-two nations were represented at the Conference and I was accompanied by Mr Richard Seal of the Commerce Department of the Government of India. The Conference and associated technical visits lasted for three weeks.

A Report was submitted to the Commerce Department and to the Flag Officer Commanding, Royal Indian Navy - regrettably, receipt of these reports was never acknowledged.

23

The Royal Indian Navy
(1612–1947) Association

by MRS PPS WRIGHT

On the 6th June 1878, the Indian Navy Dinner was held at the Criterion Restaurant in London, on the occasion of the presentation of a Testimonial to Lieutenant CR Low, Author of the 'History of the Indian Navy', which was published in 1877. This was reported in the 'The Colonies and India' on the 15th June 1878, when reference was made to the 'Annual Indian Navy Dinner' – a clear indication that this was an event which had been taking place for some years. Unfortunately, it has not yet been discovered when this annual dinner came into being – there being no reference to it in CR Low's book.

There does not appear to have been an actual Club or Association at that time – just an Annual Dinner in London, attended, one may assume, by those officers who had retired; who were on leave at the time or were in the UK for some other purpose.

The next reference I have so far traced is of the Annual Dinner and Reception of the Royal Indian Marine held at Paganini's Restaurant in London on the 25th August 1919. Another reference is to the annual Dinner and Reception of the Royal Indian Marine held at the Great Central Hotel, London, attended by RIM officers, both Active and Retired, under the Presidentship of Captain George Wilson, CIE, RIM (Retd). This would appear to be when the Royal Indian Marine Club, England was formed – the Honorary Secretary's First Annual Report was circulated for the information of members on the 1st January 1932 and contained a Provisional List of Members. Of the inaugural members, it is interesting to note that the name of Engineer Lieutenant AC Pain still appears in our list of members in 1984.

In 1931, the President was still Captain G Wilson CIE, RIM and the Honorary Secretary was Captain GS Hewett RIM (Retd). In this 1932 issue is printed a letter from Admiral Sir Humphrey Walwyn, in which he writes: . . . 'It is a great pleasure and encouragement to feel that the retired officers take such a keen interest in the Service. I can assure you that we are doing awfully well out here (Bombay) and I am really proud of them.' The letter was dated 29th October 1931.

The 1933 issue states that it is the Third Annual Report of the RIM Club by the Honorary Secretary. There seems to be no record of a second Report – this could have been more of an interim report, circulated as a duplicated news sheet, but there is no evidence of this being the case. At this time (1933) the President and Honorary Secretary were respectively,

Captain CW Hewett RIM (Retd.) and Captain GS Hewett CBE, RIM (Retd.).

It is recorded that the Second General Meeting of the Club took place on the 29th September 1933 at the East India United Services Club, followed by the Annual Club Dinner. On this occasion, there were seventy two present; the Guest of Honour being Sir H Richmond KCB, who was Naval Commander-in-Chief in India and President of the Re-organisation Committee.

The 1933 List of Members totals 194, of whom ten are still in our 1984 List of Members. In 1934, the title was changed to the RIN Club, with Captain Sir EJ Headlam CSI, CMG, DSO, RIM (Retd.) and President and Engineer-Captain A H Baker OBE, RIM (Retd.) as Hon. Secretary.

In the Order of the Day, dated 2nd October 1934, the following was published:-

It is with very real pleasure that I am able to inform you that His Majesty the King has been graciously pleased to approve the Royal Indian Marine Service being designated the Royal Indian Navy. His Majesty wishes every success to the Force in its new role.

The following reply was sent to His Majesty:-

'Flag Officer Commanding, officers and men of the Royal Indian Navy beg to tender their humble thanks to His Majesty the King Emperor for his good wishes on the occasion of the announcement of the honour which has been graciously pleased to confer upon the Service to which they belong. They desire, in addition, to express to His Majesty their loyal and unswerving devotion.'

On the 30th April 1863, the Indian Navy which, with its predecessors, the Honourable East India Company's Marine and the Bombay Marine, had constituted India's Naval Forces since 1612, ceased to exist. The seventy one years which had passed were bridged, in peace and war, by the Royal Indian Marine.

It was in the 1935 Report of the RIN Club that Articles were first published and, also, a circular was sent to all members regarding a decision on the Club tie. There seemed to be little enthusiasm for a change and it was decided to abandon the idea of a special tie for the Club. The tie was to be the Service pattern - which remains the Association's tie to this day.

The RIN Club continued to flourish, with membership increasing and, in 1939, Captain Sir Ernest Huddleston, CIE, CBE, RIN (Retd) took over as President, with Engineer-Captain Baker remaining as Hon Secretary.

During the war period, 1939 to 1946, no RIN Club Reports were published, although the Club did not in any way go into decline with Captain AG Maundrell, CB, CIE, RIN (Retd) as President and Captain PA Mare CIE, RIN as Hon Secretary.

On the 5th July 1946, it was proposed by Captain L Sanderson, CIE,

RIN (Retd) and seconded by Captain EM Bayfield RIN that an Officer of the RINR and RINVR be asked to serve on the Committee as Members. Lieutenant Commander D Leefe RINR and Commander (Sp) GE Walker, OBE, RINVR were elected as the first Reserve Officers to serve on the Committee.

A Scottish Branch was inaugurated in 1948 with Captain PH Learmont, CIE, RIN (Retd) as Chairman and Lieutenant Commander (S) A Reid RINVR as Secretary. There were two Annual Reunions - one at The Connaught Rooms in London and the other at St Enoch Hotel, Glasgow. In the three months prior to the Reunions, 160 new members joined the RIN Club. It was stated:-

> The Members of the Old Active Service, now a very small band, owe a great debt of gratitude to the Officers of the Reserves who have, so whole-heartedly, identified themselves with the aims of the Club.

At the 1949 Annual General Meeting, a motion was passed to change the name of the RIN Club to the RIN (1612-1947) Club - from small beginnings. In 1950, after an exchange of letters, an affiliation was arranged between the Royal Naval and Royal Marines Officers Club in Karachi and the RIN (1612-1947) Club. In 1951, Captain L Sanderson, CIE, RIN (Retd) took over as President with Commander (S) J Hyde, OBE, RNVR as Hon Secretary/Treasurer. 1952 saw Captain RM Philby, CIE, RIN (Retd) taking over as Hon Secretary/Treasurer. Two further motions were passed at the Annual General Meeting:-

i.   The election of Past-Presidents as ex-officio members of the Committee and

ii.   Officers' widows to be elected to Honorary Membership of the Club.

Arrangements had also been made for the official appointments of Club Correspondents by the Indian Navy and the Royal Pakistan Navy.

The following year (1953) the rule governing the election of officers' widows to the Club was amended as follows:

> The widows of the former officers to be made Associate Lady Members automatically, with the right to be notified of all social functions which they had been able to attend previous to their widowhood.

In 1955, Captain Philby relinquished the office of Honorary Secretary/Treasurer, his successor being Lieutenant Commander (E) JW Wright RIN (Retd). The annual publication, known from its inception as 'The Report', would, it was agreed at the Annual General Meeting, be designated in future as 'The Journal'. In 1958, the office of Hon Secretary/Treasurer changed hands once again and Commander JJ Carson,

VRD, RIN (Retd) took over. Unfortunately, he became ill shortly afterwards and Mr AH Hammond took over at short notice, his appointment being confirmed in 1959. Also in 1959, Captain PH Learmont, CIE, RIN (Retd) was elected President of the Club on the resignation of Captain Sanderson.

It was in 1960 that I officially took over as Honorary Editor of the Journal, although I had been greatly involved in its production since 1955, when I was unofficially editing, as well as doing all the typing. Having a free hand, I instituted the Index, which makes reference so much easier - it is a pity that I did not think of it earlier.

Commander (E) ET Elliot RIN (Retd) succeeded Mr Hammond as Hon Secretary/Treasurer in 1961. This was the year in which the late Commander GE Walker, OBE, RINVR contributed his article on the 'Gridiron'. This proved to be of such outstanding merit and interest that the 1961 issue of the Journal was in great demand, from so many sources that it was quickly out of print - even now, copies are being sought. In 1963, the Club endowed a bed in King Edward VII's Hospital for Officers, to commemorate the 350th anniversary of the founding of the Service in 1612.

On the occasion of the 350th anniversary, the format of the Reunion was changed from dinner to luncheon and, for the first time, ladies were invited to be present. There were 122 members and guests at this memorable function, with Field Marshal Sir Claude Auchinleck, GCB, GCIE, GSI, DSO as Guest of Honour. Admiral Sir Geoffrey Miles and Sir Alexander and Lady Symon were also guests of the Club. Since then, the Reunion has always taken the form of a luncheon and ladies are as much in evidence as officers.

Lieutenant Commander (Sp) J Clunie RINVR took over as Hon Secretary/Treasurer in 1963. This was the year when the Journal developed into 108 pages and I realised that we could not continue with the inevitable rise in the cost of printing such a lengthy publication. It was decided, at the Annual General Meeting, that the List of Members should be printed every five years, only amendments being given in the interim period. This caused us to 'mislay' so many members who had failed to notify changes of address, that a separate Address List was published to accompany the 1965/66 Journal.

Vice-Admiral JW Jefford, CB, CBE, succeeded Captain Learmont as President in 1964. We were most fortunate, in this year, that the Snook Sword was purchased by the Wilkinson Sword Company Ltd and was presented to the National Army Museum, on the 10th March 1965, for the display in the Naval Section of the Indian Services Room at the Museum. The inscription on the sword reads:-

Presented by the Court of Directors of the United India Company to Lieutenant Samuel Snook of the Bombay Marine as a mark of the Court's appreciation of his services when at Macao in the year 1799.

Samuel Snook joined the Honorable East India Company as a

Volunteer in 1787, becoming a 2nd Lieutenant in 1792 and a 1st Lieutenant in 1798. He rose to the rank of Commodore. He married a widow, Mrs Esther Margaret Foster, at Bombay in 1801; retired from the Service in 1816 and died in 1844.

In 1965 the title of the RIN (1612-1947) Club was changed to the 'Royal Indian Navy (1612-1947) Association' - this being considered now appropriate to our circumstances and scattered membership. Changes were made in 1967 to the conventional form which the Journal had taken since its first issue. The printers went into liquidation just as the Journal was ready for them, so we were faced with finding a new printer at short notice. We also had to face ever increasing costs and this forced us to look at the options available to us, which were:-

1.   To carry on as we were doing until funds ran out, in which case the Journal would cease to exist and contacts would be lost.

2.   To change the format entirely and merely to publish a duplicated News Letter.

3.   The Hon Editor could type the whole Journal and a firm of printers would be willing to photocopy direct from her typescript - thus saving large sums of money in typesetting.

Since, by now, it had become apparent that, with the world-wide spread of our membership the Journal had become the only stable link which kept the Association in being, we took the third option - and I seem to have been typing ever since. Without this transition, even with all voluntary financial help given by members, I fear that the Association would have been wound up by now and much of historical interest would have been lost.

At this time, we had a new President - Captain JEN Coope RIN (Retd) and also a new Hon Secretary/Treasurer, Lieutenant Commander A F King RIN (Retd) - the first time when both these important offices had changed hands at the same time, which must have made it difficult for both of them. It was at this time that I seem to have become a sort of permanent link in the chain.

In 1970, yet another break with tradition came about in the new design of the Journal's cover - depicting crossed flags. The fundamental idea was to link the dates used by the Association - 1612 and 1947, as far as possible. So, the earliest ensign known, which had red and white stripes, with the Cross of St George, was chosen to represent the beginning of the Service. This ensign was, of course, modified later to incorporate the Crosses of St Andrew and St Patrick in 1707 and 1801. One version was adopted by the Americans - soon to become the Stars and Stripes.

The other flag depicted was that of the Mughal Admiral. In those days, the senior officer did a year as Mughal Admiral, wearing his flag at the main and the Company's flag at the peak. There were some 'perks' attached to the appointment on retirement. The crest surmounting these two flags provides the link from the earliest flag, through the period when the Service provided the Mughal Admirals, to 1947. The light and dark stripes on the cover depict the RIN tie. This new cover was designed by Lieutenant Commander (E) JW Wright RIN (Retd).

1973 saw us with two more changes at the same time. Lieutenant Commander AT Bond RIN (Retd) took over as President and Commander (E) GW Watson RIN (Retd) became Hon Secretary/Treasurer - an office which he still holds today (1984). In 1978 Lieutenant Commander (E) JW Wright RIN (Retd) took over as President from Lieutenant Commander Bond. It was in this year that we inaugurated our 'Save our Heritage' appeal - some of the results of which are apparent in this volume. The object is to collect any sort of information or other 'memorabilia' which will help us to make up a permanent record of the Royal Indian Navy and its forebears for the National Maritime Museum at Greenwich and for the Maritime Museum in Bombay.

In 1980, Lieutenant Commander Wright resigned from the office of President because of ill-health and his place was taken by Lieutenant Commander AF King RIN (Retd). 1981 signalled the Golden Jubilee of the Association, it having been formed in 1931 as the RIM Club, England. For this special year, we forsook the light and dark blue cover of the Journal for a gold cover - the gift of our printers. For our Reunion that year, our Guest of Honour was Commodore KN Dubash IN, then Naval Adviser to the High Commissioner for India in London. At the Annual General Meeting in 1983 Lieutenant Commander AF King resigned as President and his place was taken by Captain WJM Teale RN (Retd) -formerly Lieutenant RIN.

In the 1983 Journal, it was a pleasure to be able to include an article by Commodore CL Sachdeva AVSM, IN, on 'The Anchor Hold' - an association set up in India on similar lines to our own. We very much hope to maintain a close liaison with this organisation and to maintain contacts with the many friends who served with us in India.

24

Sea Transport

IN INDIA IN THE SECOND WORLD WAR by SIR HENRY DIGBY-BESTE

To discuss Sea Transport work in India without some reference to the past is not possible, for, through many changes in the history of our Service in the days of the John Company; of the Indian Marine and of the Royal Indian Marine the transport of troops and stores by sea has been a major duty. Without a shadow of doubt, the Government Dockyard in Bombay, to use its old title, and the personnel attached thereto, have been pioneers in fitting out and, thus, the Sea Transport Service in India, as a Branch of the Royal Indian Navy, had a unique and proud tradition and prestige which was enhanced by the flexibility and ready co-operation with other arms of the Services and Civil Departments in India and in the United Kingdom and with the Dominions and Allies.

Up to 1943, under the Flag Officer Commanding, Royal Indian Navy, who was ex-officio Principal Sea Transport Officer in India and was responsible to the Commander-in-Chief, India, as well as to the Director of Sea Transport in London, the Sea Transport was the charge of Captain CL Turbett OBE, RIN, who was stationed in Bombay and held the dual post of Divisional Sea Transport Officer and Assistant PSTO (India).

This officer and his staff did trojan work, laid the foundations of the final efforts in 1945 and dealt under extreme difficulties with the transport duties involving the despatch of troops and stores to and from the UK, Egypt, Abyssinia, Persia and Iraq, as well as with the fighting forces in Burma during the successful Japanese push. I have no statistics by me to exemplify the volume of work done in those years, but, when the mantle of responsibility was shifted to my shoulders, or partly so, in the Autumn of '43, I was amazed at the work done with so few tools. The savagery of the war in Europe, developing into a total world war, brought in its train a new technique and, consequently, the carriage of troops and stores by sea created new and difficult problems.

After the launching of the attack and invasion of North Africa by sea and, later, Sicily, plans and preparations had to be considered for India to be a springboard for the forthcoming attack on Burma and Malaya and, eventually, Japan. This trend of events meant that Sea Transport in India was no longer a service confined to the chartering, (or impressing), and fitting-out of merchant ships for troops and stores in accordance with the old methods, but was indirectly or directly involved, in co-operation with the other services and departments, civil as well as military, with such factors as the transport of explosives in such major quantities as would have made our forebears turn in their graves; oil; the creation of new ports; fire precautions on board and ashore; watering and fuelling ships in such quantities that the normal port facilities were never intended for; small craft; crewing; seamen's welfare, especially overseas; fitting; alteration and repair of ships beyond normal facilities in ports where there were continuous demands of other, but not of a necessarily less important nature.

These few I have enumerated were not, in themselves, straight Sea Transport work, but rather that of the MWT and of Local Naval Authorities but, nevertheless, each and all had direct repercussions on Sea Transport, who had to lend a hand and, sometimes, in fact, take the lead. The indirect responsibilities, nevertheless, (I refer to tactical loading and the consequential necessary fitting-out of ships), were continually changing in the light of each campaign and so called for greater skill and up-to-date knowledge.

It was in these circumstances only that, in 1943, Admiral Godfrey asked the D of ST to send out experts, who had had the benefit of experience in mounting operations against North Africa and Sicily, to advise India. Sir Ralph Metcalf responded by asking Mr McDavid, the Deputy DSE, who was then in Egypt, to fly to Delhi, examine the existing organisation and advise. No better choice could have been made - Mr McDavid quickly assessed the problems; realised that the Indian Sea Transport was of good vintage in good bottles and that the ever-changing demands of the theatres and techniques of this total war could best be met by fortifying the Indian vintage with some old brandy that had been distilled by experience in the wars in Europe, thus blending a really heady vintage fit for the new commitments. His recommendations were accepted.

Sir John Nicholson, who at that time was a Deputy Representative of the MWT in Delhi, was appointed as Deputy Director of Sea Transport to India; a Commodore, RN was flown to India to assume the duties of Deputy PSTO, (India) with an appropriate staff in New Delhi and a small core of Sea Transport Officers, who had experience of work in France, Norway, Egypt, North Africa and elsewhere followed and the two Services - Indian Sea Transport and Home Sea Transport, each retaining their own rank, pay etc, worked as one team under the leadership of PSTO (I), who was, as before, the Flag Officer Commanding, Royal Indian Navy, whilst the DDST (I) in his post retained his previous appointment in the NWT and so was able to blend the civil and uniformed branches into one working whole.

In Delhi, plans were being discussed and made and remade daily and this entailed the closest co-operation with the Naval Commander-in-Charge, who retained a staff there throughout; with South East Asia Command and with the Quarter Master General, India. His staff were also re-inforced by experienced officers who had been in the planning and launching of the 8th Army in their history-making campaign in North Africa.

The Deputy PSTO and DDST (I) had constantly to be in the air or en route from port to port; seeing; advising; explaining or helping.

Unfortunately, I did not keep a close diary of all my travelling, but, since I went to India, I travelled some 70,000 miles by air, of which only some 15,000 miles was due to a later appointment in Australia and, to paint a true picture of the furious activities out East, some 28,000 miles were covered by rail - and this was only the writer's share. The DDST (I) was always on the go and so were many of the officers.

All the ports were staffed. During the last two years, Karachi was used as a disembarking port from the West and handled many of the larger liners - such as had not been thought suitable to use that port before. The port was particularly busy, during the early part of the war, with 'Piforce'. Captain JF Vibart CBE, RIN, returned from a long retirement, finished his sea career as Divisional Sea Transport Officer, Karachi and was greatly missed when he finally retired in 1945.

Bombay bore the brunt of the work, (though Calcutta may deny this!), - at first under Captain Turbett and then under Captain Bullock, RNR, who had seen previous service in the UK and in Egypt. In this port, the main fitting-out work was carried out and, in fact, this branch of the service became of such importance that, following the practice at home, in 1944 it was made into a separate department under Commander JC Needham, Burma RNR, with a number of officers. Later, Commander Needham went to Madras and was relieved in Bombay by Mr Murray as Deputy Principal Technical Officer.

Cochin was constantly in use as a fuelling base and for coastal craft. Madras was one of the main embarking and disembarking ports for Burma and, later, for Malaya. Vizagapatam fed Chittagong, with Calcutta and so assisted the 14th Army, while Calcutta nearly rivalled Bombay, first with the evacuation from Burma, then with the inflow of USA personnel and stores, in their gigantic task of building aerodromes for supplying China over the 'Hump' and other operations in the north-west and, later, with reliefs and troops and stores for the advance into Burma. Chittagong, under Commander Frame, was not just working to capacity, but about 100 per cent more.

The Service never had enough officers, though this was not the fault either of the DST, or of the RIN, both of whom helped to the utmost. I happen to have a list of officers in December 1944 and the following figures may be of interest:- The total number that month was 134, of which two were RN, twelve RNR, one WRNS, twenty RINR, fifty two RINVR, seven WAC (I) (Naval Wing), four Burma RNR, one Army, three Civilian, two NFS, and nine Italian POWs as technical helpers.

The great day culminated with 'Zipper', which was the code word for the attck on Malaya from the springboard of India. The actual attack did not eventuate, but all was ready with troops and stores embarked.

A few statistics, which have been taken from a report made by the NOIC, Bombay, will show the magnitude of the work undertaken, and successfully, under the aegis of the Royal Indian Navy, mainly through the Sea Transport Service.

On the 21st August 1945, there were 204 ships at anchor in Bombay and 102 at the harbour wall and in the docks. A boat pool handled 4,000 men a day. Fuel issued during that month was:-

Oil - 39,000 tons; Diesel Oil - 14,225 tons; Coal handled - 43,135 tons; Petrol to small craft - 52,530 gallons.

During the preceding six months, 1,121,897 tons of ammunition, apart from petroleum, were handled. This gigantic operation was carried out in a port which had suffered a most gigantic set-back just over a year previously, when a disastrous explosion and fire had wrecked two docks, thirteen ships and burned large areas of the docks.

(Standing, left to right) Lt(S) VH Torby RINVR; Lt(S) Satinder Singh RINVR;
Miss VE Ollenbach WRINS; Lt(S) BD Nagpal RINVR; Lt(S) RFF Bently RINVR.
(Sitting) Lt Comdr(S) TE Roff RINVR; Comdr(S) J Hyde RINVR; Capt(S) EE Brightman RN:
Comdr(Sp) E Ellis RINVR; Lt Comdr(S) CS Shukul RINVR

The Supply & Secretariat Directorate - Naval Headquarters (India) - 1944

25

The Supply & Secretariat Branch

A BRIEF HISTORICAL ACCOUNT OF ITS DEVELOPMENT by J HYDE

The formation of a 'Paymaster' Branch of the RINVR was initiated in 1936 and, in that year, ten civilians from the commercial communities in various cities in India were recruited to form the nucleus of the Officer cadre. 'Temporary' ranks were allocated on an age basis and four Lieutenants and six Sub-Lieutenants were commissioned. Training programmes were not immediately available and recruits were required to contact Shore Establishments and ships of the Royal Indian Navy and so develop an awareness and understanding of Naval Life. By 1937, training facilities were in operation and postings were made to ships and shore establishments on an annual two week period basis.

Recruitment increased during 1937 and 1938 and, by the time of the outbreak of war in September 1939, the RIN was ready for the influx of a large expansion in the number of recruits, which continued steadily through the following years. In line with the development of the officer cadre of the RINVR, so did the increase in the recruitment of Commissioned and non-Commissioned Writers and Ratings of the RIN.

On the 3rd September 1939, all officers appointed to the Paymaster Branch of the RINVR were posted to their ships and shore establishments as Secretaries, Supply Officers or Paymasters - or often a combination of all three. As befitted a new Branch, promotion was fairly rapid. In the case of the writer, the rank of Lieutenant Commander was attained in March 1942 and that of Commander in February 1944.

By 1945, the total number of officers of the Supply ;and Secretariat Branch, (as it was now re-named), had risen to just under 250 and included eleven Commanders; twenty-seven Lieutenant Commanders; over 150 Lieutenants and about fifty Sub-Lieutenants.

With the outbreak of hostilities, a large scale operation, covering the building of a number of warships for the RIN, was undertaken in the United Kingdom and Australia. In both countries, the Branch played its full part in the deputations which were sent from India. Their duties included the securing of accommodation for the many 'stand-by' drafts of officers and ratings for the manning of the new ships and Supply and Secretarial duties concerned with the running of the new shore establishments and, in due course, the commissioning of the new ships.

The UK operation commenced on 1942 and was completed in 1943, with the despatch to India of the last of the new ships - a modified 'Bittern' class sloop and the Flag Ship of the Royal Indian Navy - HMIS

NARBADA. A beautiful Scottish mansion on the Clyde had become the RIN shore establishment in the United Kingdom.

In view of the then chaotic state of the organisation and accounting procedures of Victualling and Naval Stores in the Service, the newly-formed Supply and Secretariat Duties Directorate at Naval Headquarters, New Delhi was instructed to revise, amend and simplify the existing Manuals on these subjects and, by September 1944, a revised 'Naval Stores Accounting Directive' was issued, followed by a 'Victualling Directive' in October 1944.

The RIN and, particularly its Supply and Secretariat Branch, were fortunate in having the services, on loan from the Royal Navy, of two very experienced officers - Captain (S) Brightman and, later, Captain (S) Parsons, in organising and controlling the development of the Branch. The Supply and Secretariat Duties Directorate co-operated closely with the Victualling Directorate in its responsibility for victualling stores and in the separation of the duties of Writers and Stores Ratings in each Branch.

It is interesting to observe that the breakdown of national and religious elements in the officer cadre of the Branch by 1945, showed a recruitment ratio of about 43% British, 28% Hindu and 10% Muslim. The ratio of British officers decreased in 1946 and, with the cessation of hostilities, disappeared almost overnight, with the return of the British element to their peacetime occupations.

MEMORIES OF AN ADMIRAL'S SECRETARY   *by HA McGeorge*

For many years before the War, I lived and worked in Yugoslavia where I met my wife, a Scot from Ayrshire and the thought that I might go to India and, indeed, join the Navy never entered my head. However, the immediate threat of German invasion of the country determined the future of myself and my family and, after a worrying and uncertain journey with one small daughter and very few possessions by train to Baghdad and then by Imperial Airways flying boat, we arrived in Karachi at the beginning of December 1940.

Our intention was to get back to the United Kingdom or, perhaps, go to Rhodesia and, with that in mind, moved on to Bombay and stayed initially in the Taj Mahal Hotel and the Ritz Hotel. We found, of course, that it was most unlikely that a sea passage out of Bombay could be arranged for a long time ahead and a long delay could be expected. We therefore moved into a flat to await events.

During the waiting, I met up with someone who had just joined the Navy and he told me they were looking for 'likely lads' and, as a result, I had an interview with 'Suji' Thomson and found myself a member of what was then the Paymaster Branch of the Royal Indian Navy and a VR, being appointed to HMIS DALHOUSIE on the 23rd January 1941.

I cannot remember that there was any special introduction to the mysteries of naval life, although there must have been some classes and explanations of what was involved and expected, but there seemed to be anxiety to get some life, even though very 'green' into the Navy. After a course of square bashing in the Fort, to which, as no doubt to many others, I was not accustomed, I was posted to the Signal School (HMIS TALWAR), which was then being commissioned under the command of Lieutenant Commander George Bailey. My duties were initially concerned with general accounting duties and victualling. The latter I remember particularly well, as, in enthusiasm and ignorance, I wrote a report pointing out the short-comings of the then system. I should really have known better, as the 'Wavy Navy' was initially a little on sufferance and I should not have pushed my neck out.

This changed, of course, later on, as the different approach to traditional ways was more generally accepted. It was an interesting and varied posting and my duties included the teaching of cyphering and coding to junior officers. It must have been just as frustrating for regular Officers to cope with the Volunteers as it was for the latter, brought up in a different world, to come to grips with naval routines and customs.

The Secretariat Branch (its name having been changed from Paymaster), at that time was recruited from a wide variety of professions and creeds, many accountants like myself, bankers, lawyers, insurance wallahs, etc and, while a mixed bag, formed a good bunch of men and all of them, whether British, Colonial, Hindu, Muslim, Parsi, got on well together. During my time at the Signal School, I recall a visit of the Viceroy at the time, when all stops were pulled out and there was plenty of whitewash. George Bailey was good CO, with a charming wife. He was both efficient and a good disciplinarian and was well liked.

After a period at Colaba of about six months, although I cannot remember dates, I was transferred to the Navy Office and appointed Secretary to COMRIN, Commodore AR Rattray, who subsequently became Rear-Admiral, with the appointment of Flag Officer, Bombay and me as his Secretary.

The duties of Admiral's Secretary were very varied and I was called upon to undertake many jobs which were far removed from a Paymaster's job at sea. First of all, there was the usual amount of 'bumf' which was channelled through the Secretary, having gone the rounds of the appropriate Staff Officers and to act as a 'buffer' in easing the many administrative problems which arose. Admiral Rattray really despised this side of his life, having led such a very active life in the past. He was, I think, in the Merchant Navy with a Master's ticket in sail, then in the Royal Flying Corps in the First World War and then his career in the RIN. However, the job had to be done and he did it well. He was highly esteemed and liked.

Bombay was an important centre, particularly when the Japs became obstreperous and, on one occasion, a very 'hush hush' meeting was held in the Navy Office at which the Senior Naval Officer in the Far East, Admiral Cunningham and other high ranking Service officers were present. As no outsiders could be present, I was asked to take notes of the meeting's deliberations – I aways hoped I had got them right!

As the Flag Officer, Bombay, had no regular 'Flags' at that time, I acted in this capacity on occasions and, being short in stature, found the aiguillettes (borrowed) and the sword (also borrowed), particularly the latter, something of a problem. However, the few occasions were survived without any undue humiliation.

It was inevitable that many officers who were having family troubles at home, with such long periods of separation, should seek some guidance in their personal affairs and this, alas, frequently happened and, much as one would have wished to help, there was little we could do other than try to find a source at home which might investigate and, hopefully, sort things out. My assistant at that time was a young Indian lawyer, Lieutenant (S) D B Vacha RNVR, who was a great help and a credit to the Royal Indian Navy. At that time, religious differences were overcome with comparative ease.

One of the most interesting side affairs of my job occurred when one of the Greek Naval ships sailed into Bombay Harbour with trouble aboard. The Captain was a bully and had put some of the ratings in irons and imprisoned them in the hold for an affair which many of the officers felt did not justify the treatment given. They had remonstrated with the Captain and found themselves up on a charge of Mutiny. The Court-Martial was handled by Greek officers, military as well as Naval, specially sent from Cairo. The Court was held on board the ship and the Captain was eventually sentenced in Alexandria but, being a friend of the Royal family, his sentence was soon forgotten and he was promoted shortly after. Some of the junior officers concerned were found guilty, sentenced to terms of imprisonment and sent up to Nasik jail to serve their sentences.

As Admiral's Secretary, I was able to give help in making some of the arrangements during the Court's visit and, when the proceedings were over, I received a note (which I still have) from Captain P Antonopoulos of the Royal Hellenic Navy, and who was the Senior Officer of the Court, which read as follows:-

Lt. Pay.Mast. Mac George.
In leaving Bombay I want to express to you my best thanks for all the help and assistance you have given me during my staying in India for carrying out my duties.
With my best wishes - P Antonopoulos.

A rather unusual duty for a Paymaster in the RIN.

The disaster of the Bombay dock explosion in 1944 gave many worrying moments at the Navy Office, when many of the staff were on duty during the night and giving what aid and service were possible. I can still recall seeing hundreds of Indians rushing past the office to the Docks immediately after the first explosion and then fleeing faster back the way they had come when the second of the many further explosions went off. The Supply and Secretariat Branch of the RIN was given tremendous support by the strength of some senior appointments from the Royal Navy - Captain (S) RA Braine, as Secretary to FOCRIN is a name I recall.

My progress in the Navy culminated with a 'brass hat' in September 1944 - a great fillip to my ego, by which time it seemed that the war in Europe was coming to an end and I was granted leave to the UK, on which I took my wife and daughter. I returned in May 1945 to 'finish off the Japs', having been at home for VJ Day.

By February 1946, my time for demob had come around and I sailed home, having had an experience which will never be forgotten. Shortly after my departure, I heard of the mutiny in Bombay of naval ratings and thought what a sad ending to a period, when all ranks of the Royal Indian Navy hadd worked so well together.

These are random thoughts and are mainly concerned with the duties of an Admiral's Secretary, as opposed to service afloat, but which were an integral part of the Supply and Secretariat Branch of the Royal Indian Navy. As always, after such an episode in life, members of a Naval force scatter to their different parts of the world and so often lose touch with those with whom they had close contact for many years.

26
The Tactical Unit

AT BOMBAY by AF KING

The official report of the Royal Indian Navy - January to June 1945 - contains the statement under 'Training and Education' - 'Tactical training unit weekly courses have been held. An Action Information Centre, including an ARL plot will be constructed in the tactical unit when equipment now on order is received from the United Kingdom.'

In Admiral Godfrey's personal memoirs he states on page 208, when reviewing what he had achieved during his three years as Flag Officer Commanding, Royal Indian Navy: 'One sat down with a clean sheet of paper and had to produce something out of nothing. For instance, at the beginning of the war, the RIN had no medical service, no accounting service, no welfare, no amenities, no anti-submarine school, **no tactical unit,** no mechanical establishment'. The Tactical Unit was established in Bombay in November 1944 and disbanded shortly after the capitulation of the Japanese. As I was in charge of this unit, it may be of some historical interest that my thoughts on it are recorded.

The objective was to bring the captains of ships operating in the Indian Ocean up-to-date with the tactics of enemy submarines attacking convoys or single ships operating in the area. It was primarily the idea of Vice-Admiral Godfrey, who had come to the job of FOCRIN direct from the hot seat of Director of Naval Intelligence in London and, thus, clearly knew the situation in the Battle of the Atlantic and the contribution made by the Tactical Unit in the headquarters of Admiral Sir Max Horton, Commander-in-Chief Western Approaches, at Derby House, Liverpool.

The situation in 1944 was that the war in Europe was in its final stages and the War Cabinet were now looking for more aggression in the East. More materials were to be sent out from Europe, Australia and America. This meant a great increase in the flow of men and materials by sea and an obvious increase in Naval activity, both to protect convoys and in offensive roles in support of military landings. It was clear that Japanese submarines, operating at greater distances from base than were the German U-boats in the Atlantic would not operate in an identical manner as their European partners, yet it was also known that there had been a considerable amount of liaison and exchange of information and expertise. It was further thought that a number of U-boat commanders might fight on to the end, even after their own country had succumbed, by setting up base in Japanese-held territories.

Thus, in July 1944, I was asked to set up the unit in Bombay, on the same lines as the Tactical Unit at Liverpool. The staff appointed were:- Lieutenant AF King RIN (Lieutenant-Commander) Lieutenant SM Ahsan DSC RIN, 2nd Officers WRINS E Donaghue, E Staveley, J West and EA Twynham. The party gathered together in Bombay on July 24th and flew to the UK in the middle of August in a York, being given high priority of travel. The flight took four days, changing crews at each refuelling stop at Karachi, Habbaniyah, Cairo, Tunis and Rabat, finally landing at RAF Lyneham in Wiltshire.

From the last week of August through to the end of October, the team understudied the staff at Derby House, led by Commander Duncan and learned a great deal of the Wolf Packs in the Atlantic. The routine was that Commanding Officers of escort vessels - sloops, frigates, corvettes and, occasionally, fleet destroyers - would attend for a week-long course, at which most of the time was spent on exercises using the grid-marked floor as the sea area. Each 'ship' was directed from behind a screen by its captain, who was fed with information, some relevant, some not so relevant, but all realistic and from which he had to give instructions as to his actions. the course, speed and any other action taken was then put on the Master Plot. Attacking submarines were directed by the tutor and, at the end of the exercise, the 'battle' was analysed and discussions followed on various possibilities of attack and counter-attack. Much was learned of the ways of the enemy. At this time, much information was available of enemy intentions and often of immediate actions through the intelligence being gathered from the decyphering of messages on the Enigma machine captured from the Germans in 1938.

Such intelligence as could be used without compromising the fact that Enigma was available was promulgated to ships. It was a difficult balance to maintain and it will be recalled that Churchill allowed the bombing of Coventry to take place without bringing in massive fighter cover, in order to preserve the source of his intelligence. Such intelligence as was available was given to the tactical unit, for use in the discussions and analyses of the activities of the enemy.

After this comprehensive training at the very centre of the Atlantic Battle, the Bombay team returned to base and set up their own unit in November 1944. At first, this was established in Mongini's Restaurant in Hornby Road, on the top floor. The location was acceptable for operation, but was not acceptable on security grounds and books had to be stored each evening at Naval HQ, two miles away and brought out each morning and kept under constant survey.

Courses were held, consisting of twelve to eighteen executive officers of various ranks, each week from the last week of November. The unit was transferred to a Dockyard location in February 1945 and this was more convenient for the people attending and provided much improved security.

After the defeat of Japan in August 1945, it was no longer easy to maintain enthusiasm for courses and as there were increasing numbers of people gathering in Bombay awaiting demobilisation, it was decided to set up demonstrations of a number of Naval Actions which had taken place.

'The Sinking of the Bismarck', 'The Battle of the River Plate' and others were set out, with the narrative being read from the official reports. The audiences were appreciative of such information as, of course, up to that time very few people had detailed knowledge of what really happened.

27

The Torpedo & Electrical Branches

MEMORIES OF HMIS VALSURA by GAG WILLIAMS

I was appointed to undergo the Long Torpedo course at HMS VERNON in 1943, with my fellow RIN officers, Gyan Kapoor, Heath Maskell and Dick Colls. Prior to travelling to Britain, I spent a few days in HMIS VALSURA, in early March 1943 - my first visit to the school. The Commanding Officer at the time was Commander Ward and the Executive Officer was Lieutenant Jack Bayliss.

Commander Ward, who was on loan from the Royal Navy, had selected Rozi as the site for building the RIN Torpedo and Electrical School. His foresight and vision played a very large part in the construction and layout of a very fine establishment and I can remember being well satisfied that VALSURA was to be my alma mater in years to come. I next returned to VALSURA, this time with my wife and small son, in 1945. Commander Ward was still in command and Lieutenant Colls, who sadly died of cancer a few years ago, was Executive Officer.

I was 'Whitehead Torpedo Instructional Officer,' with Torpedo Workshop and classrooms on the perimeter of the parade ground. We periodically took classes to sea for torpedo running from the ML, which was fitted with fixed torpedo tubes. Lieutenant Lodi (not Captain MAK Lodi PN) commanded this ship and 'Slim' Callaghan was his First Lieutenant.

Torpedo firing was always fun. The class prepared their torpedo or torpedoes; the Nawanagar State Railway Line provided a locomotive and torpedo truck; the torpedoes were loaded on to the truck inside the Whitehead shop and the train proceeded to the Docks. The Whitehead Instructional Officer personally drove the locomotive on these occasions, under the general supervision of the engine driver. On arrival at the Docks, the torpedo was unloaded from the truck by mobile crane, which then plumbed the torpedo tube of the ML lying alongside the jetty. There was then a rush to get to sea on the tide; fire torpedoes; recover them and return to the ML dock on the next tide. If we missed it, the ML would have to lie at a buoy.

His Highness, the Jam Sahib of Nawanagar, was a friend and ally to VALSURA. The affairs of state revolved around him and his Army background and great sense of hospitality caused him to see that VALSURA's officers were included in virtually all official and informal functions taking place in the Palace and elsewhere. Duck shooting expeditions in the season, dinner parties, cocktail parties, balls, all made social life great fun.

Commander Ward left VALSURA in 1946 and I served for about a year as Executive Officer to Commander Clark, (who died in 1956) and Lieutenant Commander Maskell, who succeeded Commander Clark. Heath Maskell and his wife, Jill, were great characters and were well loved by officers and ratings alike. They did much to make VALSURA a 'happy ship'.

For exercise, we were well organised. One could walk several miles through the game reserve to Rozi Lighthouse and back. The game reserve always fascinated me, with its wide variety of birdlife and deer. Alternatively, we could play hockey and football on our own 'sports ground', which was prepared daily by rolling and marking areas of flat baked sand in the flats outside the perimeter fence.

My memories of the two years I spent in VALSURA, from 1945 to 1947, are very happy ones. It is difficult to believe sometimes that twenty years have passed since I left VALSURA and India and I wonder whether time has worked many changes - I expect so, for change is inevitable. But of one thing I am certain - INS VALSURA is in very capable hands.

28

The Women's Royal Indian Naval Service

by PEGGY COOPER

The Women's Royal Indian Naval Service was formed for service with the Royal Indian Navy during the 1939-1945 War, to assist primarily with cypher and coding duties and, as the battle areas moved from Europe into the Pacific, so the importance of the wireless communication link through India increased and more personnel were needed. At the outbreak of war, a number of officers' wives and other ladies started work as civilians in cypher offices throughout the country, working for the Army, the Royal Indian Navy and the Indian Air Force. After some time, they were formed into the Women's Auxiliary Corps, (India). Although, in theory, an inter-service organisation, it was run on Army lines and women officers and other ranks wore Army uniform, based on that of the British Army Women's Territorial Service.

These khaki-clad subalterns, sergeants and corporals looked rather incongruous in naval offices, and steps were soon taken to create a Naval Wing of the WAC (I), with its own distinctive uniform and Regulations. Gold braid replaced subaltern's stars and crossed killicks the sergeant's stripes. As two thirds of the women who enrolled were Indian, two styles of uniform were developed - one consisting of a white sari with a blue border to suit the Indian girls and, for the British and Anglo-Indians, a uniform based on that of the British WRNS, except that the WRINS were permitted to wear the same gold braid and buttons as the RIN - by kind permission of the latter.

The creation of this new women's service produced a great feeling of esprit de corps within the Naval Establishments where they were employed, but, more importantly, after the loss of Singapore, a heavy burden was thrown on the RIN Signals organisation so that it was beneficial to recruit a number of intelligent English-speaking girls to take over these duties where possible.

In addition to cypher duties, the girls were trained and employed as teleprinter and Dome Teacher Operators; typists; telephonists; loggers; filers; message checkers; Duty Distribution Officers and clerks. In the clerical field, they helped in ships offices, worked in War Information Rooms and on War maps and, also, many were employed in Detachment and Unit offices, keeping account of pay and allowances and others were to be found working in Fleet Mail Offices.

There were WRINS at the Naval Gunnery Establishment, HMIS HIMALAYA, Karachi, where they worked on Radio Telephones; on the

Chief Officer Peggy Cooper, CBE, WRINS and
2nd Officer Kalyani Sen, WRINS; on a visit to the UK - 1945

projectors as qualified cinema-operators; on precision machines and on ordinance duties.

Some assisted at the Royal Indian Naval Tactical Unit in Bombay and some Inter-Service WRINS were employed in Directorates in Delhi, (with its large Defence Headquarters), including the Recruiting and Public Relations Directorates; Combined Operations, Inter-Services Security; WAC (I) and Organisation Directorates and, finally, in the large Release and Resettlement Departments. The responsibility for welfare and the provision of necessities in the WRINS Units was the duty of the Administration WRINS, who consisted of caterers, Quartermasters, Regulating staff, Detachment Officers, clerks and those in charge of hostels.

The WRINS furthermost outpost was Chittagong, with a complement of four WRINS officers, including one for Sea Transport. The majority were based in Bombay, but they were to be found at HMIS ADYAR, Madras, HMIS HOOGHLY, Calcutta, HMIS MONZE, Karachi, HMIS TALWAR and DALHOUSIE, Bombay and at Vizagapatam and Cochin. The WRINS started their own hostels in all the main ports and in Delhi. Here, Hindus, Parsis, Pathans, Anglo-Indians and British lived side-by-side in harmony - the only allowance made for difference in taste or religious practice were the meals - two sets being provided.

The RIN allowed the WRINS the use of all the training facilities they had themselves. The girls undertook their recruit training at their own HMIS JAHANARA, at Ahmednagar and at HMIS NALINI at Calcutta and, from then on, they could attend HMIS TALWAR, for Signals training and, finally, a Divisional Course at HMIS FEROZE, Bombay, to train them as Officers, once they had successfully passed at a Selection Board.

IN 1943, the WRINS numbered forty one officers and 204 ratings but, two years later, there were 242 officers and 746 ratings, by which time 43% of the officers, (80% among the juniors), and 77% of the ratings were Indian. For the Indian girls, it was the experience of a lifetime, broadening their outlook and helping towards emancipation - so important for their future role in India. During the three-day mutiny in February 1946, it was significant that the WRINS in all the ports stood fast and showed no signs of disaffection.

Special Regulations were created for the WRINS by reason of its composition, which differed from those of the WAC (I), who worked in Army Offices and complied with Army discipline, whereas the WRINS discipline and welfare were subject to RIN Rules and standards. In addition to the WRINS distinctive uniform, an attractive crest of blue on gold, (representing the RIN service), was designed and, within it was placed a Ganges Tern - considered appropriate, it being a bird which is a feature of the Indian river scenery.

By September 1945, the war with Japan had come to an end and, in December 1945, the India War Committee, sadly for us, decided to wind-up the Indian Women's Services - WRINS and WAC (I) - and not to continue them in peacetime, owing to the prevailing manpower position. Later, came Partition, so they have never been re-formed.

The Crest of the Women's Royal Indian Naval Service

Glossary of Abbreviations

A/S	Anti-Submarine
AWOL	Absent without Leave.
BPF	British Pacific Fleet.
CCF	Captain-Coastal Forces.
CCO	Central Communications Office.
CGO	Civilian Gazetted Officer.
COA	Chief of Administration.
COS	Chief of Staff.
CPO	Chief Petty Officer.
DG	Degaussing (method used to reduce the residual magnetic field of a ship, as a protection against magnetic mines.)
D/F	Direction Finding.
DFA(N)	Deputy Financial Adviser (Navy).
DSTO	Deputy Sea Transport Officer.
(E)	After Rank, denotes a member of the Engineering Branch.
EA	Electrical Artificer.
EO	Engineer Officer
ERA	Engine Room Artificer.
FOCRIN	Flag Officer Commanding, Royal Indian Navy.
FOO	Forward Observation Officer.
HDML	Harbour Defence Motor Launch.
HO	'Hostilities Only'.
MED	Mechanical Engineering Department.
MOD	Ministry of Defence.
MTE	Mechanical Training Establishment.
MTO	Mechanical Transport Officer.
NOIC	Naval Officer in Charge.
NSO	Naval Stores Officer.
POMMD	Principal Officer, Mercantile Marine Department.
PWSS	Port War Signal Station.
QF	Quick-Firing.
RA(D)	Rear Admiral (Destroyers).
RNAV	Royal Navy Artillery Volunteer
(S)	After Rank, denotes a member of the Supply & Secretariat Branch.
SCO	Staff Communications Officer.
SOO	Staff Officer (Operations).

(Sp)	After Rank, denotes a member of the Special Branch.
STS	Stokers Training School.
WRINS	Women's Royal Indian Naval Service.
W/T	Wireless Telegraphy.
XDO	Extended Defence Officer.

Note on References to time

Naval times always on 24 hour clock without suffix 'hours'; eg 1400, equivalent to 1400 hours or 2 pm.

Bibliography & Chapter Notes

History of the Indian Navy, 1613-1863 (2 volumes); by CR Low; published Richard Bentley & Son, London, 1877.

Official History of the Indian Armed Forces in the Second World War, 1939-1945, (Royal Indian Navy); by DJE Collins; published Combined Inter-Services Historical Section (India and Pakistan), New Delhi, 1964.

World War Two Fact Files - British Escort Ships; by HT Lenton; published Macdonald & Janes, London, 1974.

The Bombay Dockyard and the Wadia Master Builders; by RA Wadia; Bombay, 1957.

The Personal Memoirs of Admiral JH Godfrey, CB; (unpublished).

The Reports and Journals of the Royal Indian Marine/Navy Club and the Royal Indian Navy (1612-1947) Association; 1934-1985.

Chapters

2   This article by Commander DJ Hastings was published in the 1984 issue of the Journal of the RIN (1612-1947) Association.

3   Reproduced from the 1938 issue of the RIN Club Report.

4   From the address given by Captain L Sanderson, CIE, at the Annual Reunion of the RIN (1612-1947) Association in 1970.

10   From the article by Commander R Williams in the 1975 issue of the Journal of the RIN (1612-1947) Association.

11   From the RIN monthly magazine 'RINLOG', November 1945.

13   From GODAVARI's Letter of Proceedings and her Captain's private journal ("The Long Chase" by Commander AB Goord, DSC)

21   From the article by Captain FL Hemming in the 1982 issue of the Journal of the RIN (1612-1947) Association.

24   From contributions by Captain Sir Henry Digby-Beste, CIE, OBE, in the 1940-46 issues of the RIN Club Report.

27   Written by Commander GAG Williams for the Silver Jubilee of INS VALSURA, December 1967.

Note A fuller bibliography will be included in the forthcoming History of the Royal Indian Navy, due to be published in 1987:
The Royal Indian Navy - 1612 to 1950 - a definitive History; publishers McFarland & Co. Inc., Jefferson, North Carolina, USA.